ADVANCED PRAISE FOR
EARTH ANGEL WITH A GREEN CARD

Sensational! The author gives such a clear vision of every scene. It made me laugh, cry, and gave, me great suspense. The selfless life of a wonderful mother, Nena, who touched the lives of all who crossed her path. Even though she had many responsibilities to her own children and family, she wouldn't hesitate to help others in need. She gave herself completely. With the love of the good book and the Lord on her side, anything was possible with faith to see her through the task at hand. Nena turned all strangers into friends, even an officer seeking information towards the deportation of illegals. She turned his hard-core personality into heart-felt kindness. It's clear Nena's purpose in life was to shelter people from their storms. This book shows the true meaning of paying it forward. Thanks to God for sending this amazing Earth Angel for all of us to know and love.

Cynthia Schmaltz, SST

A son, surgeon, and author, Dr. Hernandez beautifully weaves together stories of his mother, Nena, to illustrate how empathy and service can transform lives and communities. Her captivating journey from rural Mexico to US citizenship is a true Good Samaritan story. The reader meets the people whose lives were changed by the simple recognition of their humanity. Nena lived and taught that whether doctor or patient, immigrant or customs officer, homeless or wealthy, human dignity transcends our conditions. This book is a welcome inspiration to put oneself in another's shoes and let kindness overcome preconception. Motherhood is the fabric of this book, and it motivates us to see all those around us not as strangers but as family.

Michael Garcia, M.D

I couldn't help but smile and chuckle while reading about Nena and Evelyn. Nena, with her light skin and freckles and Mrs. Davis's red lipstick to go with her brightly colored dress and hat. I wish I had met both of these angels. I would have enjoyed going along on their trips to the second-hand dress shop and the adventures they encountered along the way. I wish I had knocked on

Nena's door just to have the pleasure of being ushered in to share a conversation while savoring the richness of her chicken mole, or chile relleno, or maybe, just a simple gordita.

On a more somber note, Nena with her ten children, was determined to better their future by making heart-wrenching decisions, parting with Edgar, then Jorge, and Pedro. Each young man proved to be equally determined to make a better life for themselves through sheer hard work. Amazingly, these three boys, under the guidance of their elder siblings, but especially big brother Miguel, understood the sacrifices and embraced what opportunities their new country has to offer.

Angel with a Green Card and the author's first book *On the Border of a Dream* tell the story of achieving dreams through tears, and smiles, even laughter at times, but always, hard, honest work coupled with integrity. The story of Nena details the heartaches and sacrifices of a mother juxtaposed by love, selflessness, determination and commitment to better the lives of her children. As a mother, I feel her anguish, her apprehensions, and the heartaches as she parts with each child. I admire Nena's wisdom and prudence and I applaud her bittersweet legacy -Hold on to a dream and never give up, never let go; for in the end, dreams do come true.

Luiza Groover, R.N., B.S.N., M.S.N., C.N.O.R.

The book *Earth Angel with a Green Card* by Edgar Hernandez is a book of true encouragement. The author has the superb ability to make characters and situations come alive, creating an empathetic connection with the characters and their experiences. Dr. Hernandez's second book is an excellent complement to his first. While this book narrates his mother's experiences, it is evident the immense amount of influence his mother had on him as a boy, a man, and a physician. He states in the introduction that reading his remembrance of his mother and her liveliness you should "prepare to be charmed, surprised, moved, delighted, and inspired to live your life with greater joy, optimism, compassion, and selflessness." That is exactly what happened to me as I read about Nena Hernandez. So much about Nena touched my heart and impressed me, especially her "genuine curiosity and interest in even the seemingly smallest aspect of a person's life." Some may have thought she was nosey, but she knew that the key to the innermost person is seen best in the small details of one's life. Nena showed her yearning to care for others early in her life when she acted as a nurse for a young man despite having no formal education or medical experience. It was her empathy and desire to comfort others that moved her to act selflessly to assist and support those around her. Her faith and compassion led her through a life with a husband who was so full of self-loathing that he found close relationships with others difficult. She saw past that difficulty to his heartfelt desire to heal others, despite the hardship he brought to her life and the lives of her children. Nena never allowed the difficulty of her life to steal her compassion, her empathy for others, her faith, her optimism, or her integrity. Rather, she used her struggles to strengthen all that she was. As a mother she made the ultimate sacrifice of sending her children to live with others because she had faith that they would obtain a better life and ultimately be reunited again. The blessings that happened to reunite her family was something that she was so grateful for that she used that experience to bring blessings to others. Upon meeting her dear friend Mrs. Davis, she had found a partner who was just as determined as she to show kindness to others. The story of Nena Hernandez's life resonated within me as a nurse, a mother, a wife, and as a spiritual woman. I am determined to live my life "with greater joy, optimism, compassion, and selflessness."

Shahara Austin, R.N.

EARTH ANGEL
WITH A
GREENCARD
A Mexican Mother's Journey
OF FAITH, HOPE, AND DREAMS TO JOIN HER CHILDREN IN THE USA

EARTH ANGEL
WITH A
GREENCARD

A Mexican Mother's Journey

OF FAITH, HOPE, AND DREAMS TO JOIN HER CHILDREN IN THE USA

BESTSELLER
BESTSELLER
BESTSELLER

EDGAR H. HERNANDEZ
M.D., M.S., F.A.C.S.

CARTWRIGHT
PUBLISHING
Visibility • Authority • Legacy • Clients

Earth Angel with a Green Card
One Mexican Woman's Journey of Faith, Hope, and Dreams to Join her
Children in the USA

First Edition
First Printing 2018

ISBN: 978-1-7321736-3-7 (paperback)
ISBN: 978-1-7321736-2-0 (hardbound)

Library of Congress Cataloging-in-Publication Data is available.

This work was designed, produced, and published in the
United States of America by

CARTWRIGHT PUBLISHING
Visibility • Authority • Legacy • Clients

145 Corte Madera Town Center, #415
Corte Madera, CA 94924

www.CartwrightPublishing.com
415-250-6343

Cartwright Publishing is a publisher of business and professional books. We help entrepreneurs, business and community leaders, and professionals share their stories, passion, and knowledge to help others. If you have a manuscript or book idea that you would like us to consider for publishing, please visit Cartwright Publishing.com.

Cover photo: Edgar H. Hernandez
Cover design: Robin Vuchnich
Interior design: Robin Vuchnich

A Note from the Author

———≫●≪———

I have tried to recreate events, locales and conversations from my memories of them. In order to maintain their anonymity, in some instances I have changed the names of individuals and places, and/or I may have changed some identifying characteristics and details such as physical properties, occupations and places of residence.

To my entire family, the family of
Magdalena "Nena" Hernández

———

To all the wonderful women in the world—your devotion, sacrifice, and unaffected generosity to your families, children, and communities is awe-inspiring.

To women newly diagnosed with breast cancer as well as breast cancer survivors—your fortitude in the face of great pain and uncertainty is incredible.

To immigrants coming to the USA to pursue your dreams—as I know from firsthand experience, it can be scary and challenging, but it is well worth the effort. May God be with you.

———

Many women have done well, but you exceed them all.
—Proverbs 31:29

Muchas mujeres hicieron el bien; mas tú sobrepasas a todas.
—Proverbios 31:29

Power of Faith and Dreams

———

To speak is to communicate,
To read is to understand,
To write is to convey,
To desire is to succeed.
To speak, read, and write is to be literate.
To be illiterate is to be humble and
To have desire, hunger, and thirst for the power to read.
To succeed in learning to read is the power
To convey and understand all that is around us—
A powerful dream.
It's you—Magdalena "Nena" Hernández.

TABLE OF CONTENTS

———

FOREWORD...XIX

INTRODUCTION..1

PART ONE: MEXICO

CHAPTER 1: IN THE SHADE OF A TREE....................................9

CHAPTER 2: INJURY..32

CHAPTER 3: MOTHERS AND CHILDREN 47

CHAPTER 4: FAITH AND PERSISTENCE 55

CHAPTER 5: AGUA PURA..64

CHAPTER 6: LETTING GO..76

CHAPTER 7: BLUE MOON..88

PART TWO: ESTADOS UNIDOS DE AMÉRICA

CHAPTER 8: WHOLE-HEARTED 104

CHAPTER 9: CO-CONSPIRATORS....................................118

CHAPTER 10: AMIGO O ENEMIGO....................................139

CHAPTER 11: GOD'S HANDS 156

CHAPTER 12: TWO LAWS..185

CHAPTER 13: MIND AND HEART....................................212

CHAPTER 14: LEGACY 226

CHAPTER 15: NENA'S CHILDREN....................................232

CHAPTER 16: NENA'S RECIPES..236

ACKNOWLEDGMENTS 244

ABOUT THE AUTHOR..245

FOREWORD

For as long as I can remember, on every Sunday at my Abueli-ta's [grandmother's] home, I would meet someone new. More often than not, I would walk in to my Abuelita's house and see this new person sitting at the dinner table. Of course, before I could introduce myself to this new person or inquire as to how this guest found his or her way to her dinner table, I would have already had been prompted by my Abuelita or my Tías [aunts] to sit and eat. (And unless you wanted my Abuelita and my Tías to ask if you were hungry every five minutes, it was always a better idea to accept their invitation to eat).

At times, when I could be discreet, I would ask my sister Marisa if she knew who the newcomer was. As was usually the case, neither of us knew who the newcomer was, and over time, my sister and I would retell the same joke: "It is probably someone we are related to that we have not yet met."

Until I read *Earth Angel with a Green Card*, I always believed that the joke between my sister and me operated under the assump-tion that my family—the *Hernandez* family—was a traditionally large Mexican family and that the guests at my Abuelita's home were long-lost relatives. Instead, as is demonstrated within the stories told by my father in *Earth Angel with a Green Card*, my Abuelita treated everyone as if they were a part of her family. Abuelita's guests would always be provided every comfort (and would be well fed) during their visit to Abuelita's home. The conversation would rarely consist of small talk, or of matters that were unimportant or uncontroversial. Based on my Abuelita's interactions with these guests, there was simply no way these guests could not be family, and therefore, each guest was treated as such—as family.

For at least the first half of my life, I am happy to say that I followed my Abuelita's example. But, as I grew older, and as many others will learn or have learned already, treating everyone you meet as if they are family is no small feat. It is exhausting, and at times, we find ourselves holding back our energy, strength, and resources in reserve so that we can take care of ourselves and our own.

But, not my Abuelita. Despite the high cost, my Abuelita would shed tears for those she never met, provide comfort and care to children who were not hers, and demonstrate calmness in situations where any ordinary person would resort to frustration. My Abuelita had a unique capacity to understand the needs of those around her and held a strong interest in the well-being of others, including those whom she had never met. And before those strangers knew it, my Abuelita would be inviting them for dinner.

And by doing so, my Abuelita's family grew.

As told by my father, *Earth Angel with a Green Card* is the story of Magdalena Hernandez, my Abuelita, and my father's Mamá. Most, if not all, of the stories written here were based on conversations between my Father and his Mamá that took place over various breakfasts, lunches or dinners. *Earth Angel with a Green Card* consists of two parts: (1) Mexico and (2) Estados Unidos de America. Part One details my Abuelita's relationship with my Abuelo, Miguel Hernandez Cabrera. Part Two follows the death of my Abuelo, and my Abuelita's life in the United States of America.

It is my sincere hope that, after putting down *Earth Angel with a Green Card*, you discover that some part of you has changed for the better. Because if anything within you has changed, it might be traced to both my Abuelita, and the life that my Abuelita lived.

Carlos Andres Hernandez, J.D.

INTRODUCTION

"You have a cancer in your right breast, and you need surgery quite soon," I told my patient, Amy Kelly, a forty-five-year-old woman, quiet, and soft-spoken with green eyes, a smattering of freckles, and light-brown hair worn up in a ponytail.

I continued, "The ultrasound and mammogram are consistent with a localized cancer. Nevertheless, surgery is clearly warranted."

In acknowledgment of my words, Mrs. Kelly turned her lips up in a melancholic smile, all the while gazing out the window at the flowering palo verde in the courtyard of my medical practice. Her dangling earrings swayed when she turned her head back to face me. Calm and composed, she listened intently as I discussed the surgery.

"The good news is that you can keep your breast. We can remove the tumor, do reconstructive surgery followed by radiation treatments. The procedure is referred to as a partial mastectomy with reconstruction followed by radiation, and—"

"Dr. Hernández, what's your mother's name?" Mrs. Kelly interrupted me to ask.

"The name of my mother?" I repeated, puzzled. "Well, her name is Magdelena Hernández, but people call her Nena."

"Nena is lucky to have such a kind, capable, and professional son. How many brothers and sisters do you have?"

"Actually, I come from a large family. I have five brothers and four sisters."

She went on to ask, "Were some of them ever really sick? Or injured? Or in danger?"

Admittedly, I was perplexed by her questions about my family. We were deviating from discussing her diagnosis and treatment.

"Mrs. Kelly, let's return to talking about your surgical operation. As I was saying, I can remove the tumor, then we can treat you with radiation. Or you could have a mastectomy, and we could go ahead and reconstruct your breast."

I went on to discuss more specifics of the surgery, but I could tell she had no real interest in my explanation. While I could tell she was paying attention, she continued to look out the window as if also occupied by some other pressing issue.

"Dr. Hernández, about your mother—what does she look like?"

Again, I was perplexed, but I decided to respond, "To start, she has freckles like you."

"Like me?" she asked softly, her eyes beginning to glisten.

We had already talked for more than 50 minutes, which was longer than I had scheduled for this follow-up appointment. We had talked about her diagnosis and need for surgery a few days earlier. This appointment was meant to nail down the treatment she wanted and then schedule it. Still, I didn't want to rush her though I knew too that the waiting room was packed with patients.

"Where is your mother now?"

"She died a few years ago. Her grave lies under a lovely olive tree," I answered.

"Where were you born, doctor?"

Curious by her inquiries about me and my family, and how or if it all would connect to her, I continued answering her questions. "I was born on the southern coast of Mexico and immigrated to the United States when 9½ years old."

"Please tell me how she handled it when you or any of your brothers and sisters were sick or hurting."

Not wanting to be disrespectful or show a lack of concern, I avoided looking at my watch, but I was well aware of the time slipping by. Even still, I told her, "My mother was quite close to all of her children. Nurturing her children was her first priority, even with the limited resources in our small town. Sacrificing her own health and well-being was what she did when the choice was between caring for herself or for her children."

She looked at me intently and stated, "Dr. Hernández, I would really like to know more about her."

"Mrs. Kelly, I'd like to talk more about my beautiful mother, but we really need to talk about you and your breast cancer treatment. Let me say, I promise I will take very good care of you."

Once I brought the conversation back to her cancer, she shifted her gaze from me to the palo verde out the window. I wondered if perhaps she was hoping her cancer would magically disappear, or perhaps she was frightened by the idea of surgery and what might lie beyond.

Abruptly she announced, "I can't have an operation now. I'll do it later."

My response—I was stunned. Aghast. Most of the patients were overeager for me to remove any trace of cancer in them as quickly as possible, yet here was a woman asking that I wait.

Over the course of the appointment, I had begun to feel a warm connection with Mrs. Kelly, almost like I'd been hypnotized by this gentle person who resembled my freckled-faced mother.

Putting my hand gently on her forearm, I explained, "The decision is yours, but still, we can continue our conversation about your treatment options."

Continuing to gaze out the window, searching the afternoon shadows for what I didn't know, she asked, "Were you or your brothers and sisters ever seriously sick or in danger?"

"Yes, many times, but we managed to survive."

"Did your mother comfort you and your siblings during these times?"

"Yes," I answered with a smile.

"How did that make you feel?"

"I don't think we would have survived without her warm and caring love." Next I told her a story of how my mother cared for my brother Jorge when, at seven years old, he got badly burned. I also told her how Mamá cared for all of us when we all, including her, had cholera at the same time that a hurricane descended on our village.

After an hour, my secretary knocked. When I stepped into the hall to speak to her, she informed me, "I'm sorry to disturb you, but you have many patients who are anxious to see you." I told her I would try to finish soon.

When I returned to the room, Mrs. Kelly picked up our conversation, saying, "So your freckled-faced mother took care of you all, neglecting her own needs and health to ensure her children's recovery?"

"Yes, she did."

"I too need to take care of my son. Less than two weeks ago, he had a serious motorcycle accident. He broke his left femur and his collarbone, and fractured part of his spine. He's not paralyzed, and the surgeon says he should do very well, but only if someone cares for him during the next few months. I'm his mother, and I need and want to be there for him. I'm afraid my cancer surgery will have to be postponed for about six months."

I looked at her and asked, "You mean to tell me that you are willing to sacrifice your life for the future of your son?"

"Yes, doctor."

I looked at her with tears in my eyes, hugged her, and explained, "I fully understand."

She gave me a kiss on the cheek and walked out of the room.

After she left, my secretary found me to ask if everything was okay.

"Yes, everything is good. Wonderful even. That woman is a most wonderful mother. And she reminded me of my own wonderful mother."

I've never forgotten that conversation with Mrs. Kelly. It reminded me of how many extraordinary mothers there are in our world, mothers who dedicate themselves to their children and communities, sacrificing their own wants and needs so that these others can benefit. Their stories of sacrifice, love, and bravery typically don't get told. This conversation with Mrs. Kelly planted a seed in me to someday record the story of my mother, a woman ahead of her times, creative, sensitive, unselfish, humble, honest, and overflowing with integrity.

Earth Angel with a Green Card tells the story of my wonderful mother, Magdalena "Nena" Hernández. I wrote this book to lift the curtain and reveal all that so many mothers do and have done over their lifetimes without any need for recognition. *Earth Angel with a Green Card* celebrates my mother and all mothers.

As the pages of this book will reveal, Mamá was an individual deeply and sincerely concerned for others, and she didn't seek anything in return. She was a non-educated lady who practiced her faith like no other. Her ability to motivate, move, interact with, and work with people, regardless of their background, status, or attitude, was truly remarkable. Her innocence, charm, love for her family as well as all others were and continue to be, for me, memorable. Like all my nine siblings, I am happy and proud to be her son.

It was through our lengthy conversations over her amazing meals that my mother taught me how to be a better doctor, a better husband, a better father, a better citizen—a better human being. My mother didn't just teach me through her words. Her kind-spirited, selfless, and brave actions, which spanned for over nine decades, are what ingrained her lessons in my heart and mind, as well as the hearts and minds of all whom she touched.

I wrote *Earth Angel with a Green Card* based on my memory of conversations with my mother, my memory of events that occurred when she and I were together, and stories my brothers, sisters, other family members, friends, and people who knew my mother told me. I drew from all these memories to write this book.

As you *read Earth Angel with a Green Card*, prepare to be charmed, surprised, moved, delighted, and inspired to live your life with greater joy, optimism, compassion, and selflessness.

Part **One**

MEXICO

Chapter 1

In the Shade of a Tree

"Edgar, how is your patient Cynthia doing?" my mother asked me.

"How do you know about Cynthia?" I responded, surprised.

"Two weeks ago, I heard you talking to her on the phone about her breast cancer diagnosis. She was crying and very upset."

"How did you know she was crying?"

"*Mijo*, I can read you very well."

"Yes, I know, Mamá," I acknowledged.

"I'm worried about her," my mother went on to say. One thing about my mother, she wanted no one to suffer, especially mothers and children, and did all she could to minimize others' pain.

"Mamá, I want to assure you, like all the women I've operated on with breast cancer, Cynthia is a very brave lady."

As we were conversing, my mother served us the chicken mole she'd been preparing: chicken lathered in a chocolaty-looking, spicy sauce that was made up of ten-plus ingredients. The mole tasted sweet yet peppery and also tangy, all at the same time. She served it on a wide plate accompanied by refried beans, rice, and tortillas. Although my mother spent the first forty years of her life in rural Mexico cooking over homemade coals, she attributed her cooking abilities to Miguel, my older half-brother and her stepson.

9

She claimed that it was only when she arrived in the USA that she learned to really cook under Miguel's guidance.

No matter the guest—old friends, her family, or complete strangers—no one could simply sit down and have a "normal" meal with my mother. Mamá loved to cook and entertain, so a meal at her house was often a three- to four-hour affair. It would start with one meal and then move to coffee and dessert, all the while having lots of conversation. Then she'd begin cooking another meal. She had genuine curiosity and interest in even the seemingly smallest aspects of a person's life, so mealtime conversations tended to be extensive. And she was especially interested in the lives of mothers and children. So, in our regular lunches together, I would clear my schedule for around four hours in order to have a proper visit with her.

With the mole served, my mother picked up our conversation. "Tell me, Edgar, you've worked with many cancer patients over many years now. What have you noticed?"

"Mamá, I'll tell you something that I return to again and again—and that's how unbelievable it is the way patients tolerate all that doctors do to them. To make them better, we surgeons necessarily create pain and scarring. The medications we give them oftentimes make them sick. It seems that all the treatments we give them may make them sick, at least temporarily. So, these patients are in agony—yet they always smile. They never fail to show us their appreciation and desire to live.

"Really, some of the most incredible human beings I have ever met in my life are those battling and surviving breast cancer. They tolerate surgical pain, the complications that sometimes occur—redo surgery, correct drainage of wounds, infections, hospitalizations, outpatient treatments, and on and on.

My mother looked at me intently as I spoke, taking in all that I was saying.

"Mamá, something that breaks my heart but also angers me can be the husbands of my female patients who have breast cancer. I've seen several husbands leave their wives because they can't cope, number one, with the diagnosis of cancer. Or they can't cope with their wives' treatments. Or they can't cope with their wives' residual scars. I've always said that these men who run away are weak people. They're people who have no love, no affection, no spirit, and they have no tenacity to help their wives survive such a serious diagnosis and serious treatments."

My mother asked, "How can this be? How can so many husbands leave their wives?"

"Admittedly, Mamá, the majority do not. The majority surround their wives with overpowering support. But it's not uncommon to come across patients whose husbands just cannot take it. Maybe these men don't mean to be uncaring. Maybe they're just running because they're scared of the truth. They're scared death may overcome their wives. And there are lots of people who have fears like that. Or they may leave, perhaps, for reasons I may never know."

Mamá went on to say, "You are my son. As long as I know you are taking care of those patients, I know they're going to do well. There's no question in my mind. And, Edgar, I hope you talk to those patients with your heart and hold hands with the rest of the family, even the husbands."

"Mamá, sometimes husbands and relatives don't want to talk about things. They accompany their sick spouse to the appointment, but they sort of stay away. It's like they don't want to be involved, like they want to detach themselves from such a devastating diagnosis and treatment. I think they just want it to go away. So, sometimes it's very easy to talk with patients and husbands, and sometimes it's difficult."

"*Mijo*, you know how well I understand this dilemma. I recall when your father used to see patients, I took it upon myself to talk to the patient as well as the family, to explain what was happening and offer comfort and hope. Your father would do the medical treatments, and I would offer comfort and support. You see—I consider comforting—both the patient and their family—as important to a patient's recovery as the treatment to the patient themselves. And I know too how difficult it is for some relatives to cope. *Sí, entiendo bien.*"

My mother was born Magdalena "Nena" Maldonado in 1921 to Andres and Marcelina Maldonado in the southern coastal area of Michoacán, Mexico. She had two sisters, Maria and Dominga, and three brothers, Jacinto, Cecilio, and Asunción. Like her father, her brothers grew up to become *campesinos* or farmers. As adults Maria and Dominga stayed home, living and caring for their parents.

My mother was beautiful with light brown eyes, bronze skin, and a thin, freckled face. She had a precious smile. Her profile was stunning—a fine nose, slightly pronounced cheekbones, and a well-measured chin. Her eyes, eyelashes, and eyebrows were regal. She had beautiful skin, gorgeous hands, and nails she carefully tended to.

As was common for many children in rural Mexico of that time, Mamá never went to school, so she never learned to read or write. She never learned any formal math skills. When she was a teenager, she went to Arteaga, a larger town in the interior of Michoacán, to live with her tía on her father's (my grandfather's) side. At 17, she landed a work opportunity in a federal camp of soldiers, ranking military personnel, and dignitaries, in Arteaga.

At the federal camp Mamá was in charge of dining arrangements, setting up daily menus, and maintaining kitchen utensils and ingredients for everyday cooking. She managed all categories of plates, bowls, glasses, cups, and cutlery, ensuring the needed items were present and ready for use.

Because she worked around so many men, they would often ask about her, "What about Nena? Does she have a husband? A boyfriend?" She was always professional and careful to maintain her reputation as a dignified and respectable young woman. Despite requests from many to address them by their first name, she resisted. When any invited her on a daytrip to the ocean, to have lunch, or just to talk, she politely declined. Mamá kept to herself.

Her parents, Andres and Marcelina, were worried about their daughters marrying young men. As did many parents in rural Mexican villages, they considered young men unsuitable to marry their daughters. They believed young men would likely not make good providers because they typically lacked financial backing and were not mature enough to take care of wives and children. "You must look for an older man with money and status because he will protect you and treat you well. An older man will be more stable and a better provider, especially when you have your own children," they advised.

There was an auto accident at the camp. General Vargas, a dark-skinned and robust man, with a crew cut and a thin mustache who always wore a gun at his side, was badly injured. He'd been a passenger in a jeep that had rolled over, ejecting him out in the process. Then the vehicle had landed on the general's leg. Miraculously his leg didn't break, but it was severely scraped and burned.

Though General Vargas had visited multiple doctors from the bigger city of Uruapan, the injured area wasn't healing. It was infected, even weeks after the accident. So, he decided to try out the services of an Arteaga man who practiced both medicine and dentistry.

Through a window in the dining hall, Mamá saw the man enter the camp, walking up its dramatic drive. Trees lined the drive on both sides, and because they were old and tall, their tops seemed to embrace each other, making a green, living tunnel around the driveway. The man wore a double-breasted suit and a hat, which was customary dress at that time for educated men from cities. His gait denoted focus and energy.

When this man passed the dining hall, my mother noticed the hair protruding from his hat was dotted with gray. He had a wide mustache that covered his entire upper lip, a pocket watch in his vest, and a shirt collar slightly stained by sweat, but still clean.

Soon thereafter, Mamá was called to the clinic. Upon entering, she came upon General Vargas, whose left leg was propped up on a chair, and the man, who immediately said to her, "My name is Miguel Hernández Cabrera, and I'm here to treat General Vargas"—he paused to take a drag from a cigarette—"And I was hoping you could assist me."

"Yes, Dr. Cabrera, as you wish."

"Miguel, call me Miguel," he told her. He then turned to General Vargas to continue their conversation, all the while smoking the cigarette. "Yes, I was able to get most of the information from the jeep driver. You're lucky the jeep didn't crush your bones or even crush you, sir. Also, the driver told me you already consulted with several doctors from Uruapan?"

"Yes, three different doctors. Each of them gave me ointments to put on the wound, but, as you can see, it hasn't improved. Actually, it's gotten worse."

Miguel nodded his head in confirmation and proceeded to examine the leg. He asked the general to flex his leg muscles and then move his toes and ankle.

Next, he directed his attention to Mamá to inquire, "Do you have starch and lard?"

"Yes."

"Also, please get some white bandages and sterilize them."

14

"Can you tell me how to do that?" she asked.

"Take some clean white fabric. Cut it into one-inch strips. Boil water and mix in two spoonfuls of salt and one cup of alcohol after it finishes boiling. Then place the bandage strips into the water."

When she returned with the sterilized bandages, Miguel proceeded with the treatment. He removed syringes and needles that had been sitting in a small metal container of boiling water. He filled the syringes with a local anesthetic.

With a sterilized syringe in one hand, he told the general, "I'm going to inject some anesthetic into your wound. It will hurt, but it will make what I'm going to do next much less painful." With the general's consent, he injected the anesthetic into the 10-by-4-inch wound on the general's upper left leg.

Vargas grimaced and then asked, "Are you from Arteaga, Miguel?"

"No, sir. I've actually only been here for about four months, but I like it very much. This is what we're going to do now that your wound is totally numb. It's what the previous doctors didn't do and should have—thoroughly clean it. I think there's still debris in there, and that's why an infection has developed and festered."

At that, Miguel scraped the wound with a sterile, sharp spoon, all the while pulling out small bits of rock, dirt, and organic debris that had been buried underneath the poorly-healed tissue. During this process, the wound oozed blood.

The general stared down, stunned by what he saw emerging from his wounded leg.

Miguel then dabbed the area with a clean white cloth and used silver nitrate to cauterize the wound's edges. He then instructed Mamá to continue the dabbing while he prepared a mixture of lard, starch, and powdered antibiotic. It had a very unique smell, almost chemical-like.

He didn't speak much as he worked. It was apparent he was very concentrated on the task at hand. Also, he smoked continuously. When he finished one cigarette, he'd soon light another.

Miguel, next, applied the paste-like mixture to the wound before covering it with strips of the sterilized bandages Mamá had prepared.

Once Miguel finished, he remarked, "If what I did doesn't help to heal your wound, the next option is to remove pieces of skin from another place on your body and graft it onto the wound area. However, I think the scraping and local debridement and treatment should stimulate granulation tissue to heal it."

General Vargas spoke, "Thank you, Miguel, and thank you, Nena."

Miguel immediately responded, "Sir, it is I that thanks you. I am honored and humbled that you have given me the opportunity to care for you. If you like, you can leave the dressings in place for two days and go to the city where you could have a real doctor treat you."

"Thanks for your suggestion," the general began, "but I prefer to stay here and have both of you take care of me. I'm very impressed, and I feel confident that I'm going to get better. What I saw you do today was never done in all the treatments I had from the doctors in the big city, so I think I'm getting some excellent care from you."

Miguel turned to my mother to ask, "What did you say your name was?

"My name is Magdalena, but everyone calls me Nena."

"Nena, you saw what I did. Do you think you can have another batch of sterile bandages ready for me tomorrow, so we can dress the general's wounds again?"

"Yes, I can do that," she affirmed, daring to look him in the eye for the first time. For a quick moment, the two looked at each other, eye to eye.

Mamá then exited the clinic. She was hurrying away to fetch Miguel a cold lemonade. By the time she returned, he was already gone. Through the window, she saw him light up a cigarette and walk through the tunnel of trees away from the building.

She could tell that the general was genuinely impressed by Miguel Hernández Cabrera, and she, herself, was intrigued by him. Over the next few weeks while treating the general, they worked together frequently. Each interaction only increased her fascination.

"I've been told he's treated a lot of people in the area, and folks really like him," remarked a staff member about Miguel Hernández Cabrera.

"He's a doctor but does a lot of other things like dental work and complicated surgeries," someone else added.

Another staff member interrupted, "Not what I heard. A drug-store owner told me he's a drunk and doesn't even have a medical or a dental degree. Apparently, his drinking was so bad that he was thrown out of *escuela dental y médica*, and no other school would take him. So, he decided to locate here, hoping no one would find out that he's a bogus doctor."

"Well, I think he's a gentleman. And General Vargas certainly seems to be improving," the first staff member responded.

Mamá didn't contribute, but she listened intently, wondering about Miguel Hernández Cabrera's true story.

Weeks later, when General Vargas, Miguel, and Mamá were convening in the clinic and the general's leg wound was healing nicely, the general began, "There's something I want to admit to you, Miguel. Before I first reached out to you, several members of my staff urged me to try another doctor in the city instead. Evidently, some people love you, and others are very skeptical."

Miguel admitted, "What you say doesn't surprise me."

"What I want to tell you, though, is that I've concluded that this town is lucky to have you."

At these words, Mamá looked at Miguel and smiled. She wasn't sure if the smile was appropriate, but it was her way of showing that she agreed with the general.

The general continued, "Please tell me how it is you came here and why."

To give Miguel the space to answer this personal request, Mamá made to leave the room, but Miguel gestured for her to stay as he proceeded to speak, "General, I'm indebted to you for allowing me to treat you despite others urging you to seek a city doctor. As I said before, treating you is an opportunity that means the world to me. Now that people know you trust me with your life, this has given them confidence to support me. Before, many were reluctant to acknowledge me when I passed. Thank you again, sir." He paused to light a new cigarette before continuing.

"I'm 49 years old. I started smoking when I was 17, so it's been 32 years now. Initially, smoking seemed to calm my anxiety. Over the decades I've found myself smoking morning, afternoon, and evening. I even wake multiple times in the night to smoke. My drinking is a similar story. It started casually, but over time I've found myself drinking more and more."

My mother was well aware that she was listening to privileged information. She wasn't sure why Miguel wanted her to remain in the room, so she felt a combination of nervousness and privilege about being there.

Miguel continued, "I've even tried to put on aftershave to mask the cigarette smell, but I don't think it helped since most people could tell or see"—he gestured to the cigarette he was smoking—"that I'm a heavy smoker. I was admitted to the University of Mexico, Michoacán, an institution that offers a dual medical and dental certification. It offers a program where students gain expertise in both disciplines, that way the program's graduates are adept medical doctors and dentists. Since many doctors and dentists typically want to stay in cities, rural areas are in great need of them. This special program is aimed at those who want to practice in rural areas. That's what I intended to do after I graduated. However, a year and a half before finishing, I was called in by the dean of the university. The dean expelled me for what he termed, my 'complete disregard for the code of conduct,' meaning my heavy smoking and drinking.

"Many students smoked and drank, but none like me. I showed up to classes and even internships at hospitals with alcohol on my breath. I smoked no matter where I was—during autopsies, labs, lectures, and when seeing patients. Quite a few nurses, doctors, and patients noticed. I was given a warning, not once, but twice. That's when the dean expelled me."

Mamá noticed she was experiencing a mix of feelings in regard to this man's revelations: disappointment, anger, and also compassion.

The general urged, "Go on."

Miguel took a long drag of his cigarette and exhaled the blue smoke in one long breath then continued, "Six months after the expulsion, when I was still contemplating what I should do next, I found myself at a bar. I sat down, lit a cigarette, and started a conversation with a couple sitting near me. The man was an elderly retired doctor, his wife a nurse. The three of us hit it off really well. We smoked and drank as we talked. I told him what was going on with me, including my smoking and drinking addictions. This retired doctor listened and then told me, 'I have a clinic where I act sort of as the administrator. There's another doctor there. I want you to work with us too. You'll do mostly dental, but some medical work too.' And so, I ended up working at this clinic—for the next 15 years.

"During that time, I became quite an experienced and skilled medical and dental provider although I never held the title of doctor or dentist. All I did was treat people. I got a weekly payment from the clinic owners, and they treated me very well and gave me a life that was very rewarding. I learned a lot. Next, I went to work in another clinic for three more years.

"During those 18 years, I was married twice, but tragically I lost both my wives to postpartum sepsis. I have six children, and they are living with relatives in various parts of Mexico.

"During all those years, I continued the heavy drinking and smoking. I went on to work in more small clinics as an assistant to doctors and dentists. I tell you—I always considered myself more skilled and experienced than the licensed doctors and dentists whom I worked for—and I felt devastated that I'd failed at getting my degree. I felt like a real failure. A loser. And I still do. I'd look at those doctors and see their lack of experience and understanding—as a matter of fact, I often was the one to do the procedures, and the mediocre doctors took all the credit—so, I felt like a serious loser, and this led to great bouts of depression, which in turn drove me to drink and smoke even more.

"On one level, I thought smoking and drinking would calm me during my episodes of depression and lessen my rampant suicidal urges—but on another level I knew it was only making things worse. But I was—and am—addicted. I developed a very uncaring attitude as to whether people liked me or not. A take-it-or-leave-it attitude.

"Last year I found myself in a clinic in a village, and I was working on a patient who'd injured himself by falling from a fence and cutting his leg on dirty barbed wire. Over the course of treating this man, he told me about Arteaga and how the rural villages of Michoacán are in desperate need of a man of my experience and skills, even though I'm not certified. It was because of this man and his urging that I ultimately landed in Arteaga to practice medicine and dentistry."

At that, Miguel finished his story. The only sound in the room was his inhaling on a cigarette and exhaling of blue-grey smoke.

Mamá was mesmerized by the man's testimony and honesty. At the same time, it dawned on her what the puzzling yet particular odor that accompanied him was—the scent of fermented alcohol and nicotine.

Finally, General Vargas spoke, "Miguel, honesty is good for the soul. It makes you a better person. We will be calling upon you for anyone here in the camp in need of dental or medical care. You are the man for the camp. I appreciate your testimony and bid you respect."

As Miguel moved to give the general a firm handshake, he winked at my mother.

"You see, General, I don't take credit for what I do. I always thank patients for giving me their trust. If they address me as 'Dr. Hernández,' I correct them, saying, 'Just call me Miguel.' "

"Then, Miguel, you are my doctor of record, and you will be assigned to the camp here."

Mamá, having born witness to the heart-moving scene, with wide eyes stood up and spoke. Emboldened, she voiced to Miguel, "Thank you, *señor*. Thank you for your kindness. You are a rare man, and I have great respect for you," and gave him a hug.

At this the general remarked, "I think there's something between you two, and may God love you for that."

Miguel winked at my mother, touched her on the shoulder, bid the two farewell, and made his exit.

The sounds of emphatic pounding on the doorway of the camp's main hall rang out in the night. There was shouting, "*Ayuda! Necesitamos ayuda medica! Es una emergencia!* Help!"

Mamá opened the door to find a party of men carrying someone. They explained that it was Luis. He'd set up his telescope on a cliff and had accidentally fallen over its high edge during his stargazing. Luis seemed to have landed on his face. He was only 24 and had been handsome. Now his face was deformed, an unrecognizable pulp, the nose and mouth orifices effusing blood. The place where his face had been resembled a deflated beach ball. Plus, he couldn't walk. One of his legs and an arm seemed to be injured.

Mamá opened the camp's small clinic and instructed the men to place the young man on the table. She sent someone to find Miguel.

In the meantime, she prepared a large vat of water. Once the water started boiling, she added salt and alcohol to it. She boiled more water in a smaller pot—for the sterilizing of syringes—to which she also added alcohol. She tore strips of fabric to act as bandages and absorbent cloths and prepared to sterilize them.

Miguel, wearing a three-piece suit and hat and smelling of cigarettes and alcohol, arrived at the clinic. He had just finished treating a young child with a lacerated lip.

With a nod of the head Miguel acknowledged Mamá and all she'd prepared, and then he turned to the patient. With a cigarette vibrating in his mouth, he began evaluating Luis, who was in apparent agony.

Miguel tried to give Luis a liquid medication for the pain, but the young man indicated that he could not swallow. Saliva and some of the liquid medication dripped from his mouth in a steady stream, combining with the blood spouting from his nose and lips, to make a morbid fountain. His ability to talk was minimal and apparently painful with his jawbones, facial plates, and teeth rattling as if very loose, disconnected, no longer locked into correct alignment.

"Let's try this again, *mijo*. Try to lift your tongue, so when I spoon the medicine in, it can sit in that pocket underneath the tongue. Try to keep it there for as long as possible—we'll tilt your head back a bit—even just a few seconds, so your body can absorb it and it'll ease your pain," Miguel explained to the young man.

Mamá moved into the kitchen to prepare more vats of boiling water.

Miguel entered with multiple instruments. As he placed them into vats, he instructed her, "After ten minutes I want you to use this large clamp to remove each instrument and immediately dip it into this canister containing alcohol. This ensures they're all sterilized. Then bring them to me."

Back in the clinic, Miguel sat the patient up in a semi-backward position. Two men helped Miguel cut away Luis's clothing. Miguel continued the evaluation. He started at Luis's head, noting some cuts in the scalp and forehead, and severe bruising on the face. He examined all the young man's extremities, tapped his chest and abdomen, and was able to confirm a fractured right leg and left arm, as well as multiple facial fractures, fractures Miguel described as "of the Le Fort variety." While performing the examination, Miguel would pause to take a drag of his cigarette.

My mother returned with the sterilized and alcohol-soaked instruments. She saw Miguel take a cloth, soak it in warm water, and tenderly clean the patient's face, ears, and eyes. He examined the eyes and ears, to ensure they were functioning.

Calmly, steadily, and without a hint of nervousness, Miguel filled the sterilized syringes with an anesthetic and told the patient, "In my twenty-plus years of medical and dental work, I've helped many people with even more severe facial fractures than what you've suffered—and they all recovered beautifully. Many had minimal scarring as well. So, while what I'm about to do to you now will hurt, I promise, it will make you better."

In response Luis nodded slightly.

Miguel then placed injections on the angle of the young man's mandible, cheeks, and in multiple locations on his face. He must have injected the area in seven to ten points in order to numb all the particular nerves in the face, so that what he had to do next would be as painless as possible.

Next, Miguel explained, "Your facial bones have separated, and to fix them and heal them, we're going to have to wire your face back together. I'm going to place holes through your skin and into your bones. I'm going to pop out the bones on your face and reset them. You see, facial bones are not fused. They are flexible, but yours have separated and moved apart too much, so I need to put them back in their correct position. You're going to be feeling a lot of intense pulling and shoving, but hopefully that's all you'll feel—and I promise, this is going to make you better."

All the while, Mamá stayed busy, keeping up with clean and warm sheet segments to wipe away effusing blood and other fluids, and maintaining the supply of hot water mixed with alcohol.

The men who were helping Luis were perspiring. They radiated anxiety and confusion. However, Miguel was totally composed. His steady hand and steady concentration gave everyone confidence.

Miguel smoked throughout all the hours of the surgery. He talked, puffed, and worked steadily. He told the young man, "I'm going to pop out your mandible. It's broken in half. I will place a small wire in it." So, he placed a small hole through the skin of the lower cheek, and, gripping with his left hand, took what looked like a long, sterilized nail with a tip that resembled a screw. He screwed it into the bone and pulled it. A cracking sound issued.

To set the mandible back together, Miguel took another nail-looking instrument with a hook and a hole at its end. He placed a wire into it, put it right into the bone, and then pulled so that the wire looped through and came out the other side, sort of like he was making a sewing stitch. After that, he used forceps to turn the wire, as if tying a piece of thread, until the two bones were secured in the correct position. Next, he cut the wire with a pair of scissors and bent it back. The ends of the wire stitches were visible on the outside of the skin. That was so that after several weeks, when the bones were set and healed back in the correct places, Miguel could easily locate and remove the wire stitches.

Then Miguel explained, "I'm going to wire your upper and lower jaw together, which means you're not going to be able to eat, but I'll explain how to handle that later." He again placed the long nail with the screw end into Luis's cheekbone above the upper lip and pulled the wire through. In this way, piece-by-piece, Miguel wired the bones of Luis's face back into place.

The whole ordeal lasted about three hours. At its completion, Miguel told the patient, "You will not be able to chew for several weeks. Your mouth is wired closed, so you will have to suck everything through a tube. Do you recall that cracking sound that took place on the right side of your cheek? I pulled out one of your teeth. Do you know why I did that? Because I wanted to make a hole there for a tube to go through, so that you can take in liquid nutrition through that hole while your jaw is wired shut. Normally, it's one of the front teeth that gets pulled for such a hole, but I don't know how to build a brand-new tooth at this time, so I've taken out a side tooth. Also, with both your front teeth still intact, you can maintain that handsome smile of yours! Later on, you can have some type of crown or bridge made to fill the hole from the missing side tooth. The important thing—you'll still have a beautiful smile for all the young ladies, and also you'll be able to drink through a tube for the next several weeks."

Miguel winked at Luis, and Luis reached for the man's hand and gave a slight wink in return. Miguel endured the young man's hold for a moment before stepping back.

Mamá was stunned by the whole ordeal, stunned and deeply moved, for Miguel had reorganized the young man's drooping and inconceivable features back into the semblance of his face. He had achieved what everyone else had thought impossible. She was completely convinced that not only would this young man survive, but he'd probably have very little scarring too.

Miguel approached Mamá to ask, "Can you be responsible for finding bamboo? We need several thin tubular pieces to fashion into straws. And, we'll need thicker pieces to make into splints. And let's wait until we have the straws made before we let his mother see him. She needs to understand why the straws are necessary and how to use and clean them. We're going to have to teach her a lot, and she'll likely already be overwhelmed just by looking at her son with all those wires sticking out of his face."

Mamá took it upon herself to make the bamboo straws. She knew it was the tops of bamboo stems that were most thin and pliant, thus most straw-like. She instructed a local workman to locate and cut off the five thinnest bamboo tops he could find, each at about ten inches long.

Once she had these, she stuck a long metal icepick through each hollow, ensuring there were no obstructions on the inside. Once satisfied, with sandpaper pieces of various grades that the carpenter had sold her, she worked on each tube, sanding away at the bamboo ridges to make it into a single smooth piece. Next, she took that same icepick and placed its lower end into a fire so that it became red and hot. She pressed the hot pick into the side of a bamboo tube, about 2½ inches from its end, and then pulled on the ends to slightly wrap the bamboo around the contour of the hot metal. In this way, she created a curve in the bamboo tube, somewhat similar to the way modern-day straws have bendy necks. She ran water through each bamboo straw, and even sucked water through each one, to ensure they worked. Finally, she sterilized them in boiling salt water.

In the meantime, Miguel worked on the patient's fractured arm and leg. First, he had a man with an axe split the thick bamboo pieces Mamá had supplied, making each one into two thick split halves. Miguel then pulled Luis's left arm, gave it a twist, popped it, and reset the fracture. He placed the first pair of thick bamboo halves right up against Luis's forearm, on opposite sides, to make a kind of splint, and wrapped it all tightly with long strips of home-made bandages to keep it immobile. He did the same thing with the leg, this time placing four long bamboo halves around it to work as a splint and wrapped it all tightly. In this way, Luis became almost totally incapacitated. He could not walk, use his left arm, or open his mouth to eat solid food.

After this Miguel went outside and stood against a tree. As he stood in the tree's shade, lit cigarette moving from his hand to his mouth, Mamá approached. Looking him in the eye, she told him, "You're God's gift to our town. You are amazing." Then she gave him a hug.

As a general rule, Miguel Hernández Cabrera did not like to be thanked or praised for his services. Typically, he would walk away when people tried to embrace him or thank him. Often this created an awkward or bewildering situation because the grateful person, or people, wouldn't understand what was happening. This tendency that others found so strange was due to Miguel's extreme feelings of personal failure that he suffered because he failed to earn an official medical and dental license.

However, when Mamá spoke to him and hugged him underneath the tree at the clinic, he remained in place, perhaps stunned or humbled by this shy and dignified young woman's act of bold sincerity.

Soon after he told her, "It's time to bring in the patient's mother. I'm going to need your help."

Mamá went to the main dining hall to fetch the mother. As Miguel had warned, the already distressed woman broke down in violent sobs when she saw her son—bruised, bound, wired, exhausted, and traumatized. She wailed in horror at what she saw, fearful of the wired Frankenstein's monster-like face, "My handsome boy! *Mi hijo guapo! Qué pasó con mi hijo?* What's happened to him?" But at the same time she was aware of how lucky it was that her son was alive, "*Gracias a Dios* that you are alive!" Then just as quickly she'd move back to a state of fear and weeping, "He's going to die. He's going to die, isn't he?"

Because Miguel had prepared her for this outburst of oscillating emotions, Mamá was ready to reassure the woman and dispel her fears. Mamá's own compassionate nature had already prepared her to embrace the woman, hold her hand, and comfort her.

With the mother's hand in hers, Mamá firmly told the woman, "He is not going to die, but you are going to have to work very hard to keep him alive. You see his leg and his arm? He cannot move them because of those fractures. He will need you to assist him until they heal. Also, to save his face, Miguel had to perform surgery on it. He's had to wire Luis's mouth shut. Luis depends on you, on your love and devotion, so that he can become whole again. And you must believe that he will become whole again. His face will heal, and he will become handsome again. You must be strong and ready to assist him."

With the five bamboo straws that Mamá had fashioned in his hands, Miguel entered the clinic, immediately introducing himself to the mother, "*Hola, señora.* My name is Miguel Hernández Cabrera. I'm the one who performed surgery on your son's face and made the splints for his arm and leg. Because I had to wire Luis's mouth shut, he cannot eat solid food for several weeks. In order for him to heal, he's going to need to ingest nutritious liquid meals. You're going to have to give him as much fluid as you can because that's his only option for attaining nutrients. He can drink in the fluid with these bamboo straws that Nena made for him."

To Mamá, he asked, "Can you teach her how—and what—to feed her son?"

"*Claro que sí*. It will be my pleasure," Mamá responded, both to Miguel and the distraught woman.

Mamá showed the woman the hole in the side of Luis's mouth where the end of a straw was to be placed. Next, she explained to the mother that because Luis's jaw, face, and whole neck area were so weak and damaged, he didn't yet have the full capacity to suck up liquids through the straw; instead, the straw would be turned up-wards and connected to a funnel. Luis would have to crane his neck up and back, and the mother would need to slowly and carefully pour the liquid nutrition into the funnel, which would then travel downwards into the straw and continue right down into his mouth and down his throat. It would be her care, plus the funnel and straw and Luis's craning neck, and—of course—gravity that would supply the young man with the needed nutrients. And it would take time, perhaps an hour of slow pouring, three to five times a day, for Luis to receive the necessary amount of calories.

Mamá next led the woman in brainstorming the options for rich and nutritious liquids that she could prepare: coconut water, guava juice, watermelon juice, rice water, mango juice, milk, and broth from fish, shrimp, or chicken. "You can even grind shrimp and fish and add a little broth to it to make a slurry that he can in-gest through the straw."

Mamá instructed the woman on how to clean the straws to make sure they stayed sterile and how to use an icepick or a long piece of wire to rid them of any debris that might clog them.

In this way Mamá tried to move the mother from fear and over-whelm to hope and competence. Even still, the woman was badly shaken. She found her son's face, with wires protruding from the skin in at least ten different areas, foreign and frightening. She found the funnel and straw and craning back of her son's head and neck intimidating and unnatural as well. On his part, Luis found the required craning of his head and neck—for hours at a time every day—very uncomfortable, but he didn't complain because he knew his life depended on it.

For the first four weeks Mamá ended up visiting their household each day and staying for at least two of the feedings to try to normalize the woman's take on her son, provide comfort to them both, and ensure he was taking in enough nutrients and healing well. Miguel, as well, checked in on the patient a few times a week to ensure he was healing properly.

Eventually the day arrived for Miguel to remove the wiring. In a way it was quite similar to the surgery itself. Needles and instruments had to be sterilized. Miguel injected anesthetic in locations all over the young man's face. With the face numb, Miguel then carefully removed each of the many wires, all the while smoking cigarette after cigarette.

Once the wires were out, including the wires that had held the jaws shut, Miguel instructed Luis, "Slowly and carefully, *mijo*, move your jaw." Tentatively Luis opened his mouth and closed it, jutted out his lower jaw and brought it back in.

His mother, Mamá, and Miguel in unison exhaled sighs of relief.

Miguel spooned up some tender pieces of coconut yolk and handed the spoon to Luis who put it in his mouth. Not having eaten anything solid for many weeks, the young man closed his eyes and chewed, evidently savoring the experience. With a big smile on his face, he opened his eyes and made to reach out to touch Miguel's arm, while saying, "*Muchas—*"

But Miguel immediately pulled away.

However, the mother caught him from the other side and wrapped her arms around him, weeping, and declaring, "*Señor, salvaste a mi hijo*. You are a miracle worker, a true gift of God. *Eres bendecido*. I am sorry I doubted. *Muchas gracias.*"

Like an animal in a trap, Miguel endured her embrace and her thanks. But once she'd finished, he was quick to tell her, "You see

Nena there? She came to your home every day for at least a month to make sure he stayed alive and in good spirits and to help you feed him. You thank her. She helped you keep him alive. I only did an operation that needed to be done."

And so began Magdalena Maldonado's life with Miguel Hernández Cabrera, the ever-smoking, alcoholic genius of a man. A man whose fighting mission was to keep people alive in effort to survive his own self-defined tragic and miserable life.

In 1941, when Mamá was almost 20 and Miguel—my father—almost 50, they married. That's when she became Magdalena "Nena" Hernández.

Chapter 2

INJURY

"Eat your meal, Edgar, or else the enchiladas will soon get cold and soggy," my mother chided.

"I know, Mamá, but I lose my appetite when things don't go well with my patients," I explained.

"I know, *mijo*. Last year you lost eight pounds over the death of a trauma patient."

"Yes, I remember."

"Edgar, tell me what's going on. Let's talk," my mother urged.

I explained, "This morning an elderly lady was brought to the ER by her son. She was very frail but had been living on her own. Her son was supposed to be helping her, but he hadn't been checking in on her much. When he finally visited her, she complained about abdominal pain and diarrhea. That's why he brought her to the hospital. Since I was the surgeon on call, I was the one to see her."

"Edgar, I know how serious that can be for an elderly person. Tell me—what did you do? What did you discover?"

"Her body was a disaster. Her kidneys had shut down, and her heart was failing. But her son was very wound up and demanded we do everything to save her. I strongly advised against operating on her, explaining to him that she would likely die from the anesthesia alone—and he went off on me. He started yelling out insults at me and all the staff."

"Oh how difficult—for you, for her, for him . . ." my mother uttered.

"I recommended that we give her fluids and antibiotics before we do anything else, in hopes of reversing the damage to her organs. I told him again that she could certainly die on the operating table, and I did not want to harm her. Even the anesthesiologist told him the same thing. Eventually, we convinced him.

"With fluids and antibiotics, we managed to resuscitate her, and unsurprisingly, she was in a terrible state. She was completely dazed and responded poorly to questions. We took her to the intensive care unit and vigorously supported her. I stayed with her, hoping we could stabilize her, so we could take her to the operating room and give her a better chance of survival. I knew for certain that she needed an operation because her abdomen was very tight."

Though tears had formed in her eyes, my mother told me, "Don't forget to eat too, Edgar."

I took a bite of the enchilada, and while I could intellectually recognize it was amazing—as always my mother had lightly fried each tortilla before stuffing it with shredded chicken, diced onion, a bit of oregano, and a tinge of vinegar, and smothered it in cilantro-laden *salsa verde*—my heart was simply not into eating.

"It's great, Mamá. I just cannot eat," I maintained.

I continued to talk to her about the elderly patient, "So, over her five hours in the hospital, this woman maintained that poor response. Finally, she collapsed and died. And on the one hand, I know that my team and I did all we could, so I don't feel bad about our part. What makes me feel terrible are the son's cruel comments about our care. Yet I didn't dare tell him that her death was likely due to his neglect. Frankly, she looked poorly cared for, as in, no bath for weeks and soiled with her own stool all over her body. He hadn't visited her for weeks. If he had brought her in earlier, probably she'd be fine, but I didn't dare insult him or hurt his feelings or hand a guilt cloud over to him. I held back from pointing this out to him. And it was hard."

"I'm proud that you didn't hurt this man by criticizing him for neglecting his mother. I agree, there's no need to cause him more pain, even in the face of his behavior. I'm proud of you, *mijo*."

Then she went on to say, "What happened to you at the hospital this morning reminds me almost exactly of what happened to your father and me at one time. Let me tell you about it."

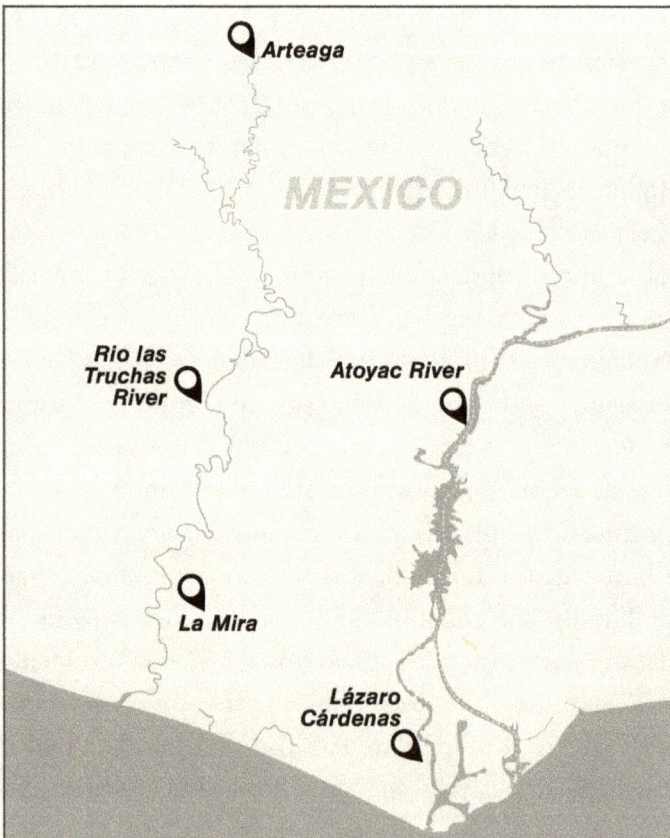

Mamá and Papá had their first child, my oldest sister Surama, in 1942. Pedro was born in 1945 and Jorge in 1947. All the while they continued living in Arteaga where Papá was practicing medicine and dentistry.

A knock on the door, any time of day or night, soon became familiar to Mamá in her married life. It was someone seeking Papá to visit a sick or injured person. Papá's life was a busy one. He was always around and always on call. The people of Arteaga seemed to respect and trust him with their lives, despite his drinking, smoking, and at times awkward behavior.

In 1949, in the night, my father was called to the home of the Ayalas, an influential family in Arteaga. It was Rosa, Mr. Ayala's elderly mother, a woman in her 80s, who was ill. Extremely ill. When Papá reached her, she was confused and complained about abdominal pain. She was pale and her pulse was rapid. Papá learned too that she had been sick for five weeks already. Only now had the Ayalas sought out medical care.

Papá knew there was very little he could do for Rosa, and likely very little any medical team could do for her. He explained, "Doña Rosa is in a very fragile state. While she certainly needs surgery on her abdomen, she's so weak that it's highly likely she won't survive the surgery. It's likely she wouldn't even survive receiving anesthesia for the surgery."

"So what will you do? What will you do to save her?" they asked him.

"What I'm trying to say is that I don't think it is wise to do anything. If you are set on doing something, I recommend you take her to the hospital in Uruapan, but I fear the journey will be very painful for her, and she'll die on the way or at her arrival. The most humane thing is to allow her to die as comfortably and peacefully as possible surrounded by her family at home."

When my father left, he had a heavy heart, knowing that the elderly *señora* would likely die that night because the family had waited so long to seek out medical help.

As he'd expected, within hours, the elderly woman died.

After the funeral the *chisme* began flying around Arteaga:

—"Miguel Hernández certainly proved he's not a real doctor. He said he didn't know how to help Doña Rosa, *la pobrecita*. He just let her die."

—"We were wrong to trust that Miguel Hernández. Apparently, when he doesn't feel like it, he won't help people. That's what he did to the Doña Rosa, may she rest in peace."

—"He should be arrested. Imprisoned. What he did—or rather, didn't do, is criminal. It's murder."

When Papá was out and about, people wouldn't greet him. They ignored him, like he was invisible. He received death threats. When he was working with patients, they and their families treated him coldly.

Mamá and my older siblings were shunned too. Surama and Pedro were insulted and ostracized by other children, and even the teachers, at school.

Mamá decided to visit the Ayalas in effort to rectify the situation. She tried to make them understand that Papá and even her children were being singled out unfairly because of some unfounded gossip. "Let's have a public reconciliation—where you and my husband stand before the people of Arteaga and assure everyone that there's no problem, that you all are in support of one another."

Mamá went from home to home trying to share our family's take on what had happened with Doña Rosa that night. Her efforts, however, were to no avail.

"Miguel, we must leave this town. It's gotten too difficult for Surama and Pedro. I dread Jorge growing up here too. And, frankly, it's become too dangerous for you. Remember General Vargas's friend you treated a few years ago—the man with that terrible rash on his back and arms? I remember him telling us about a village called La Mira that desperately needs a doctor-dentist."

So, they moved to La Mira.

Prior to departing, many of the townspeople begged Papá to stay. They realized what a great loss the people of Arteaga would suffer with his departure.

La Mira, too, is in the state of Michoacán. It was a tropical village that has since joined with other nearby towns and villages, like Playa Azul, to form the big seaport city Lázaro Cárdenas.

La Mira sat by the Pacific Ocean and had two large rivers that ran parallel and framed one of its sides. These rivers emptied into the Pacific. The larger of the two rivers was the great Río Balsas, also known as the Atoyac, the largest river in Mexico and one of the largest rivers in the Americas.

During the rainy season, Río Balsas, as well as the second smaller river, Río Las Truchas or "Trout River" that ran parallel to it, sometimes would overflow, which flooded La Mira. Residents recalled having swum down pathways they regularly walked. Cattle, goats, chickens, horses, trees, homes, and even people got pummeled and dragged away in the swiftly moving floodwaters. Many lives were lost in the floods.

Like all mothers in La Mira, Mamá frequently warned my siblings and me to stay away from the Río Balsas since it was very dangerous, "*Mis hijos, tengan cuidado.* It may look welcoming on a hot day, but it can pull you in and drag you out to the ocean, never to emerge again."

One of the extraordinary occurrences that La Mira inhabitants and visitors alike marveled at was the exploding waters of the great Río Balsas and the smaller Río Las Truchas. At one point, just as they emptied into the Pacific, all three bodies of water—the two rivers and the ocean—met to create an unforgettable, violent show of slamming and smacking. This happened at Melchor Ocampo. It was a spectacular scene, with the whacking and whirling waters from both rivers sending mighty towers of water exploding upwards, about thirty feet in the air, as the rapid, vicious river waters tumbled into the ocean. It was as if a water H-bomb had been detonated.

As La Mira was a tropical place, the prevailing tree, by leaps and bounds, was the palm. There were palm trees everywhere— lining the dirt roads and paths, in backyards, in front yards, lining fields, and clustering in groves. Only once you left La Mira would you start seeing other types of trees. As such, the people of La Mira put the palm to good use. While the walls of homes might have appeared to be made of adobe, in fact, underneath the mud mixture, making up the bulk of the wall, were palm trees and leaves packed together. Mud was used as a kind of mortar to glue the palm pieces together, and the earthen adobe-mixture was applied as a coating, to make a thick and smooth wall that protected families from the heat and rains. The fibers of the palm were woven into circles about a half-inch thick to make *petates*, the bedrolls that people slept on. Benches were made of palm trees, and when your hand brushed against the sides of the bench, you could feel the fuzziness of the skeleton of the palms. Even popsicle sticks were made of palms.

The fishermen of La Mira fashioned small kayaks out of the palms. They'd cut the thickest palm they could find, typically about three feet in diameter. Then they'd painstakingly remove its insides, hollowing out any interior fibers to make a half-moon-shaped space in the interior. With their palm-tree kayaks, nets, and hooks they'd fish on the Río Las Truchas.

For the most part, the men of La Mira were *campesinos*—subsistence farmers. Their standard attire was a white shirt and white pants that tied at the waist with a cord. The clothes were made out of the strong, rough white cotton material also used for making sacks that held grain, fruits, and vegetables. *Campesinos* tended to wear a machete strapped to their hip-area and hanging at their side. At sundown each day, the *campesinos* would walk home from the fields, often in single file. Their silhouettes, with their machetes protruding off at one side, were striking, like a line of canoes, each with a paddle dangling off to a side.

When Papá, Mamá, and my older siblings moved to La Mira, Mamá's parents, Andres and Marcelina Maldonado, along with her sisters, Dominga and Maria, moved there also. As a *campesino* himself, Andres, or Abuelo, as we grandchildren called him, wore the traditional attire. Papá, however, maintained his urban apparel—suits, button-down shirts, and hats.

The kids of La Mira also wore clothes made of the white sackcloth material. On their feet, the children wore sandals called *huaraches*. This was the clothing my siblings and I were accustomed to.

Mamá, my aunts, and my grandmother wore the traditional women's garb—an ankle-length loose cotton dress with a square collar and billowy short sleeves. The cotton dresses came in brilliant colors—green, turquoise, magenta, orange. The women embroidered exquisite arrays of flowers, also of all colors, onto the front of these cotton dresses.

While my family first moved to La Mira, Papá also bought a small coconut planation outside the village. This land received run-off water from the Río Balsas, making it ideal for the growing of various fruit trees. Coconuts, guavas, mangos, and pineapples flourished on the land. Abuelo had a small plot of land too on which he raised corn, jicama, tomatillos, watermelons, and varieties of green chiles that he sold in La Mira's small outdoor *mercado*.

Fruits, vegetables, and seafood—lobster, shrimp, crab, oysters, clams, trout, *huachinango, pargo, corvine,* and *langostina*, a giant variety of shrimp with huge claws—and corn tortillas, pinto beans, and rice were the standard cuisine of the people of La Mira. Chicken, beef, pork, and milk were considered luxuries.

Because La Mira was rural and remote, it did not have electricity or running water. There was a generator the townspeople put to use sparingly, only for special events. For example, during some holidays, the generator was used to power lights in the *zócolo*, or town square, at night. Telegraphs and telephones hadn't yet reached La Mira. The written letter was the means of long-distance communication.

Here, in La Mira, Papá, Mamá, Surama, Pedro, and Jorge made their home. Within a few months of arriving, another child was born—me—in 1950. In 1952 Lupe was born, Asunción in 1954, Reyna in 1956, and Manuel in 1958.

Just as in Arteaga, where knocks on the door at any time of day or night was the norm, the same soon became true in La Mira. However, now that Mamá and Papá had their own thriving bevy of children, sometimes those knocks were not about a fellow villager in need of medical assistance; they were about one of us who'd landed an injury.

One fine day, seven-year-old Jorge and I, at five, were returning home from our young boys' adventures. As was not uncommon, we noticed a tall, dark mountain out in a field off the path. It was a mound of manure.

"*Hermano, crees que yo puedo saltar sobre eso?*" Jorge inquired.

"No. Probably not," I replied.

At that Jorge set out sprinting. He took a mighty leap—and ended up landing right in the middle of the manure mound. However, as was the practice, earlier that morning a farmer had set the manure on fire. Burning manure ended up making it into a dust that made fabulous fertilizer. So Jorge landed not in the middle of a mountain of manure, but in the middle of a stack of scorching dust and burning coals.

"Awwwwwwwwwww-eeeeeeeeeeeee!" Jorge shrieked.

Arnoldo, a young man who was working nearby, heard the screams and rushed to pull Jorge out. Jorge's shrieking continued. From his knees to his ankles, the skin of his legs had been cooked and had simply peeled away. Strands of tissue dangled in clumps and tendrils.

Arnoldo raced to the village with Jorge in his arms, wailing, and I ran on his heels. We were running to our home.

I remember hollering, "*Jorge se quemó! Jorge se quemó!* Jorge got burned!"

Abuelo, heard the shrieking. "*Que pasa?* What's going on?" he inquired.

He quickly determined what had happened when he saw Jorge in Arnoldo's arms. Jorge was shivering and drowsy. Out of it. Exposed pink flesh with drooping strands of tissue made up his lower legs. There was the smell of burnt flesh.

Abuelo joined us sprinters.

Mamá, who'd heard the commotion, was standing at the front door. When she saw Jorge in Arnoldo's arms with Abuelo and me trailing close behind, she uttered, "*Dios, ayúdame. Dios, ayúdame.*"

And then she got down to business, instructing, "Arnoldo, set Jorge on the table. Papá, get me sheets and hot water."

Abuelo asked, "*Donde esta Miguel?* Where's Miguel?"

"In Capilcan. He went there to see a sick patient," Mamá answered. Capilcan was a village about an hour away walking or twenty minutes by horse. There were only paths, no roads, to reach it.

Mamá went on to say, "Don't worry. I know what to do."

Once at home with our mother, Jorge's screams subsided into tears, dramatic tears. She gave him two spoonfuls of a liquid medication that Papá would give his patients. "This is to ease the pain, *mijo*," she explained.

Mamá comforted my brother and washed his wounds. Gently she cleaned away the debris and dirt, extricating grass, rocks, charcoal sediment, and dead skin to expose the raw, pink flesh underneath that wept blood and fluids. Next, she cleansed the vulnerable flesh with warm salt water, the sting from which caused Jorge to screech and yelp afresh.

"Now we will dress the wounds. This will feel uncomfortable, Jorge, but we must do it to protect your vulnerable legs, so they can heal," she told him. She took long segments of fabric that Abuelo had cut and sterilized to make into bandages and carefully wrapped them around each lower leg, covering each once completely. All the while, Mamá spoke softly to him, trying to comfort him and ease his fear and apparent agony.

After a few hours, she told Jorge, "*Mijo*, it's time to change your dressings. It will be painful, but it's what we must do to ensure your legs heal properly—and not become infected. Let's give you some more medication to help with the pain."

Even still, because the cloth bandages had adhered to his wounds, removing them first entailed saturating them with warm salt water and then slowly extracting them from the wounds' outer layers. Again, Jorge experienced severe stinging when Mamá gently applied the salt water first to remove the bandages and next to clean. Finally she applied more bandages. Jorge cried in agony—as if re-experiencing the trauma afresh. Healing him would entail a lot of effort and would cause him a lot of pain.

When Papá returned from Capilcan, after examining Jorge, he remarked to Mamá, "*Muy bien*. You did great work. My assistant is learning well," and he winked. He went on to prepare an emollient cream made up of powdered antibiotics, a pinch of starch, and a spoonful of lard.

With the ever-present cigarette in his mouth, Papá proceeded to apply a smooth layer of the cream to Jorge's burnt lower legs. During the application, a segment of ash fell from the end of the cigarette onto my brother's cream-slathered leg. Though he was suffering from the awful burns, Jorge managed to giggle.

Surprised and delighted at Jorge's giggle, Papá jokingly remarked, "Yes, *mijo*, what's wrong with a little ash?"

Jorge then managed to smile at our father's kind words.

However, our mother did not smile. Not amused, she shot our father a stern look, and he immediately began wiping away the bit of ash. Jorge managed a third smile but then quickly grimaced, for the pain was very intense.

Over the next six weeks Mamá took charge of Jorge's care. Twice a day she performed the procedure of removing the bandages, cleaning the burn areas, applying the special cream, and reapplying the bandages. For my seven-year-old brother it was utter torture, and he'd sob and holler in distress, but Mamá never lost her patience. She always worked carefully and offered Jorge sweet comfort, for she understood how confusing and painful the twice-daily ordeal was for him.

Because both of his lower legs were so thoroughly burned, tender, and in pain, Jorge couldn't move around easily, so Mamá carried him from place to place. When he needed, she'd carry him to the outhouse. He spent a lot of time lying on a *petate* with his legs propped up for comfort. Mamá encouraged me, my sisters, and brothers to visit him or play in the room near him, so he'd not feel isolated.

Prior to Jorge's injury, Mamá herself had been enduring a terrible toothache. She had cracked a tooth, and Papá planned to patch it with mercury, but the mercury had yet to arrive from Uruapan. Because La Mira was so remote, really only accessible from a dirt road approximately 50 miles long, that in rainy season was impassable, it was expected that deliveries would take a while. Luckily it wasn't rainy season, but they still anticipated it would take around six weeks for the mercury to arrive. Mamá's goal was to hold on for six weeks because she really wanted to keep the tooth.

Initially the cracked tooth area was simply uncomfortable and very sensitive to temperature extremes when she was eating or drinking. Over time, though, an infection developed in the pulp of the tooth that, over more time, spread to the surrounding gums. Though she didn't discuss the pain she was feeling, it was evident to the rest of us. She emitted low moans as she went about her housework. She often would hold her jaw and press it with her hand to try to relieve the discomfort. Always a dedicated Christian, Mamá prayed even more often, asking God to give her the strength and patience to bear the agony. Because of Papá's serious substance addictions, Mamá refused to take painkillers stronger than aspirin.

All the while, she stayed dedicated to Papá, us children, taking caring of the household, and assisting Papá with his work when necessary. And, of course, caring for Jorge. With one baby wrapped to her back and another wrapped in her *rebozo* on her chest, she performed her duties—sweeping the compacted mud floor of the house, fetching water for the household, hand washing our clothing, preparing the fire for cooking, going to the *mercado* each day to buy food, cooking three meals each day, and redressing and cleaning Jorge's burnt lower legs.

At six weeks the mercury still hadn't arrived. By this time, Mamá's cheek was very swollen. She could no longer eat solid foods. She would smile and laugh with us children, comforting us and encouraging us, and not showing the debilitating pain she was experiencing. We overheard Papá talking to her about her deteriorating health. We were worried too.

"Nena, it's not wise to wait any longer. Your overall health is decreasing from this tooth infection. You've lost a noticeable amount of weight. Your complexion is off. I'm worried. We can't wait for the mercury. It's time we pull the tooth," he advised. But our mother refused, confident that in just a day the mercury would arrive.

After eight weeks and no mercury, Papá discovered that an abscess had developed on her neck, which required draining.

"I'm going to Uruapan myself to get the mercury. I'll return in four days," he informed her, but she balked.

"Miguel, what if Jorge develops an infection when you're gone? It's too much of a risk. He could die."

"Nena, you are caring for our son so carefully and diligently, I am almost certain that won't happen. However, I do worry about what will happen to you because you are the one with the serious infection," he replied.

With the ever-present cigarette in hand, Papá downed a shot of tequila and then stood to inform Mamá, "It's time we extract the tooth. You know how this procedure works because you've helped me do it many times over the years. Let me get ready. This time you're the patient."

This is how it worked. First Jorge, Surama, Lupe, Pedro, Asunción, and I hugged our mother. Meanwhile Papá placed a bucket of hot, steaming water onto the table. In it he poured a cup of alcohol and a spoonful of salt, and mixed the contents. On a similar table to his left he had a syringe with a long needle that he'd just removed from a small pot filled with hot water and alcohol. He loaded the syringe with anesthetic.

He explained, "I'm going to stick this needle into the side of your jaw to numb it." She didn't even flinch when he injected her. Instead, immediately afterwards, she turned to us children and smiled, wanting to ensure that we didn't feel scared.

Papá took a swig from a tequila bottle then a long drag from his vibrating cigarette. After that, he asked, "Ready?"

"Yes, Miguel, do it."

At that he punctured the lemon-sized red abscess on her left mandible. Puss came rushing out. He irrigated the area with hot salt water and packed it with some cheesecloth in order to stop the oozing of blood. After that, he pulled out the packing and reapplied it again.

"I'm sorry to have to do this to you, Nena."

She waved her right hand twice as if to say, "Don't talk about it. Proceed. I'm ready."

She looked at Jorge and me and winked in an attempt at decreasing our anxiety and assuring us that she was okay.

After placing a clamp onto Mamá's tooth, our father pulled, extracting the tooth.

In quick response, Jorge hobbled out of the room, sobbing. I made to hug Mamá but ended up crying and fleeing the room too.

Papá took up a clean cotton cloth and proceeded to dab at Mamá's face, carefully cleaning it. Her eyes were closed. Her face muscles finally relaxed.

Later, Mamá and Papá found Jorge crying on a *petate*. "*Todo es mi culpa*. It's all my fault," he blubbered to them.

"*No, mijo, eso no es verdad*," Papá told him, "It's not your fault. *Es simplemente parte de la vida*."

"*Tu padre esta correcto*. It's the will of God that we're all alive and together," Mamá added, holding my brother in a close embrace.

Chapter 3

Mothers and Children

It was around 7:00 a.m. when I entered the house. Mamá was sitting with her Bible. Her Bible was like her third hand, or second heart, and had been that way for decades, even before she'd learned to read it.

"*Buenos días*, Edgar," she began, "I thought we were having lunch together today?"

"Mamá, breakfast will be sort of like lunch for me. I've been up for the past 24 hours, at the hospital, and I haven't had a decent meal in all that time. I'm beat," I explained. This was in 1983 when I was finishing my surgical training and working long hours.

Mamá was up and going, even before I finished speaking. Frying pan out and warming on the stove with a touch of oil in it. Tortillas, eggs, tomatoes, onions, and peppers gathered on the counter. Cutting board in place and sharp knife in hand.

"Sit while I prepare *huevos rancheros*," she told me.

Huevos rancheros—just what my body and soul craved: a fried egg sitting on a lightly fried corn tortilla. All that topped with my mother's special spicy tomato salsa—chopped fresh jalapeños, onions, and tomatoes combined with Ortega brand green chiles, also diced. My mother included a healthy portion of black beans with it too. *Delicioso*.

I should note that in Michoacán, Mamá used turtle eggs when making *huevos rancheros* because chicken eggs were rare. However, the opposite was true here in the USA.

"What is it? What's wrong? I can tell it's more than just being tired," she remarked as she diced the vegetables.

"You're right. I feel stressed. Sad. A bit frustrated," I admitted.

"*Dime. Estoy escuchando.*"

"A beautiful mother had twins, but one of them died during delivery. At the same time, she lost her uterus from a rupture. It was devastating. Bloody and painful, and also just sad."

"Are you delivering babies, Edgar?"

"No, Mamá, I got called in because after the hysterectomy, they couldn't stop her bleeding, so they needed a surgeon. I had to ligate two major vessels in the pelvis in order to stop the life-threatening hemorrhage. Plus, this lady has a breast infection and can't breastfeed the surviving twin."

"How difficult. How terrible. For her and her family—and for you and the staff. *Mijo*, it is very sad. Will she be okay? How is her family?"

"They're doing okay, considering."

"Did you talk to her personally?"

"Yes, Mamá. I spoke with her about the reason for the surgery."

"Will you be seeing her again?"

"Yes."

"Good. Please hold her hand because she's suffering. I know you probably already know this, *hijo*, but for a mother, the death of a child is practically insurmountable. We who have lost a child avoid discussing it because it's so devastating. Immediately there's often a severe depression, and over time it's a wounded mind, body, and heart. An aching echo of all that was lost. All that could have been. A scar that never fades."

In Arteaga, Mamá and Papá had another baby, Edmundo, born after Jorge. However, at 17 months old, Edmundo died. His cause of death wasn't known. Mamá never discussed Edmundo. She was too heart-broken—even decades later. To others it might seem like he'd never existed, but she never forgot him.

In rural Mexico in the mid-20th century, the death of children was not that uncommon. Considering the scarcity of antibiotics and doctors, people's general lack of education about the spread of infection, and people's tendency to believe in myths and old wives' tales, the prevalence of young children dying during that time period is not so surprising, but still bitterly upsetting.

It was March 1952, and Mamá and her friend Concha, with their *rebozos* covering their heads, walked in the group of mourners. It was already the sixth funeral for a child that year, and the year was only in its third month. The second child had died in her sleep, and no one, not even my father, could determine the cause of death. The other child deaths, including this one, were due to scorpion bites. In our area scorpion bites were the prevailing cause of death in little children but not so much in adults, although on occasion they were lethal for adults too.

Several of the mourners carried empty glass cola bottles now full of petroleum. The local myth was that the way to cure scorpion bites was to bathe the person who was bitten in petroleum and that would rid their body of the poison. My parents tried to educate people that this wasn't true, but many folks clung to the belief.

Some of the mourners carried candles, some carried flowers, and others, including Mamá and Concha, carried baskets of food: tortillas, *tamales*, *empanadas*, and *gorditas*, a very thick tortilla that's cut in the middle and filled with beans. As was customary, the funeral was held in the home of the family of the deceased child. From a distance, the home shone from the light of the many candles placed in its small windows. The sound of melancholic chords—an off-key violin—reached the mourners' ears.

Outside the adobe casita the male mourners gathered. They were sipping glasses of spiked punch and eating. Inside, atop the kitchen table, sat a tiny wooden box, about three feet by 1½ feet. Surrounding the child's coffin stood many more lit candles. Flowers of multiple varieties—cactus flowers, roses, bougainvillea, oleander, lemon and orange tree blossoms, and river and pond lilies—adorned the room, as well as palm branches that people used to sit on.

The women gathered inside the casita with the grieving mother. Mamá noticed women wiping themselves with petroleum-dabbed rags. They believed this protected them from any remaining poison from the scorpion that could be tainting the atmosphere.

Standing in the corner of the room of mourners, with eyes fixed on the tiny coffin and a violin in his hands, stood Santos Ortiz. Santos Ortiz was the town hermit, bogeyman, and mystic all rolled into one. He hadn't exactly spoken in years. He did not work. He lived alone in a small hut of mud and sticks he'd built himself. He showed up at a different home each day, and the family in the home—though most were afraid of him—gave him food and water.

What he did do was play the violin—and chant—at the funerals of children.

And that's what he was doing at this funeral.

"*Ángel, ángelito del cielo, ángel de los ángeles, ángel de Dios, ángel del Cielo, ángelito inocente, miembro del Cielo visitante a la Tierra, que no olvidas, que las alas te levantan al Cielo,*" Santos Ortiz rasped and warbled. His chants were always about God's tiny angels, angels briefly visiting a family and then ready to return to God and Heaven. He repeated the dirge several times, accompanying it with his crying violin.

He didn't play actual tunes on the violin. Instead, Santos Ortiz made his violin weep dejected arrangements. His violin prayed, shouted, whispered, and purred beautiful, angry, begging, haunting, and dissonant soundscapes.

Santos Ortiz was always the first to arrive and the last to depart at a child's funeral. He preferred standing in a corner, not speaking—except to chant—rarely smiling, and not making eye contact with people. He tended to keep his eyes on the coffin.

One of the few people who never showed fear or distrust around him was Mamá. She never simply handed him a plate of food when he showed up at our doorway. She invited him into the house and had him sit at the table and eat with all of us. When his white sackcloth clothing was terribly dirty or in need of repair, she was the one to wash or mend it, or replace a worn-out garment. At funerals Mamá made up a plate of food for Santos Ortiz and stood next to him, encouraging him to pause from his music and eat.

In turn, she was one of the few whom Santos Ortiz trusted. He dared to look her in the face. He sometimes would nod his head in acknowledgement of her. He even spoke to Mamá on occasion, referring to her as an "*ángel de Dios*." Mamá would smile warmly at him in response.

Mamá took it upon herself to organize support for any mother who had lost a child, and this was particularly important when there were a number of children in the family of the deceased. Mamá recognized a mother needed time to mourn, so she would organize the women in the community in shifts to keep the mother's house going, preparing food, collecting water, caring for the children, cleaning.

One time in the kitchen Papá found two large glass containers of milk. He was about to pour some into his coffee. "Wait, Miguel. I don't think that milk is for you," Abuelo told him. Apparently, it was for several babies in town whose mothers couldn't offer them milk because the mothers were suffering from cholera. Mamá had found women who were breastfeeding and organized them to donate breast milk to these children in need.

Of course, even my siblings and I were susceptible to unexpected injury, disease, or even death. The one difference was that our parents were more educated on how to appropriately deal with most illness and injury. When I was very young and accompanying Abuelo to the seashore, a scorpion stung me in the hand. In response I passed out, and my body began convulsing. While locals pressed Abuelo to bathe me in petroleum, he refused and instead carried me to where the waves crashed onto the beach. The ocean water cooled my feverish body, and the convulsions eventually subsided. Miraculously I survived, but Abuelo was very shaken.

Women dying from complications related to childbirth was the leading cause of death in Mexico in the 1930s, '40s, and '50s, with postpartum sepsis the main culprit. What this infection entails is a dangerous bacteria infecting blood vessels and preventing them from constricting. With the blood vessels dilated, the blood pressure plummets to dangerously low levels—and eventually causes death. With antibiotics and excellent medical care, postpartum sepsis is treatable. However, in Mexico in those decades, both of those were scarce.

It was postpartum sepsis that had killed my father's first two wives. And, in La Mira, even under Papá's care, women dying due to postpartum sepsis (or other complications from childbirth) was not uncommon. Many children lived with their grandparents because their mothers had contracted the lethal infection.

One very early morning, before dawn when it was still dark out, Mamá woke to the noise of urgent knocking on our door.

"Yes. Tell me," she declared as she opened the door.

"We need Miguel. It's Chucho's wife."

"We're on our way."

Like Abuelo and most of the men of the village, Chucho was a farmer. But Chucho was also a chief of sorts among La Mira's farmers. The local ranchers and farmers consulted with Chucho before making business deals. They respected him wholeheartedly. He knew the middlemen buyers from the nearby towns and cities. These were the buyers that would purchase crops, meat, and produce from La Mira growers to sell to other companies and businesses either to sell or to further process. Chucho knew everything about these buyers—their needs, their prices, and how to handle them—so local growers first consulted him before making any deals.

Often, all the farmers and the ranchers would meet with him at his home to discuss strategies for business. He talked about pricing and the time for selling crops, advising, "When we are together, we are in control. When we falter, the buyers will pull us apart." Chucho was ahead of his time in this regard.

By the time my parents arrived, Chucho's wife had already died. It was postpartum sepsis. Chucho was devastated. She'd died after giving birth to twin daughters, so now his daughters had no mother and he had no wife. Plus, he had lost his only two sons years earlier, one from an infection and the other from falling off a wild horse.

Though Mamá had seven children of her own, she cared for Chucho's twin girls, Andrea and Carlina, as if they were her own. My parents insisted that Chucho and the babies move into our home. And for five years, we all lived together in the same household. Mamá made sure the twins had sufficient milk, and she nurtured them, ensuring they received lots of love and attention. It was only after five years, when Chucho decided to move back into his own home with the twins, that Asunción and I realized that Andrea and Carlina weren't our sisters.

Mamá knew that she was actually blessed to have carried and given birth to all her children without having endured any complications. Of course, Edmundo's death at 17 months was always devastating for her. She did (eventually) have ten children.

Reyna's was a memorable birth. It was on January 6, 1958, a particularly cold, rainy, and dreary day, that Mamá gave birth to Reyna. Asunción was only 2½ at the time but very aware that because of the new little creature, her own life had somehow changed, probably not for the best.

My 2½-year-old sister had an idea. "Mamá, why don't you take that *chiquilla* outside and down the road? Maybe she'll walk away and find a home," Asunción suggested.

Smiling, Mamá unwrapped the blanket from around Reyna's little body to show it to Asunción. "*Mija*," Mamá began, "do you see these tiny legs and feet?"

"*Sí*," Asunción begrudgingly admitted.

"She is so small. She cannot walk."

"Hmph," Asunción muttered in response.

"Will you go outside and call Edgar in for me?" Mamá then asked Asunción.

"But, Mamá, it is very cold outside. And it's raining," Asunción quickly replied.

"Yes, that's true. I don't think your baby sister would like to be outside either. What do you think?"

"Mamá, that's true," admitted Asunción.

In this way, Mamá taught Asunción empathy, something she herself had in abundance.

Chapter 4

FAITH AND PERSISTENCE

My mother held my suit jacket in one hand and scanned it for lint. With her free hand she picked off a few stray bits. Then she inspected its buttons, ensuring that each was secure. After hanging it in the closet, she swiped her hands down it twice to press out any possible wrinkles.

Once the jacket was hanging to her satisfaction, she turned to me to ask, "How are you, Edgar? Are you hungry?"

"Yes, indeed. *Tengo mucha hambre.* What does the celebrated chef have for the daily special?"

"A delicious beef soup and fried shredded beef tacos with a sauce of fresh green tomatoes."

"Fresh tomatoes? Not canned?"

"Edgar, the neighbors have given me some beautiful green tomatoes from their garden. I like the way the sauce tastes when the tomatoes are not ripe."

"Incredible. I'm looking forward to it, Mamá."

"While I'm heating up the food, I'm going to get you some *agua de tamarindo.*"

For those who don't know, *tamarindo*, or tamarind, is a pod-like fruit. It looks sort of like an oversized peanut in its shell. When you open the brown pod, you find big seeds and an orangey-brown sticky pulp. Like many Latinos, my mother makes a drink from it by piercing a few pods and dropping them in a pot of water. She boils the whole thing to make a brown broth. Then she mixes in more water and lots of sugar. After that she chills it, so when it's ready to serve it makes a sweet, tangy, tart, cold beverage.

"What's going on with your work lately, Edgar?" she asked after setting a tall glass of *agua de tamarindo* before me.

"Today a middle-aged man came to see me for a follow-up visit. Earlier he had a tumor in his cheek, so I had to remove half his face. Then he had to get a lot of reconstruction done."

Always intrigued and concerned for others' well-being, she asked, "And how is he handling things?"

"He seems good. The reconstructive surgeons took living skin and tissue from the interior of his thigh and covered the cheek area with it. Although he has an obvious scar on half his face and some of his neck, he's grateful to be alive."

Then I went on to ask my mother, "You told me the incredible story of how you and my father worked together to heal the young man who fell from the cliff and severely damaged his face. Did you work with other patients that needed facial work?"

"Oh yes, *mijo*. Yes, indeed. I recall facial surgeries as well as important dental work"—she paused for a moment, deep in thought—"When I reflect on that healing work, something I realize is that it always brought us back to faith. Never lose faith in what you do, *hijo*. As a surgeon, you are a great healer, and faith in what you do is paramount in the outcomes of your patients. Let me tell you some of our experiences, so you can see what I mean."

She told me about an older man from our village, Señor Soto, who had a small pimple on the lower left side of his face. Señor Soto decided to visit my father when he noticed the small pimple was unusually sore. However, Papá was out visiting a patient, so Mamá advised him, "Please, Señor Soto, return tomorrow morning. Miguel will be here to see you. It's very important he sees you because it's possible that a dangerous infection could happen." Before saying goodbye, she even gave the man some antibiotic anointment to put on the pimple.

Señor Soto did end up returning, but not the next day. Instead, it was ten days later. The small pimple had grown in size from about a quarter of an inch to 3½ inches, and it seemed to be consuming much of his chin and part of his neck. The tissue there had turned black.

Without hesitation my father informed Señor Soto, "You have a tetanus infection with multiple layers of bacteria eating your skin. It's very dangerous. I'm very sorry to have to tell you this, but it's most likely fatal. There's little that can be done. This is very unfortunate."

My father, my mother, and Señor Soto were shocked and grief-stricken.

With all the strength she could muster, my mother held one of Señor Soto's hands and said to both him and Miguel, "The Lord will guide us to your survival. We'll treat you with antibiotic drinks and ointments. We'll clean it daily. We will not give up, and we will not leave you alone. We must be persistent. We must have faith."

My father looked at my mother and reflected, "Do you remember how I regularly scraped General Vargas's leg wound to rid it of its festering infection? That's what we'll try with Señor Soto's face. We will do some deep scraping and cleaning."

Mamá started the sterilization process. She got a big vat of boiling water mixed with salt and alcohol going. In it, she set a metal canister that would hold the equipment to be sterilized. She also sterilized syringes, needles, and bandages.

After Papá anesthetized Señor Soto's infected area, he scraped away all the black, dead tissue that covered half of the left side of his face all the way down his neck and collarbone. Next Papá plastered the area with a mixture of lard and antibiotics, which was mainly sulfa drugs and tetracycline powder, the only antibiotics they had, and a pinch of starch. Finally, he bandaged the area. The bandages were held in place with a string that went over and around the face and neck. Papá instructed Señor Soto to return the next day for another treatment.

To Mamá, Papá confessed, "Nena, this is an infection made up of a combination of deadly organisms: strep, clostridia, and tetanus. These organisms are probably going to eat that man alive—and fast. Without treatment the death rate is almost 100 percent, and even with treatment, it is likely he'll die. I'm only telling you this to prepare you for the pain and gruesomeness you are going to witness when he returns for more treatments."

"But, Miguel, we must try, *sí*? We can't just give up."

"*Sí, estoy de acuerdo*. We won't give up, but still—we must prepare ourselves and him."

Mamá took it upon herself to treat Señor Soto's wounds every day: scrape, clean, apply antibiotic ointment, and bandage the area. However, after three days, the infection spread out almost twelve inches across his face and also down his neck, and it was beginning to descend down into his upper chest.

Mamá was discouraged, but she didn't give up. She did all she could to stay positive with Señor Soto and at the same time keep us children away, so we wouldn't have to witness his evident suffering.

After two weeks, the infection ceased worsening. After a month, it actually seemed to be improving. After seven weeks, Papá was confident that Señor Soto would heal and live. That's when he decided the wound was ripe to receive slivers of skin to promote healing. He took quarter-inch bits of skin from the man's chest and placed them onto the wound to make a kind of skin graft. Though

Señor Soto from then on sported an awful scar, he was alive. It was a miracle.

Everyone in La Mira had been praying hard for Señor Soto to survive. Mamá had prayed with his wife and children. Everyone had prayers for him. Mamá led me and my brothers and sister in prayer too. We prayed that the treatment would be vibrant, that it would penetrate his tissues, and that it would turn from being a man-made treatment to a divine one. God heard us and delivered on our prayers.

I was six years old when I pointed out to my mother, "Those men don't have any teeth."

"*Eso es correcto, mijo.* Did you know that all the people in La Mira depend on them? They are very important men. Every day they bring wood, *leña*, here to sell to us. Tell me, why is *leña* so important?"

"*Leña* provides the energy for cooking. Without *leña*, we can't eat," I answered matter-of-factly.

In La Mira, as was true in most households in rural Mexico, the cooking was done on wood-burning stoves. Mamá used about six pieces of *leña* each day, two for each meal. Each morning she'd wake around 5 a.m. to start the logs. You see, you can't just light the *leña* and start cooking. First you must turn it into coals, which takes around 45 minutes. Once the logs become coals, then they are ready to be used for cooking.

As the logs were getting heated into coals, Mamá used that time for other chores. She'd sweep the hard-packed dirt floor of the kitchen. She'd take the *nixtamal* she'd made the night before and grind it. *Nixtamal* is the term for corn kernels that have been soaked for hours in hot water so that they become puffy, looking sort of like soggy pieces of popcorn. Each morning, Mamá would take a heavy stone rolling pin-type instrument to crush, smash, and grind the *nixtamal* on a *metate* to transform it into a dough that's called *masa*.

When the coals were at the right temperature, she'd place a hot plate, similar to a griddle, on top of the porcelain stove frame. Next, she'd pinch off chunks of *masa*, press them into flat, round disc-like shapes, and cook them on the hot plate, so her family could enjoy corn tortillas for breakfast. She actually made corn tortillas in this way three times a day, for every meal.

The surface of the hot plate was large enough to also accommodate a pan for heating beans at the same time that the tortillas were cooking on it. Mamá typically scrambled three eggs and mixed them with the beans. This, along with *café con leche*, one-third coffee and two-thirds milk, was the customary breakfast in our household. The portions were small, but that was normal for our family.

It's true what I'd said—for rural Mexican families like ours to consume cooked food, we depended on the *leña* that the Lencho men, a father and his two sons, brought to our village each day to sell. Granted, sometimes farmers would carry home a bundle of *leña* they'd gathered after finishing up their daily work in the fields. The problem was that after a long day's work, a load of *leña* was the last thing they wanted to have on their backs. That's why most families bought *leña* from the Lenchos.

My mother had been concerned about the Lenchos for a while. At this point it had been about a year since she had urged them to let my father examine their teeth. His conclusion: "They have a condition called *hipoplasia del esmalte* [enamel hypoplasia], meaning the enamel that covers and protects their teeth from erosion is defective." As a result, the father lost all his teeth at around 20 years old, and by the time each of the sons turned 20, the same happened to them.

"Señor Lencho, let me talk to Miguel. He knows dentists in Morelia that can make dentures for you and your sons. What do you think?" Mamá suggested.

"Nena, I would appreciate it very much. Really, it's my sons that I worry about. Currently, they aren't attracting any girlfriends, so they'll never be able to get married. This means I'll never have any grandchildren. I'm going to admit something to you—I am incredibly envious of your father and how he has so many grandchildren. I want that too. Unless my sons have teeth—or dentures—I don't think I'll ever get to enjoy grandchildren," he confided.

"Yes, grandchildren are indeed a delight to *mi papá*. You deserve to enjoy them too, señor. I will talk with Miguel, and we will see what we can do," she told him.

Their enamel problem went beyond just their teeth. Their faces were unusually thin and slim, and their skeletons looked weak. To aid them, my mother took large calcium pills ordered especially for them, ground up the pills, and mixed the powdered calcium with rice water. The Lenchos would drink this special beverage as a supplement. Every Friday there would be a stack of wood in front of our house that we children would carry back to the kitchen for later use. That was their way of saying thank you.

To get the Lenchos' dentures made, my mother had to convince my father to accompany them to Morelia to get dental measurements. Because La Mira was so remote, a journey to Morelia took 2½ days, in just one direction. Because my mother was so determined, my father took the time and effort to make the many voyages to Morelia with these men to ensure the fittings were correct.

After four years and several long journeys to Morelia and back with Papá, the three Lencho men finally got their dentures. It took a lot of faith, planning, and persistence on everyone's parts, but eventually it happened.

After they got their dentures, the father and his two sons dared to smile. And later, the two sons got married and had families of their own—that's when Señor Lencho became an *abuelo*, and his smile became broad, proud, and full of joy.

Formulating liquid medicines—similar to how my mother ground up the calcium supplements and mixed it with rice water for the Lencho men—was among her regular duties with my father's medical and dental work. Regularly they would receive shipments of tetracycline powder and bags of sulfa antibiotic, and it was my mother's job to make these into liquid antibiotics. She recalled patients complaining, "Doesn't your husband have anything that tastes better? This powered liquid is disgusting," or "I'd rather die than drink this awful antibiotic."

She was careful to show concern and firmness in her response: "This medicine is what is available here. Yes, the antibiotic tastes terrible, but it's going to cure your problem. Without it, you'll not do well." If the person continued to complain, she would remind them, "You are certainly welcome to take a truck to the city and seek medical or dental care there."

Mamá experimented on her own, trying to make liquid mixtures that tasted better. She tried mixing the antibiotics with coconut water, *tamarindo* water, pineapple, guava—almost anything to improve the taste. It was difficult to hide the bitterness of the drugs, but she tried.

A crucial aspect of making the liquid antibiotics was timing. Papá taught Mamá that it had to be ingested within 24 to 48 hours, or else it would spoil. So, she had to be very organized, determining which patients needed which medication mixtures, the amounts, and the times particular patients would be available to pick them up. All the while, she had to make sure the mixtures stayed sterile, which was very tricky in such a small house with so many of us young children as well as patients coming in and out.

Keeping all of the medical and dental equipment and supplies clean was paramount. Dust, fungus, germs—there were so many contaminants to guard against. Even before Mamá used them to hold the mixtures, the individual glass jars with their metal lids had to be in stock, on hand, and very clean. She would sterilize them in boiling water, salt, and alcohol before filling them with the liquid antibiotic mixtures. They kept hundreds of those jars in the bedroom, and we children knew never to touch them.

My father was all about healing. Logistics were not his thing. That meant it was up to my mother to do inventory. Though she couldn't read or write and hadn't learned math formally, she was in charge of inventory and money. When the fabric salesman came to La Mira once every few months, Mamá had to figure out how many rolls of fabric they would need to buy from him to make into bandages that would last until his next visit. She had to make sure they had enough space in their metal containers to store the fabric as cleanly and dust-free as possible. Tetracycline, sulfa, lard, starch, syringes, needles, glass bottles, alcohol, scalpels, scissors, mercury—there was a number of things to keep up with.

Paying for supplies was always a problem. Papá tended to be oblivious to money—both the cost of supplies as well as collecting payment for his services from patients. Many payments were made in goods—bags of corn, a chicken, a goat. But there were small amounts of money too. Mamá would pool the money together, and when she had enough, she'd visit storeowners in town who would make orders for them with the bigger suppliers from the city. Though she couldn't write words or numbers, she could count money and keep mental records of how much was owed for orders. While there was no paper trail or records, she kept a tally in her mind.

There were many times when my parents didn't have the money to buy supplies. That's when Papá was forced to go to friends and acquaintances who owed him favors. Indeed, many people owed him favors. So while there were many times when things were tight, Mamá held firm in her belief that the Lord was on our side and would always provide for us and protect us.

Chapter 5

AGUA PURA

Over a wonderful meal of enchiladas with red sauce, Mamá asked, "What are you doing at the hospital these days, Edgar?"

"I'm treating a young man named Eduardo who has a severe infection in his intestines," I told her.

As per usual, my mother wanted to know more about this man: how old he was, where he came from, if he had a mother, a wife, any children, his work, where he lived in the area—she wanted to know every detail about this man.

Anytime a conversation started about any person, Mamá wanted to dwell upon every detail about the individual. It didn't matter if she was talking to someone outside on the street, in the grocery store, or at her kitchen table, she was hungry for details. She asked a lot of questions. Sometimes I would joke with my sisters, telling them, "I love Mamá, but she is probably one of the nosiest ladies I've ever met in my life!" and we would all laugh together. It was all in good humor because she was simply a highly interested and compassionate individual.

Plus, she was concerned that her children, even when we were adults and on our own, be surrounded by wonderful people. She wanted us to be surrounded by wonderful people, and she wanted us to behave like wonderful people, even when interacting with unkind and difficult folks. Since we were small, she regularly advised my siblings and me, "Even if someone is mean to you, you must make every effort to be nice to them. In this way, you can provide them the kindness in life that they've probably rarely had before."

To satisfy her many questions about Eduardo, I told her all I knew: "He had diarrhea for ten days prior to coming to the hospital, and he was dying. His system shut down due to a lack of fluids. He had diarrhea, nausea, and vomiting, and he hadn't been drinking fluids at all. He'd been working on a farm, and he thinks he drank contaminated water. He was having fever, chills, and abdominal pain as well."

"*Dios, ayúdalo*," Mamá began and then asked, "Is he going to survive?"

"Yes, I believe so," I answered, "but he may lose his colon."

"*Por qué*? Why would he lose his colon?"

"Because the diarrhea has destroyed a lot of the texture and the wall of the colon, and sometimes the bad bacteria stays in the colon, so we might have to remove it. If so, he'll have to wear a bag in his side for a while."

"A bag in his side?" Mamá asked but then continued, "I know about those. The ones today are very sophisticated so that the contaminants don't spill out and infect the user. I remember your father would fashion similar kinds of bags back in rural Michoacán. He instructed the patients to put starch and lard around the cavity where it was attached to the body, so the contaminants did not eat their skin."

"Really?" I marveled.

"Yes. Just like your Eduardo, we dealt with a lot of complications due to water contamination, even cholera."

"Tell me what you remember, Mamá," I urged her.

These are the stories she told me.

It was unusually cold and windy. Papá and Abuelo were in Petatlán, Guerrero, a small village on the other side of the Río Balsas, when the rains started. Once the rainstorm unexpectedly and rapidly morphed into hurricane conditions, Mamá knew there was no way that Papá and Abuelo would be able to return home anytime soon.

It was windy with relentless rain. The dark sky was spread heavy with lightning and whistling wind. It looked like nighttime, yet it was daytime. Mamá started to light candles and kerosene lamps when leaking in the roof began. The single small stream of rain into the house's interior soon became two, then ten, then thirty separate streams of cold rainwater pouring inside. Only one small bedroom was spared.

My siblings—Jorge, Lupe, Asunción, and baby Reyna—and I were complaining of upset stomachs when Mamá gathered us into the small bedroom. We huddled and cuddled with her on a single *petate*, trying to stay warm and dry.

We were scared, and our sickness became progressively worse— diarrhea, nausea, vomiting, pain, and fever. Mamá could tell that she too was getting hot with fever and nauseous, but we also needed her. Keeping us warm, clean, and hydrated became her focus.

"*Dios, ayudanos*," she prayed. "My children are burning up. Shivering. Jorge looks pale, and he tells me he feels like he's spinning."

Mamá thought about Papá and how he would treat patients with similar symptoms. Next, she realized we only had tetracycline on hand, so that was her only option in terms of medication. She mixed the powdered antibiotic into rice water and gave it to each one of us to drink.

For three days we took refuge in the closet-sized space. For three dark days storms raged outside our home, and inside our home a vicious sickness wracked our bodies. Hydration, medication, cleanliness, warmth, comfort, and prayer—no matter how delirious she felt Mamá was determined to maintain this focus.

When any of us kids felt a spell of diarrhea coming on, we would tell Mamá. She'd whisk off the cloth wrap around our waist, so that we were bare-bottomed. Then she'd quickly scoop us up and run us to the front door. There she would hold us out and away from her so that the rainwater streaming over the side of the lamina roof would wash clean our soiled bottoms and legs. Then she'd pat us dry and return us to the closet, with our lower bodies wrapped in a clean, dry cloth. She performed this routine many, many times over those three days.

When she was most desperate for comfort, she grasped the Bible she kept next to her underneath the blanket, feeling its heft impart vibrations of peace and hope to her.

When the storm broke, our illnesses broke too. The sun came out, and we emerged from the small room.

Within hours Papá and Abuelo returned home, and it was one of the few times Papá gladly reciprocated the embraces my siblings and I gave him. Apparently he had been shaken too.

After describing our severe illness to Papá and how she'd used tetracycline as a treatment, Papá told her, "Nena, we're seeing many cases of cholera, likely due to water contamination. I imagine you and the children contracted it, and tetracycline is the only antibiotic we have to treat it. You probably saved their lives."

Although La Mira was situated next to two rivers and also very close to the ocean, access to water was an ongoing issue. In our first six years in the village, our family got our household water as all the other families did. This is how it worked: about a mile from the village near the mountains lay a fountainhead amongst the rocks. Really, it was only a trickle of water that ran out of a crack in the rocks and filled a small cavity, about 1½ feet cubed, of smooth rock.

The women of La Mira would fill a large clay jug, or *olla*, with this clear, clean mountain water, place the *olla* on their heads, and make the mile trek back to their homes without spilling a single drop. My mother and the other *mujeres* of La Mira, walking in a line with the jugs on their heads, made an unforgettable picture, almost like a moving picket fence. The women retrieved water several times a week in order to have the water needed for drinking, cooking, washing dishes, cleaning, and watering plants.

Near this spring was a creek where the bathing took place. When the women were bathing, they would stand side by side to make a curtain of bodies to block off a pool of water. This gave the woman who was bathing some privacy. Each woman took turns bathing and standing in this protective line.

About this ritual my mother warmly recalled, "Often we teased the lady who would be bathing. There was a lot of laughter. *Muchas bromas.* Also, there were more serious discussions. We would talk about things that bothered us, about things that concerned us. We talked about our husbands, about our children. There was no hidden agenda."

All the while we children would be playing together as our mothers bathed in a nearby pool in the creek.

About six years into our life in La Mira, my mother told me, "Edgar, your *padrino* [godfather], Edgar Schwartz, will be arriving soon. He will be living in La Mira for several years. You don't remember him, but he is a wonderful man. You are named after him. He is the one who baptized you. He and your father have remained very good friends in the years he's been away. Your grandfather refers to him as a great philosopher. Your *padrino* loves our family and the townspeople here, and we also love him."

Edgar Schwartz, or Padrino Edgar, as I called him, first came to La Mira from Germany to excavate the precious metals in the local mountains. The German company he worked for mined for metals all over the world. After they tested samples of soil from the La Mira area, they understood it was rich with nickel and silver, so they sent Edgar Schwartz to set up and run a mining operation.

My godfather was red-haired, tall, about six-foot four, and muscular, with a well-trimmed beard. He brought with him six identical outfits of khaki pants and khaki shirts and wore one each day. They were custom-made to fit him perfectly. They were so well-pressed that even when he was working in the dusty, dirty mines, they showed no wrinkles. He had three different pairs of boots, all brown, thick, and military-looking, plus a brown belt.

Padrino Edgar had a long, narrow nose that began up between his eyebrows. He had fine, thin features and slightly long ears. He had a pleasant smile but would only smile when necessary. He seemed to never waste a smile. It had to be for a specific reason. Otherwise, he had a serious look. He walked straight, never hunched over. His posture, stance, and walk resembled a soldier's.

He spoke excellent Spanish. He was very kind to people and loved children. He was married but didn't have any children. His wife was a teacher in Germany. His parents had also been teachers.

When he first came to La Mira, he did not have a place to stay, so my father offered him a small segment of our house to live in. He ate his meals with my family. He and my father hit it off really well. Even when he had living quarters of his own, he came to our house several times a week for socializing, dinner, and even breakfast.

My godfather was returning to La Mira to continue the work that he'd started several years prior in the very rich mines. In addition to his mining work, he put his many skills and great energy to work to help all of us in La Mira. For example, the local farmers had tried to raise cattle for beef and milk, but they'd never been very successful. Fortunately, there was never a shortage of fish and seafood for everyone. Even still, Padrino Edgar thought that he could make the beef industry work better. He invested his own money and conducted trainings with many of the ranchers to create a cattle-breeding area and a system for better production of cattle. The cattle ranchers often cited Señor Schwartz (this is what everyone in La Mira called him except my parents who addressed him as "Edgar" and me, who called him "Padrino Edgar," as I already shared) as a *regalo de Dios*, a gift from God, and commented how La Mira was very lucky to have him.

A few months after his arrival, when my godfather was having dinner with us, lentil soup followed by *aporreadillo*, a dish composed of bits of dried jerky mixed into eggs and simmered in a red hot-sauce and then served over white rice, my mother spoke up, "Miguel and Edgar, there's something on my mind I'd like to discuss with you both."

"Of course, tell us," they both urged.

"As you know, cleanliness and hygiene are of utmost important to good health . . . and to me. In our years in La Mira we've contended with several outbreaks of cholera probably due to the ingestion of contaminated water. On top of that, we women spend so much time and energy getting water into our homes, time and energy that we could dedicate to other tasks. For these reasons, I think it is time that La Mira has its own running water system. Miguel, with your organizing abilities, and Edgar, with your engineering skills, we could make it happen."

In this way, Mamá initiated the project of bringing water to La Mira.

Papá was the one to organize the town meeting. The men gathered at the front of the room. The women behind them. Papá and my godfather presented to the people. In their presentation they were careful to credit Nena for having the vision for the water system in order that the village enjoy better health and hygiene.

After several town meetings as well as meetings with regional officials, Padrino Edgar was delighted to report, "We have been given full support. Miguel and I, Andres, and many of the townspeople, as well as the women, were able to convince the higher-ups to give us the miles of piping we need to build a water system." That was a day of celebration, after which followed many months of strategic planning and hard physical labor.

The planning: my godfather determined that we would excavate the rocky area in the mountains around the main fountainhead where the women had been collecting water in order to find more wellsprings. Then we would build a large, deep cistern to collect all that spring water. Next, we would funnel the water out of the cistern and into pipes that would carry it to La Mira. The diameter of the pipes would decrease as they got nearer and nearer to town. Because the origin of the water was up in the mountains, the whole system could run on gravity. No pump or electricity was needed.

Residents wouldn't have running water in their homes; instead, there would be several stations around the village where residents could retrieve water. However, he did make an allowance for my family to have a faucet inside our home because, after all, that's where La Mira's medical and dental clinic was located.

After creating a detailed map of La Mira, my godfather was able to determine how many miles of piping would be needed: approximately six miles. Additionally, he conceived the idea of having regular pinpoints above ground along the water pipes, so if there were problems with pipes, like clogging or corroding, they could use the pinpoints to locate the piping underneath. Each pinpoint consisted of a top hat-sized piece of concrete to designate the area where a pipe was buried.

To keep the water free from debris, he included in his design a series of strainers. He created a system of layered strainers, one atop another, at strategic points in the water piping. These strainers would catch leaves and other debris but allow water to pass. Equally important, he designed it so these strainers could be taken out and the debris removed, a task the women of the village decided to make their own.

Once Padrino Edgar completed all the planning, he made the orders for pipes, joints, taps, bags of cement, and tools. As he explained, "We don't need to order any sand. We have plenty of sand here at the beach, which we'll use to make mortar."

The day the trucks full of pipes and materials arrived in La Mira was a day of excitement. There were pipes of all sizes, some six inches in diameter. They were all galvanized and quite heavy.

I remember my godfather instructed me, "Edgar, you're going to help me count. You're going to count out all the faucets, every one of them. You have to count them accurately because if something is missing, it will create total chaos and stall our project." And so he and I counted them.

Because most of the men of La Mira were farmers, their land and animals demanded their attention every day. For this reason, my mother organized the women, under the direction of the engineers working with my godfather, to do the labor for the laying of the pipes. The women decided they would use their afternoons and all day Saturday and Sunday. Mamá helped organize the women in teams of four to dig the trenches in designated segments. The women's older daughters were organized in teams to prepare and deliver food and water. In addition to digging the trenches, Mamá also organized the women to lay the pipes.

The pipes were so heavy that it took a lot of effort to move and place them. When a pipe accidentally fell onto one lady's foot, she walked with a limp for two months afterwards.

Another side effect of all the hard labor was severely blistered hands. At one point my mother's hands were so mangled that she told my father, "Miguel, I'm not going to be able to make the *masa* to make the tortillas. I'm going to need you and the children to do it for a while." While most women in rural Mexico in this time period wouldn't dare say something like that to their husbands, my mother was different.

At our next meal, my older sister Lupe, who was still quite young, ended up being the one who made the *masa* and patted out tiny tortillas. After my mother took a bite of one, she turned to Lupe and said, "*Qué rico*! This is the best tortilla I've ever eaten!"

Little Lupe beamed.

Suddenly, my father piped up, "Of course it is. I'm the one who made it!" and then he smiled and winked at us. The rest of us just laughed at his unexpected joke.

It was a massive effort that took months of dedicated work and organization to complete. And finally, they finished it.

El día de agua, the day we opened the valves to bring running water to La Mira was one of grand celebration. When my godfather spoke at the celebration, he reminded everyone, "It was Nena who conceived this project, and it is through her persistence and organization that the ladies of La Mira completed it. I am impressed by all of you, and we are all indebted to the Nena's fortitude."

Next, he took a clay *olla*, held it up above his head, and declared, "Never will the beautiful ladies of La Mira have to carry jugs of water on their heads again." With that, he flung it onto the ground, so that it broke into many pieces. My mother sprinted to our home and retrieved an *olla* and she too held hers above her head and dashed it on the ground. Everyone clapped and laughed. The ladies of the village lined up next to my mother in order to take a turn to give her a hug and a thank you.

Also, more and more ladies retrieved their ollas to do the same. There must have been 20 or 30 *ollas* that got smashed that day in commemoration of the village's big achievement.

My mother's quest—or battle—to maintain cleanliness and excellent hygiene was ongoing. On Sundays, she sat all of us children in a line on a bench. Mamá would cut our nails and clean them until they glistened. She frequently told us, "Your clothes may be old, but they will be clean, and you too shall be completely clean."

It was after one such weekly cleaning session that Mamá met with my godfather to discuss another idea: "As I recall, you once told us that you helped create some waste water systems in rural areas in Germany when you worked there as an engineer. Am I remembering this correctly?"

"Yes, I did a lot of work with sewer systems. Not just in rural areas, but in many German cities, especially when I was younger." He explained that when he was just 12 years old, he worked in some of the sewer systems with engineers, so he knew a lot about the required engineering.

"I worry about the bad bacteria and contaminants in our outhouse. Even with our wonderful new water system, worms, dysentery, and even cholera are at times problematic in La Mira. Could you design a sewer system for me and my family? I would feel so much better if our home offered the most hygienic toilet possible to my family and to our patients."

Once Mamá made this request, Padrino Edgar was ready to embark on the project. Because he had worked so much with tunnels and also had developed septic tanks, he decided that for the special outhouse it would be far better to tunnel the waste about 25 feet away from the source, into a cement tunnel or shaft that would serve as a kind of septic tank. He explained that the waste could stay in the shaft for years as long as we treated it periodically with acid.

With my godfather's ingenious design my mother finally had an outhouse that provided excellent hygiene. Amazingly, it also didn't smell. Potentially harmful bacteria were minimal. The structure could endure rains and offered great privacy as well.

Because we had our own water tap in our home, Mamá taught us to keep several buckets filled with water in the new outhouse. Whoever used the toilet would then use the water from a bucket for flushing. This too was novel in the village.

Actually, our bathroom was so unique that during the first weeks after it was built, I gave regular tours of it to people from the village. "Maybe I should sell tickets to people to come and see it because it's just so popular!" I joked with my mother.

She told me, "*Mijo*, I think it is wonderful that you explain our special outhouse to everyone. You might not realize it, but just as your father and I try to do at the clinic, you are educating people about how to be clean and hygienic. You are teaching them how to have good health. Before you know it, *mijo*, you will be a doctor or a dentist too."

Chapter 6

LETTING GO

As I stood to leave, my mother asked, "Why are you going so soon?"

"So soon? Mamá, we've been talking for about three hours. I must return to the hospital to close up a patient's abdominal wound."

"What's this patient's name? Tell me a bit about this patient before you go."

"The patient is Greg, and he's 17. He was ready to go on a mission for the Mormon Church but was in an auto accident and ruptured his colon. I need to place it back into his abdomen."

"Back into his abdomen?"

"Yes. His colon was torn from the impact, so I repaired it, pulled it out, and then will return it at a later time, which entails a second surgery."

This procedure is called an "exteriorization of the colon," which means I actually patch the colon inside the abdomen. Immediately afterwards I make a hole in the abdominal wall and then pull out the area of the colon that was patched. That way, if there's a problem with the repaired area of the colon, it doesn't leak inside the abdomen. After the patient starts having bowel movements and passes gas, I can slightly open the abdomen again to return the colon back inside to its regular location. Then, after that, if the flow of liquids and stools travels right into the rectum without any harm to the patient, we know the patient is fine.

"How is Greg's mother?" As always, my mother wanted to know about my patient's parents and family.

I replied, "She's not too happy. I don't think she likes me very much."

"Why?"

"Because I said to her it's highly likely her son will be able to go on his mission four weeks after the surgery as he hopes to. However, she wants me to justify a cancellation of his mission to East Asia—or, at the very least, recommend a several-month delay—because she doesn't want to risk him having problems or complications while he is out of the country.

"From the start, Greg has been adamant that he go on this mission trip. As he explained it to me—his passion is to save people by allowing them to understand and love the Lord. He's been longing to do this mission for his whole life. Mamá, Greg has explained to me the importance of this mission the first time we met in the ER and every time we've met since then. His blue eyes are piercing when he talks about it. He feels the Lord will care for him. He will not take no for an answer.

"I've had to tell him, 'I understand, but I'm in the middle of two strong individuals—you and your mother. Your mother cares about you and doesn't want anything to happen to you while you're gone.' He responded by saying, 'Dr. Hernández, this mission is the most important thing in my life. I practice and live to spread the word of the Lord.'

"When I've explained to him that it's not like his mother never wants him to go on a mission and that she'll accept a three-month recovery period, he reminds me, 'Yes, doctor, but you told me from day one, that I'm strong and healthy and I should heal and recover quickly. You told me that you expected I'd only need four weeks to recover.' "

After carefully listening to my extended explanation of Greg and his mother, my mother suggested, "*Hijo*, why don't you talk him into staying here a little longer and doing his mission at another time?"

"He has an overwhelming desire to serve the Lord. He's insistent . . . Frankly, Mamá, I'm surprised by your response. When I was 9½ years old and I came to you and Papá, saying I wanted to leave La Mira, so I could fulfill my dream of becoming a surgeon, you were ready for me to do that. So, how can you ask me to talk Greg out of his unselfish dream?"

She paused, deeply thinking.

Finally, she responded, "Edgar, he's right. I think you should support him. You should talk to his mother and tell her your story."

I smiled at my mother, my counselor, as she looked at me, touching me on my forearm.

Then she went on to explain, "The reason I wanted you to talk him into staying a bit longer, Edgar, is that it is so, so difficult for a mother to release her children out into the world. And when it seems premature because the child has been ill or injured, like in Greg's case, or when the children are very young—it is even harder for the mother. So, while Greg is right—and I agree that you should support him—I know it is excruciating for his mother. Next time you visit, I will share with you my own experiences with this painful letting go."

A few days later, over a savory meal of chicken mole, my mother shared with me her experiences.

My mother started by reminding me that she encouraged four of us, three of my siblings and me, to leave our home in La Mira to live with our close relatives—adult children from our father's previous marriages—in other parts of Mexico and even abroad.

When people would ask her how she could allow four of her children to leave at such early times in our lives, Mamá would respond, "It's never been easy to let them go, but their future is what I most care about. Yes, it's at the expense of my loneliness and heartache, but I would do it over and over if it meant a better life and future for them." This was a common question people would ask, and she always responded in the same manner: she would sacrifice anything so that her children could have the most opportunities for better lives.

The first of us children to leave was Surama at 12 years old. Mamá encouraged Surama to go and live with Avisac, my father's adult daughter from a previous marriage, in Zamora de Hidalgo. In Zamora de Hidalgo, the capital city of Michoacán, Surama would have much better educational opportunities than what the village of La Mira offered. In a way, Surama's leaving was similar to what my mother had done as a girl when she left her family and village to live with an aunt in Arteaga.

Even still, Surama's departure was a trial for Mamá. In the beginning, she cried frequently and at moments when she least expected—though she knew it was for the best. After receiving letters from Surama in the months after her departure, Mamá's sadness found some relief.

In 1955, when Pedro was ten, Mamá encouraged him to go to the United States to live with Olivia, our adult half-sister. Again, the village school in La Mira offered a limited education. Mamá figured the Phoenix-area schools where Olivia lived would certainly offer Pedro more learning and a greater number of opportunities for a good life.

My mother always felt secure with the family members whom we children were going to live with. However, that moment of parting was like tearing a limb from her body and leaving her disabled. She actually said "disabled" because it would take her weeks to months to get over it, to heal that wound. She healed with the clear understanding that us children would be well-cared for and would enjoy more prosperous lives in these other places.

In 1956, Alberto, one of Papá's adult sons from a previous marriage, visited us in La Mira. Alberto was an anthropology professor in Vera Cruz. Alberto agreed to allow Jorge, 8 years old, to join him and his family in Vera Cruz.

After Jorge left, it was Lupe, Asunción, Reyna, baby Manny, and me in La Mira with Mamá and Papá. I remember being distraught at Jorge's absence that I lost my appetite and ended up losing five pounds. So, not only were these departures painful for my mother, but those of us children remaining found it incredibly difficult too.

All the while, my father's smoking and alcohol abuse continued, leading to increasingly poor health, which in turn encouraged more smoking and drinking. He continued treating patients, but he was having greater difficulty meeting financial obligations. Papá was always busy, helping people, but his earnings were miniscule since most people could not pay. Often, he did not have enough money to buy the medications and materials needed. Even the small coconut farm that he'd bought when he and my mother first moved to La Mira did not provide us the extra bit of income needed so we'd have enough to eat.

So, while Mamá always explained to people that she allowed some of us children to leave La Mira to bigger cities in order to get better educations, so we could have better lives, there was another factor involved that she didn't discuss: she and my father simply didn't have the resources to feed all of us.

Miguel, Jr. had successfully navigated the complicated immigration process in 1952 and had been living in the US for many years, working as a successful craftsman of Navajo jewelry in Phoenix, Arizona.

It was 1957 when he received a letter from Chucho in La Mira. In the letter, Chucho described Miguel, Sr.'s extreme deterioration: stunning weight loss, yellow, translucent skin, a shuffling walk, trembling hands, and coughing fits that could last thirty minutes in which Miguel struggled to breathe and hacked up globules of dark blood. Chucho revealed his worries about the financial state of Mamá and us children: we were already scraping by, and once our father passed, our survival was even more questionable. Chucho urged Miguel, Jr. to visit La Mira, so they could discuss the situation and come up with a plan. Thus, Miguel, Jr. made the five-day trip to La Mira, riding many buses, taking a train, and eventually sitting in the bed of a pickup truck to reach the village.

Papá, Mamá, and we children were overcome with joy at Miguel, Jr.'s arrival. I was eight years old at that time, and I remember being mesmerized by this adult older half-brother whom I was meeting for the first time.

On the first full day of his stay in La Mira, Miguel, Jr. and I visited Chucho. During this visit, Chucho explained that he'd witnessed our father enduring an absolutely relentless and horrifying coughing fit. It happened when Chucho brought a man to Papá who'd fallen off a carriage and injured his leg. While Papá was cleaning and closing the leg wound, he started coughing severely. Additionally, during the fit, his color changed from blue to gray to purple to ash.

"The man whose leg was wounded became so frightened of your father. I didn't know what to think myself—I couldn't tell if it was the man or your father who needed the most help. Really, I was horrified. I didn't know what to do, and that's why I wanted you to return to see for yourself what's been going on," Chucho lamented.

A week into his visit, Miguel, Jr. finally witnessed one of these coughing episodes. Papá coughed and coughed and coughed. Meanwhile, his whole body turned blue. He seemed to be choking. His face was frightening. His eyes became noticeably more sunken in, and his eye sockets seemed to get bigger and bigger. With all the shuddering, shaking, and thumping, it didn't seem possible that his frail, degraded body could continue to support him. He seemed to be coughing out his last bit of life.

Reyna and baby Manny became so terrified that they hid.

Miguel, Jr., very afraid as well, rushed to comfort our father, to try to help in some way, but Papá pushed him away. This back and forth went on repeatedly. It was a ghastly scene. After Papá gulped down a small jolt of liquor, the coughing finally subsided.

Later, Miguel, Jr. and Mamá had a talk. Mamá revealed all the concerns she'd been holding back, her worries about us children, the family, our livelihood, and Miguel Sr.'s likely fast-approaching death.

Because Miguel, Jr. had a successful job in the USA, a house he'd just started renovating, and a car, he couldn't stay long in La Mira. Before his departure, he and Chucho made a plan. They knew they wouldn't be successful in convincing Papá to stop, or even decrease, his smoking and drinking, but what they could do was ensure a small nest egg for Mamá and the rest of us in preparation for his death. The plan: Chucho would sell a small coconut farm that Miguel, Jr. owned for a good price, and he'd give that money to Mamá to use immediately.

I remember Miguel, Jr. was careful to tell Chucho not to let Mamá know that the money was from the sale of his farm. He didn't think she'd accept it if she knew that. Plus, my older half-brother was a very humble and thoughtful man, and he didn't want my mother to feel awkward at all about accepting the money.

The day my older half-brother departed La Mira was bitter-sweet. The sweetness came from his having visited at all. The bitterness was about his departing. I was particularly distraught, for I'd made a deep connection with my older half-brother, so much so that I even got the dream in my head that someday I wanted to leave La Mira to live with Miguel, Jr. in the USA. I was very, very upset to see my kind, thoughtful, and talented older half-brother depart. The rest of my family was very sad also.

In the months afterwards, Papá's health, which had seemed to have already hit rock bottom, managed to decline even more. Mamá discovered he'd been secretly taking some type of potent pain medication that was usually taken by the spoonful; he was drinking it down, straight from the bottle.

Mamá lamented, "It's some type of strong pain medication your father gives to patients when he has to do a procedure on them. Now he drinks it like it's water."

The violent and bloody coughing episodes became more fre-quent. My father's activity level dramatically decreased. He left home less and less. Eventually he did not go outside the house at all. His appetite was poor, and his overall ability to move became so restricted that it was striking and pitiful to see.

About a year and a half since my older half-brother had visited, when I was a nine-year-old, I approached my parents. Although I'd dreamed of going to the USA to live with Miguel, Jr., in the letters we received from him, no such possibility was ever mentioned, so I decided to seize another opportunity.

"Papá, Mamá, there's something I want to talk to you about," I began. "As you know, my godfather is returning to Germany in a few months. He told us that I'm welcome to return to Germany and live with him and his wife. He says they are happy to raise me like a son and that his country can offer me an amazing education. I would like your blessing to do this."

Papá responded, "*Hijo*, I'm going to die soon, very soon. It's unpreventable at this point, so I think it would be a good idea for you to leave with your godfather. I trust him completely. I know nothing bad will ever happen to you as long as he is with you. If I had to bet on someone becoming successful, it is you, *hijo*. Go and make us proud."

With tears in her eyes, Mamá agreed, saying, "I want the best for you, *hijo*, and it will be best for you to leave with your godfather. No matter how far away you go, we will reunite again *si Dios quiere*."

Within weeks of this conversation, we woke one morning to discover that Papá had died during the night.

Papá's funeral and burial were lovely. There were many flowers. The people of La Mira and other villages came together and, one-by-one, expressed to Mamá their sincere friendship and unending support for us.

Mamá wept at the passing of our brilliant, generous, and afflicted father. She understood that his death was for the best because it meant his suffering had ended. She told us children that she hoped his journey would be a good one and that he would be amongst angels. However, Mamá had no illusions that her life without him would be very difficult.

Because Miguel, Jr. had been hospitalized in Phoenix with a serious infection at the time of our father's death, he didn't arrive in La Mira in time for the burial. Instead he arrived two weeks later. Within hours of his arrival, Miguel, Jr. visited the grave of our father to talk, weep, ask for something, and make a promise: "Papá, I will miss you greatly. Although I have been away for many years, I always thought of you. You were always on my mind. I will be taking Edgar with me back to the United States, and I want your blessing. Also, I promise to you that I will do all it takes to bring

Nena and the rest of the children to the United States as well. We will all be reunited there someday."

In this way, the first step of my great dream—to move to the USA to live with my older half-brother and to study to become a surgeon—was taken.

Additionally, though he was saddened for himself and his wife at the missed opportunity, my godfather understood that it made the most sense for me to live with my older half-brother in the USA.

In this way, Mamá said goodbye to me, her fourth child, to leave her home at a young age. She let me go to pursue my dream and to enjoy tremendous opportunities in the United States.

Before Miguel, Jr. left with me, he approached my mother and promised, "Nena, I will send for you and all the children. I will work to pay for the documentation, so all of you can come to live in the USA with Edgar and me. It may take several years, but I promise it will happen."

With the death of our father, my departure to the USA, and the departure of our close family friend, Edgar Schwartz, to Germany, the year 1959 proved to be a difficult one for Mamá. Luckily, she had the emotional support of her father, mother, and two sisters, as well as Chucho. As far as financial support went, Chucho sold our father's small coconut farm. The money from that sale would last Mamá about two years. Also, my godfather had insisted she accept a gift of a thousand pesos. Only after stubborn insistence on his part did she accept.

Frequently when people would kindly remark to Mamá, "We really miss Edgar," she would respond quietly, "Yes, I do too. Very much," not knowing which Edgar they were referring to. To Mamá, both Edgars—me and my godfather—in a sense, had become the same person. When someone would say, "I wonder how Edgar is doing," she would respond, "I'm sure he is doing very well," without even asking which Edgar. She worried about both of us and prayed we would be safe wherever we were.

Approximately a year and a half after my godfather left La Mira, an engineer who worked in the mines came to see Mamá. He delivered some terrible news: at a construction site my *padrino* had fallen off a scaffold to his death. My mother never learned where this had happened or any more details about his death. All the people of La Mira were stunned and numb over the news. Mamá mourned his death like it was the loss of a family member.

Mamá regularly received joyful news from me. I would write letters, and even though I was just a child, I would send small money orders, money that I earned from working with Miguel, Jr. in the jewelry store and from a weekend paper route. Each money order ranged from $7.00 to $12.00.

As Lupe later explained to me when we were both adults, "Every time a letter from you came to us, we would sit around the table waiting for one of us to read it. Then we would see this interesting-looking paper with numbers and writing in English on it. It was a money order. Mamá would look at the Bible by her side, always longing for the time when she'd be able to read it. She would touch it and rub it gently as if she were trying to pull words from it. She would caress it as we children would listen as one of us read your letter."

As expected about two years after Papá's death, the funds were running out. Mamá's friends and our relatives would help out when they could. Abuelo was a pillar of support, but his farm was plagued with disease and crop production had taken a big hit. To make ends meet, Mamá knew she had to do something outside of the home, so she started doing housework for the better-off families in La Mira: washing clothes, ironing, and doing other household chores.

My mother took great pride in her ironing skills. She would set four irons on a hot plate over a fire. The irons' hot handles were covered with thick rags. She would iron with one until it became too cool, then exchange it for another, and so on, until she finished. It was tough, straining work that entailed regular hand and arm burns, but she never complained.

Mamá's days had always started very early, cleaning me and my siblings, feeding us, sending us to school, and making food, with no electricity or gas, only running water and her ability to make coals from placing logs on the fire. To this daily routine she added on her work in other people's homes. It was her persistence, energy, and faith that allowed her and my siblings to survive.

Even still, it was a vulnerable position that Mamá found herself in: a working widow with several young children. In order to better protect my siblings, Mamá agreed to marry Alejandro, a mason. From the beginning, she was very clear with him, "When the time comes that my children and I will be reuniting in the USA, I'm going to be leaving. If you and I have any children, they'll come with me to the United States. You will not be going with us." Alejandro agreed to her conditions.

Chapter 7

Blue Moon

Ames and I had been at the hospital for almost three days straight. We'd done well over thirty operations and supervised the interns and second-year residents in a few small ones as well. We didn't feel tired; on the other hand, we were hungry.

As we approached the house, Ames asked, "Is this a restaurant?"

"Not exactly, but the cooking is unparalleled. We're actually going to my mother's," I answered.

Ames was a great cook himself. He made excellent egg rolls and would bring in batches while on call. Plus, he was always ready to eat!

Upon entering the house, we found my mother reading the Bible. She wore a flower-covered apron over her dress, and her hair was neatly pulled back. She immediately stood to greet us, "Come in."

"Mamá, this is Dr. Yee, he works with me."

Ames immediately added, "Please call me Ames. I'm a third-year resident, and Edgar is my chief resident. He's like my boss."

"*El patron*," my mother commented jokingly. Then she continued, "Please call me Nena. Welcome to my home."

My mother gave me a warm hug, as was customary. She took my white coat and started inspecting it for lint and smoothing out any wrinkles as she went to hang it, all the while telling Ames, "Please, hang your coat here."

"Something smells wonderful. *Muy rico*," I commented as I led Ames into the kitchen.

Near the stove we found a well-organized workstation. There were pans ready to go on the burners. On the left side was a stack of tortillas, and on the right sat separate bowls containing chopped lettuce, tomatoes, powdered cheese, and shredded chicken mixed with a tinge of vinegar and oregano. Tall glasses of sweet tea sat on the table, waiting for us.

I explained to my colleague, "Ames, you are about to see a master chef at work."

In a wide pan covered in a scant layer of warm olive oil, my mother placed two tortillas and fried them lightly. Next, she put them into a saucepan of *salsa verde*, but only for a moment. Quickly she removed them to two separate plates and placed atop each one layers of shredded chicken, lettuce, tomatoes, and a sprinkling of cheese. After this she rolled each filled tortilla. The enchiladas were bathed in more *salsa verde* with additional lettuce and a sprinkle of cheese on top. She spooned a side of rice and refried pinto beans onto the plates and then set the plates before us.

Ames noted, "Ten minutes to do this—wow." And after taking a bite, he added, "Incredible. *Muchas gracias*." Then Ames mused, "The enchiladas I usually eat are baked in the oven. I guess so the cheese on top melts—but these stovetop ones you've prepared are extra special."

Mamá explained, "In my opinion, the oven ruins enchiladas because they sit too long in the sauces, and the tortillas turn to mush. When the tortillas are crispy, enchiladas are exceptional."

Ames confirmed, "Yes, I agree. Edgar talks a lot about your cooking. Now I see what he means."

Suddenly Ames's beeper sounded, so he asked, "Nena, may I use your phone? I have to call the hospital."

"*Por supuesto*. It's right there," she answered, pointing.

After a few minutes speaking, Ames held the phone out and told me, "They want to speak to you, Edgar." His face was scrunched up with worry.

"*Todo no está bien*. Something's happened with a patient, *si*?" my mother asked him.

"Yes, something distressing has happened," Ames confirmed.

When I set the phone's receiver down, my mother insisted, "Edgar, tell me what's going on. Please."

"Mamá, I don't want to worry you," I replied, hopeful that just this once she'd let it go.

"No, *mijo. Diga me*. Please tell me," she urged.

"Earlier today, a family travelling in a truck hit an elk, and everyone was hurt badly. They ended up getting flown in to the hospital. Ames and I already did a lot of surgeries on them, and the staff called to let us know what's going on with them," I told her, hoping this response would suffice.

"And?" she pressed.

Ames answered, "The father and one of the children actually died on scene . . . And we just got news that the mother died in the hospital. Only one child made it, and that child is quite ill."

My mother began weeping. Then she stood, took her Bible, and exited the kitchen, making her way outside to the backyard.

Ames turned to me, offering, "I'm sorry, Edgar. I should have kept my mouth shut."

"Ames, it's okay. My mother wouldn't have let us leave until she knew. Just give me a minute."

In the backyard I found my mother praying silently with tears streaming from her eyes. She held her Bible close to her heart. When she opened her eyes and found me next to her, she hugged me and spoke, "This is so upsetting, so sad . . . I am reminded of 1966—that awful car accident. Yet, we only got a scratch or two, but . . . but why, Edgar? How? This poor family . . ."

I looked at my mother's scalp and touched her forehead where the well-healed cut from that 1966 accident was located.

She urged, "*Anda, hijo*. Go and take care of who is left of the family."

Here is what happened in 1966.

———————

It was 1966. Pedro decided to stop in Culiacán, Sinaloa, for gas and maybe a short nap. After all, Miguel cautioned him many times to be careful not to fall asleep while driving. At this point, Pedro had been driving for around 14 hours without stopping to rest. It was nighttime, and he was exhausted.

The gas station attendant had questions for him: "I've never seen a car like that. What kind is it?"

"It's a Mustang," Pedro answered.

It was a big deal for Pedro to have that orange Mustang. What happened was that one of Miguel's colleagues, who was also a good friend, had a son who'd bought the orange Mustang. The son was 25 months into the 36 months of payments necessary to pay off the car when that son got drafted into the military. So, rather than allow the car to get repossessed (and lose those months already paid), Miguel advised Pedro to take the car and pay off that final year of payments. As this was also the time when my siblings in Phoenix were working very hard to raise the money to fund the immigration of our mother and other siblings as well as pay for the remodeling of the house, Pedro would have to work even more hours to also fund the monthly car payments. As I said, having this Mustang was a big deal for Pedro.

And Pedro lived up to the challenge. I remember one time, it was very late on a Saturday night and Miguel was asking us if we knew where Pedro was. Olivia replied that she thought Pedro was at a get-together with friends, a small party. In the end, Miguel found him at the jewelry shop, using a special saw for cutting fine metals. Pedro wasn't relaxing at a party; he was working late into the night on a Saturday! While all of us were renowned for our incredible work ethics, Pedro was the hardest working of all of us, something he certainly showed here.

"Where are you from? Where are you going?" the gas station attendant went on to inquire of Pedro.

"I live in the United States. I'm driving to a small town on the coast called La Mira. It's in Michoacán. I'm bringing my mother and siblings to the USA."

It had been 12 years since Pedro had left Mexico to live in the USA, and 7½ years since Miguel had promised Mamá that he'd send for her and the rest of the children and reunite everyone in Phoenix.

During those 7½ years, Miguel worked impossible hours at the jewelry store, first to raise the money needed to fund my legal immigration, a process that proved very complicated, much lengthier than expected, and more expensive as well. For a little less than a year, I even lived in the USA without proper documentation, but after almost getting caught and deported on two separate occasions, we decided it was better for me to live in Nogales, a town just on the Mexican side of the border, while we waited to receive the additional certificates and letters needed to complete my paperwork.

After about two years, we finally had the needed paperwork, and I was able to enter the USA legally. With this hurdle completed, Miguel set to work earning money to renovate the small house and pay for the gathering of documentation and other immigration-related fees for Mamá and the seven children still in Mexico. In 1965, with the house renovation almost complete, Miguel was able to bring Surama, who'd been living in Zamora Hidalgo, and Jorge, who'd been living in Vera Cruz, to Phoenix with the appropriate documentation. A few months later, Olivia and Pedro moved into Miguel's house from where they'd been living outside of Phoenix.

Finally, with Miguel, Olivia, Surama, Jorge, Pedro, and I all living together under one roof, we went to work to raise the necessary funds to bring Mamá, Lupe, Asunción, Reyna, Manuel, and Salvador—one of two sons Mamá had with Alejandro, her second husband. The plan was for her other son, Jose Angel, to come at a later date.

Once we raised the necessary money, Miguel came up with a plan. He would do as much of the documentation process as possible beforehand, so that when Mamá and the children arrived at the Consulate in Nogales, they'd only have to spend minimal time there completing the process. Miguel had filed the applications so that the children could come to the US with student visas and Mamá as a legal resident. The plan was for the children to file for permanent residency within two years. Doing it this way would save time as well as money.

At this point, Pedro would drive to La Mira to retrieve them, leaving on a Friday morning and arriving in La Mira on a Sunday night. His route was to go from Phoenix to Nogales, Hermosillo, Los Mochis, Mazatlán, Guadalajara, Morelia, Uruapan, Arteaga, Los Coyotes, and then finally La Mira. It was around 1,600 miles one-way. Pedro would leave with the family early Monday morning and plan on reconvening with Miguel in Nogales that Wednesday night. Miguel hoped to complete their successful immigration by that Friday. It was an ambitious plan.

When Pedro left us that Friday morning in Phoenix, he was very nervous. Nervous and exhilarated. He later told us that upon turning on the radio, he heard the bopping of his favorite song: "Blue Moon" sung by the Marcels—

Blue moon, you knew just what I was there for
You heard me saying a prayer for
Someone I really could care for

Pedro got a huge smile on his face and a feeling of joy and cer-
tainty in his heart. Next, he did one of his signature moves: he adjusted the rearview mirror, so he could see himself in it. Then he
pulled out his comb and ran it back through his hair, first on the left
side and then the right, Fonzie-style. After this, his face split into a
"looking pretty good there" kinda smile. Yes, Pedro knew there'd be
a lot of driving ahead, but it was going to be a great road trip.

When Pedro stopped in Culiacán for gas, he was well on his way
to La Mira.

The gas station attendant, a thin man with a light complexion,
well-shaven and about five feet, four inches tall, asked Pedro, "How
old are you, son?"

"I'm 19."

"You are very mature for someone so young and on such an
important voyage. I'm impressed."

"Thank you, sir," Pedro replied and then asked, "Do you think
it's possible I could park my car here and take a short nap, for a few
hours?"

"Do you see all the people around us?" the man asked.

At these words, Pedro turned around and saw that a number
of people had gathered. Their eyes were on him and the orange
Mustang.

"I don't think they've ever seen anything like your car. I find it
concerning. Do you agree?"

"Somewhat . . . Yes, I guess I do," Pedro consented and then
asked, "What's your name, sir?"

"My name is Gregorio. I already know you are Pedro."

Puzzled, Pedro inquired, "How do you know my name?"

"I heard that little guy call you 'Pedro' from inside the car."

Pedro was perplexed because he didn't have anyone traveling with him, but he didn't press the man.

"I tell you, son, how about you park the car around back and cover it with a tarp, so you can sleep soundly for a few hours, and we won't have to worry about anyone bothering you or your car?"

"Thank you, Gregorio. I appreciate your kindness and concern." Pedro moved his car to the spot Gregorio indicated. With the man's help, he covered the car with a tarp and then napped until about 1:00 a.m. After he woke, he found Gregorio to thank him and then continued on his way.

From Los Coyotes to La Mira it was about 50 miles of dirt road, the part of the trip Pedro had been most worried about. For one thing, if it was raining, then this road became impassable. Pedro and Miguel consulted with me to see if I could remember whether there would be rain this time of year. I recalled that it would be dry, so it was an ideal time for Pedro to make the drive. The second issue with the dirt road was that it was craggy and uneven. Though the Mustang was a sleek vehicle, it wasn't built for bumpy terrain. Because of its low-lying chassis, the car was quite vulnerable to getting stuck or damaged on its underside. On top of this, vehicles on this road, even traveling at low speeds, kicked up a lot of dust, which could be problematic. Pedro would have to carefully navigate the dust, especially dust from other vehicles, or else it could block his view and possibly cause a collision or some other type of accident.

My memory of it being the dry season proved correct, so the road was passable—as long as Pedro drove slowly and carefully, which he managed to do.

When near La Mira, Pedro turned on the radio, hoping to find some kind of reception. Upon moving the dial, the great Mexican *charro* Luis Aguilar's crooning of "Una Luna Para Ti," which translates as "A Moon for You," reverberated from the speakers. Pedro smiled to himself, for he determined this was another great sign in that it complemented his landing upon "Blue Moon" as the introductory song of the road trip.

Upon arriving in La Mira that Sunday night, the orange Mustang, apart from a thick coating of dust, arrived unscathed. Pedro emerged from the vehicle wearing his customary cowboy boots, feeling exhilarated in spirit and exhausted in body. Many people from La Mira surrounded his vehicle, curious and amazed by it. Next, everyone surrounded him. There were hugs, kisses, tears, and laughter. Kids were jumping around, overjoyed to see Pedro.

Mamá was there. She held Pedro in a long embrace. He'd left her a ten-year-old boy and returned to her a young man.

"Mamá, we don't have much time. We're going to have to leave early tomorrow morning, so we can arrive in Nogales on Wednesday to meet Miguel there," he explained.

Mamá was already prepared. As Miguel had advised, with Chucho's help she'd sold our family home for around 3,000 pesos, which equaled around $250. Pedro had with him $700. That total was what they were using for traveling expenses and to add to the immigration fees.

Pedro took some time washing the car of all the dust while Mamá said her last goodbyes. Chucho and the twins, plus our grandmother (her mother) and our two aunts (her sisters) were among the most difficult. Sadly, Abuelo had died a few years earlier.

Monday morning, with only a few belongings, Mamá, Lupe, Asunción, Reyna, Manuel, and Salvador, who as a baby was strapped to Mamá's chest in her *rebozo*, piled into the Mustang and set off on their long one-way trip.

Lupe, never having encountered seatbelts before, asked, "Pedro, what are these straps for?" While he carefully navigated the dusty, craggy dirt road in the low-lying Mustang, Pedro explained to them about seatbelts and had everyone buckle themselves in.

Years later, as a medical intern and then a surgeon in the ER, I came across a lot of people injured or even killed due to car accidents. In particular, I remember Beatrice and her parents, Randall and Kathryn. These three were driving along a highway when suddenly a wall of dust descended on them. They couldn't see anything and had a nearly fatal wreck. A helicopter had to airlift them to the hospital.

When I met her, Beatrice was out of control, screaming, "Much dust! A lot of dust! We couldn't see anything!"

Randall was in the direst condition. Beatrice and Kathryn were more stable but still very bad. Their injuries were extensive: broken arms, broken legs, a ruptured spleen, a ruptured liver, and an injured intestine. Plus, lots of lacerations to their bodies' exteriors.

After a lot of work on our part and weeks in the hospital, all three survived. But it was horrific. And Beatrice's screaming about the dust brought me back to that 50-mile dirt road—and all the dust that got kicked up on it. So many of us in my family had to pass through that curtain of dust—and how blessed, how incredibly blessed we all were to have made it through it safely.

Once on paved roads, Pedro was able to drive much faster. When they reached Culiacán, he stopped at the same gas station to get gas for the car.

While Mamá and the children stretched their legs, used the toilet, and sipped on cold drinks, Pedro sought out the person working the gas station. He wanted to see if the guy knew if Gregorio was around. Pedro noticed a line of people waiting to speak to the attendant, so he hesitated, not wanting to bother the guy or delay his family's progress.

Because Gregorio had been so helpful, Pedro decided it was worth waiting in the line to inquire about him. Finally, it was his turn to speak to the attendant.

"I was hoping Gregorio would be working today. I wanted to let him know that I made it. He isn't inside or nearby, is he?" Pedro asked.

The man's forehead showed lines of confusion when he replied, "Gregorio who?"

"You know—the guy who works here. I was here three days ago, and Gregorio was on duty. He helped me out," Pedro explained.

The attendant told Pedro, "*Amigo, no hay ningun Gregorio aqui.* There is no Gregorio that works here."

Pedro was surprised—and puzzled.

Before returning to the car, Pedro walked to the back of the gas station. He blinked his eyes a couple of times to try to clear his mind and his vision. Surely he hadn't dreamt the whole thing, he wondered. Imprinted in the soil, he could make out the distinct tire tracks of his Mustang. He smiled, recognizing that it was, indeed, not a dream.

Only two years later did Pedro, unable to get it out of his head, finally confide this Gregorio episode to Miguel.

Miguel responded, "Pedro, did you know that in 1959, when Edgar was living here without his documents, he was nearly deported two different times. Each time, the officers hunting him were within arm's reach. They saw him and could have grabbed him as they'd done to others in the raids, but for some reason, they chose not to. Two times officers looked at Edgar and just walked away.

"Pedro, the thing is, it's very rare that men are able to make such noble and kind decisions—at least not on their own. That was God intervening. God or his angels were taking care of us by protecting Edgar.

"And what happened with you and Gregorio—that was one of God's angels taking care of us by protecting you."

"Yes, I'm in agreement," Pedro confirmed.

"But, Pedro," Miguel continued, "listen carefully. I don't recommend you speak to anyone else about this episode. There are so many non-believers in this world. I worry they would ridicule you, or it would harm you in some way if you tell anybody."

Only 50 years later did Pedro ever confide this incident a second time, and that was in a conversation with me. I too agreed that Gregorio was an angel, protecting Pedro as I had been protected in those two raids.

It was just outside of Los Mochis, right after nightfall, that the car, traveling at around 65 miles per hour, collided with something. When the car came to a stop, the windshield and hood were bathed in blood and organic matter. The front end was bashed in, obviously severely damaged. Smoke filled the air.

The blood and organic matter on the windshield and hood were from a cow that had unexpectedly trotted onto the highway. The Mustang had collided with it.

"*Mamá, esta bien?*" Pedro managed to ask.

"Yes, *mijo*, I'm fine. I think we're all fine, *gracias a Dios*," Mamá responded, coming out of the daze she'd been in. Mamá eventually determined the blood covering her and baby Salvador was from a cut in her forehead, which she got when her head slammed into the dashboard from the unexpected impact.

She hugged Pedro, and the children ran to her. They hugged in a huddle. Soon they saw people coming towards them. Two men pulled the cow's corpse to the side of the road. Others approached. They started to take the cow apart, butchering it, because, for sure, nothing would be wasted.

Pedro asked if anyone had a bucket of water that he could have, so he could fill the radiator and for future refilling. A man gave him a large canister of water and told them to continue on their way.

As they drove away, Pedro saw from his rearview mirror that the men were cutting apart the cow.

Pedro stopped regularly to refill the damaged radiator with water.

On Wednesday night, as planned, Pedro, Mamá, and the children arrived in Nogales to find Miguel awaiting them with six folders. Because Miguel was so experienced at this point with the immigration process, having done it himself and having aided a number of our siblings already, including me, he had every document needed. The files were complete.

Miguel stayed with the family while Pedro continued on. Pedro wanted to get the Mustang repaired and also immediately get back to work to pay for the extensive repairs. This is just another of the many times that Pedro showed himself to be inexhaustible in his ambition to work hard, even under very difficult circumstances.

That night in the hotel, Mamá washed all the children's clothes in the sink. It was very important to her that they looked immaculate in their interviews. Thursday morning, she ensured each child had bathed thoroughly, their nails were flawless, and their hair combed and orderly. Mamá and the children were glistening for their Thursday and Friday immigration-related tasks. On Thursday morning they went to get their physicals and skin tests, as required. The next day they had their interviews. The process went like clockwork.

In the late afternoon of that Friday, they handed the officer at the border their documentation. After reviewing it, he returned it to them, stating, "Congratulations, you are now legal residents of the USA."

Just as Miguel had done with me, he took everyone to the Dairy Queen in Tucson and ordered burgers, milkshakes, and French fries to go. About fifteen miles past Tucson, at a line of trees at the side of the road, Miguel parked the car. Everyone got out and sat on an old 1½ -foot wide tree trunk to eat and take in the setting sun.

Miguel explained, "First with Edgar in 1959 and a second time with him in 1961, we sat on this very tree trunk and enjoyed burgers, milkshakes, and French fries from Dairy Queen. Now, we are completing that circling by doing the very same thing, right now, with you all. *Gracias a Dios.*"

Late that evening, Miguel, Mamá, and the children arrived at our Phoenix home. Surama, Jorge, Olivia, Pedro, and I ran out of the house to embrace our mother and siblings. It was a scene of tremendous joy—crying, hugging, laughing, and more crying—reminiscent of the welcoming Pedro had received in La Mira just a few days earlier.

Miguel told us all, "I told Papá that I would not rest until all of us were here together. That promise has been accomplished. I thank the Lord for giving me strength, and he did. Now we live together, and we should love each other. We will succeed in life. Let me show you your new home."

He then took Mamá by the hand and walked her into the house with the rest of us following. Once inside, Miguel pointed out the floor of orange-and-white checkered linoleum tiles that spread throughout the house. The five bedrooms: Surama and Olivia shared one; Pedro, Jorge, and I shared another. The rest of the children would share one. Miguel had his own. And Mamá would have her own. As she'd never had a bedroom of her own, Mamá teared up—in awe of this blessing.

With everything Miguel showed her, her amazement and emotion only became heightened. The two bathrooms, inside the house, one that had a bathtub and the other a shower. The living room area. The kitchen—with its stove, fridge, and appliances. It was a tiny, humble home that felt like a palace to all the family, especially to our mother. She was openly weeping by the end of the tour, thanking Miguel and all of us for our hard work and thanking God for the blessings He bestowed upon her and our family.

After the house tour, we sat to eat our first meal altogether. Miguel first said a prayer, a prayer for unity—unity in the world and continued unity in the family. Then he spoke about the power of faith—faith in God, in fellow human beings, and in hard work— and how it had led to the achievement of bringing the family together. He praised and thanked the American Consul, immigration officers, and one person after another. He must have named thirty people. It took him a long time to thank everybody.

The rest of us sat in awe at the wisdom of Miguel's words. His message overflowed with gratitude and sincerity. He talked about integrity, the integrity of the immigration officers and the integrity of the American Consul. He was eloquent.

After his moving introductory words, we enjoyed enchiladas and ice cream.

Miguel made sure to ask Mamá, "What do you think of the stove?"

In response she burst into tears.

Miguel told her, "You'll never again have to make *leña* into coals and cook over a fire. You've done it for so many years, and you cooked thousands of meals for these children. Thank God for that. And now, your life will be easier."

In that moment the yoke of toil and suffering seemed to slide off Mamá's shoulders to reveal a younger woman, full of even more love and hope. No more making logs of *leña* into coals. No more cooking over an open fire. No more ash and smoke. Now she could put a match to the stove, it would light up, and she could cook meals in minutes.

With tears streaming from her face, Mamá thanked God for the wonderful gift of life, for allowing her years of sacrifice and hard work to have paid off, and for bringing the family back together in a new country where opportunities abounded.

Part **Two**

ESTADOS UNIDOS DE AMÉRICA

Chapter 8

WHOLE-HEARTED

"Mamá, Mrs. Cane had one of her 'scholar days' a few days ago, and she invited me to speak to her students," I shared before savoring a spoonful of *chiles rellenos*.

While many people may have had this dish before, in my years in the United States, I've never once encountered *chiles rellenos* the way my mother prepared it.

Her *chiles rellenos* was a complex and divine soup—yes, a soup. First, she made the stuffed peppers (she roasted green *chiles guajillos* and *chiles pasillas* and then stuffed them with a mix of onions, tomatoes, shrimp, and cheese). Then, after dipping the stuffed peppers into an egg and flour batter, she lightly fried them and set them aside. Next, she prepared a soup from a chicken broth base to which she added diced fresh serrano peppers, onions, tomatoes, and garlic. She stirred in some flour to thicken the soup as well. When it was time to eat, you'd receive a bowl of soup with a lightly fried stuffed pepper in it and *salsa verde* on top. It was time-consuming to prepare, but it made an incredible meal.

"*Qué bien*! Tell me, how is Mrs. Cane doing? It's been a year or two since you last visited her, correct?" my mother asked.

Mrs. Cane had been my eighth-grade teacher about eleven year earlier. Since even before I'd been in her class, she was holding "scholar days." These were special days on which she invited certain

104

former students who were already in college, graduate school, or pursuing their careers to speak to her current class. The speakers described their study paths and career choices. They answered students' questions. And they all emphasized hard work—"If you are willing to work hard, you can achieve your goals."

Mrs. Cane had invited me several times to speak at her scholar days over the years. In this instance, I was in my second year of medical school.

"Mrs. Cane must be in her late seventies now," I answered my mother, "and she's doing great. She's continues to teach with as much vigor, enthusiasm, and discipline as ever."

"What did you talk to her students about?"

"I explained to them how I immigrated to the US—even how I lived here without proper documents for almost a year at one point. Then I told them about my longtime life goal—to become a surgeon—and how I never lost sight of that goal even when money, gang problems, and other things seemed like insurmountable obstacles. I told them that as soon as I left high school, from that point on, I had been going to college year-round and working at the same time. And that I'd gotten my college degree and master's degree in just four years. Then I told them about applying to medical school and what it's been like so far."

Mamá inquired, "How did the students react? Do you think you inspired them?"

"That's just it, Mamá. I remembered being a student and listening to people like me come and speak, so I knew how important it was to emphasize to them what Mrs. Cane and those other scholar day speakers had emphasized to me."

"And what's that?"

"I ended my talk by telling them that when I was in the eighth grade with Mrs. Cane, she taught us her philosophy of unity, helping one another, and setting big life goals. I told them how she'd taught me and my classmates the beauty of discipline, honesty, and responsibility. And I explained that her teachings never left me and that they were a key to my success. And with Mrs. Cane, they were getting the path to success clearly laid out for them. All they had to do was commit to it."

"Yes, Edgar. Mrs. Cane is a beautiful lady. An incredible teacher. We are so blessed that you got to be in her class," Mamá observed.

"I've always told you, Mamá, that you and Mrs. Cane are two branches from the same tree. I wanted to tell those students about you too."

"Edgar, Mrs. Cane is a teacher. She turns her students into thinkers, readers, analysts, and writers. Me—I've never even gone to school. You are very kind, *mijo*, but her branch is on a much thicker, taller, and more glorious tree."

I disagreed. Completely. Let me explain: perhaps more importantly than her academic instruction was Mrs. Cane's philosophy. For the year her students were together with her, everyone was a tight-knit team. The classroom philosophy that we all functioned under was that it was our collective responsibility to help those among us that were struggling, for whatever reason. And that tenet worked. We were amazed at how well our classmates that had been lagging and had had poor grades and attitudes in previous years performed with Mrs. Cane. It seemed like whomever she touched turned into an excellent student and an empowered person.

In essence, she could awaken the most reluctant or unconfident student and make them outstanding. She always said she just had to make sure that all students first felt good and loved themselves so that they had confidence in themselves. After that, learning was easy.

Plus, her enthusiasm and discipline, both personally and what she expected of us, were remarkable. Even when she had a cough, was sneezing, was sick with the flu, she never missed work. She wanted to show us what hard work was all about, explaining, "You can't let the small things in life get you down. A cough or a sneeze shouldn't sway you from your commitments." She proved it to us herself, and we knew how strong this lady was.

Plus, Mrs. Cane not only opened up our minds to what we could do in the future for ourselves and our communities, but we also learned the importance of generosity, kindness, and sharing. That's what the constant teamwork taught us.

Though my mother was certainly too humble to see herself in this way, it was evident to all those around her that she too embodied this same noble and beautiful philosophy. It's evident in how she raised my siblings and me, how she supported my father, and how she worked tirelessly for all the residents of La Mira. Then, even when she came to the United States, as alien, big, and intimidating as it might seem, my mother embraced this new country, its people, and its customs whole-heartedly. She didn't stop her quest of empathy, generosity, kindness, and sharing, not for a moment, no matter the person or the circumstances.

My mother's daily schedule didn't change drastically once in Phoenix. As in La Mira, she woke early, around 5 am—but in Phoenix it wasn't the crowing of roosters or rays from the rising sun that woke her. It was the sound of Pedro's three favorite songs: the Marcels singing "Blue Moon," Gene Chandler singing "Duke of Earl," and the Penguins singing "Earth Angel." Pedro had these songs on 45s, which he'd play consecutively each morning. For him, the music got his day going with a punch; for the rest of us, it was Pedro's particular alarm clock for the household.

Pedro had made it his morning routine to play the songs consecutively in two rounds while preparing the lunch he'd bring with him for the day: an egg sandwich (we didn't have the luxury of affording meat). However, once Mamá arrived at the house, she considered it her duty to prepare all the food for the household. We were studying, going to school, and/or working, so Mamá considered it her duty to support us at home by preparing all the food—no matter what.

When Mamá heard the Penguins crooning, "Earth angel, earth angel, the one I adore," that was her cue to get out to the kitchen to make Pedro's sandwich for him. But, as this sandwich-making had become part of Pedro's morning routine for a few years at this point, he didn't want to simply hand it over to Mamá. What ended up happening was a kind of well-choreographed dance or mock-fighting scene that the rest of us found really funny to behold. There Pedro would be, cooking his eggs at the stove as he sung along to whichever song was playing. Mamá would emerge to take up a spatula of her own, and the two of them would jockey for the prime position in front of the frying pan, both armed with spatulas and ready to turn the eggs. When the toast popped out of the toaster, Pedro pounced on one piece while Mamá grabbed the other. Pedro would open the fridge to grab the mayonnaise and mustard, all the while Mamá arms would be snaking under and around his to snatch whichever bottle he hadn't already taken ahold of. While Mamá was indeed our Earth Angel, she was certainly a wily and persistent one—whom we all adored!

Once Mamá and Pedro managed to get his egg sandwiches made, Mamá then woke my siblings and me to get the bathing going and supervise the cleaning of nails and brushing of hair and teeth. Jorge, Lupe, Reyna, Asunción, Manuel, Salvador, and me—that's seven children to consider—so it took planning. She prepared breakfast for us and sent us off to school.

Next, she would clean the kitchen and begin preparing lunch. Similar to La Mira, our schools in Phoenix were close enough that we walked home to eat lunch. In the afternoons she cleaned the house, washed and ironed clothing, shopped for food and other items, and prepared dinner. After dinner and homework, it was time to put us all to bed. Keeping this 12-person household running was nonstop, full-on work.

The older children and stepchildren, Miguel, Olivia, Surama, and Pedro, would help Mamá when they could, but they were working fulltime themselves. Because they'd pooled their money to pay for the immigration fees and still owed money for loans they made to finance that, as well as paying weekly and monthly expenses (the mortgage, car payments, electricity bill), money was scant. Those who could work had to. Olivia worked in the clothing department of Sears. Surama worked with tailors in a bridal shop. Miguel continued crafting silver Navajo jewelry. Although Pedro had wanted to be a dentist, he ended up quitting school to contribute money first to the fund for the immigration process and then simply to the running of the 12-person household. Like Miguel, Pedro learned to craft exquisite silver Navajo jewelry. Within just a few years of starting, Pedro became a master. Over the course of his career he became sought-after to craft the finest jewelry. People searched him out to commission him to make pieces that featured very precious and rare stones. His abilities and success were remarkable.

While Mamá's daily schedule mirrored that of hers in La Mira, how she went about doing her tasks was drastically different. Of course, in Phoenix she had a stove that was ready to go with the strike of a match, but that was just one of the many new time- and labor-saving conveniences. The refrigerator was a sensation to her: she didn't have to go to the market daily. Also, she could make a vat of beans, keep them fresh in the refrigerator, and simply heat them as needed. The same with tortillas. There was no need to soak the corn, grind it, prepare the dough, shape and pat out the discs, and cook them three times a day before meals. She could prepare many, keep them in the fridge, and reheat them as needed. Plus, there was a blender, a toaster, an oven, and a washing machine—the kind with wringer rollers. There were several running water taps inside the house: a sink, right there in the kitchen, the sinks in the bathrooms, as well as running water in the tub and shower. Extraordinary. No more toting water from a single faucet to the *pila* or the outhouse.

My mother actually wept when Miguel showed her the electric iron and ironing board. No coals, coal dust, or heavy, caustic irons. Incredible.

It should be said that living in a house—a whole city, even—with electricity was, itself, new, wonderful, and amazing to Mamá.

While these conveniences certainly decreased the time and intensity needed to perform each task, because she was running a 12-person household, the size of each task made up the difference. She was always busy. There was always something more to do.

Even with so much to do, Mamá was always meeting new people—in the neighborhood, at the grocery store, at the school, the library, everywhere. Even when meeting folks for the first time, she invited them to come over, or come in, for a meal. Lengthy meals with lots of conversation were a real joy to her.

One time she opened the door to find a young man standing there on the porch. He was selling quails that he'd hunted himself. Mamá invited him in to sit and have a meal and a talk with her. She learned that he was a Mexican immigrant who was working in the farmland outside of Phoenix, helping set up elaborate irrigation systems. It was intense work, and because he also had a family, he was searching for ways to earn additional income. That's why he was selling the quail.

After the delicious meal and friendly conversation, the young man tried to give my mother some quail, but she insisted she pay for them. Additionally, she gave him several bags of clothing that we had outgrown. It was a satisfying get-together for the both of them.

We were particularly pleased with our dinner that evening: quail with tomatillo sauce served with beans and rice.

Before Mama and my siblings arrived in Phoenix, Miguel had already opened our home to folks he'd come across who were experiencing difficult times. These people would stay for a few days to a few months. Typically, they were undocumented immigrants trying to start new lives in the United States, working and sending money to their families, whether those families were in the United States or in their home countries. So, when Mamá invited the many new people she was meeting into our home for a meal or to stay for a time, she was continuing with a practice Miguel had already started.

The garage at the back of our house was equipped with mattresses, so that guests (Mamá always referred to these people as our "guests") could sleep in it. They typically left very early in the morning to work and returned late in the day after work. My mother made food for them that they'd take to work. She also invited them to have dinner with all of us in the evening. Miguel and my mother never asked for compensation, but most of the people insisted on giving us something, whether it be small food contributions or services, like helping clean, cook, or do repairs.

As my mother said to our guests, "My children and I are so very lucky to have landed here in the United States with this home, jobs, and schools. We are in debt for the blessings we've received. That's why we've opened our home to you. It's our privilege."

The guests came from a variety of backgrounds. There was a teacher that stayed with us. He crossed the border illegally and needed a place to stay while he waited for an acquaintance. He wrote poems. He sang. Sometimes he stood and gave poetry recitations to us after dinner. After six weeks, his acquaintance finally arrived and the two left to New Mexico.

Daniel Thunderbird, an elderly Native American, lived with us for two weeks. About half a block away at a neighbor's, Mamá found him a tiny guestroom that he could live in for a reasonable rate. He stayed there for years and ended up becoming our good friend.

Leonard Uskilith, a Navajo man who was going through very hard times, stayed with us for about six months. He'd had serious drinking and smoking addictions, but he changed that quickly once he was with us. As Miguel was fluent in Navajo, the two could communicate easily. Leonard learned to cook Mexican food from Mamá and to speak some Spanish as well.

When my mother came across Jonathan Wyles, an elderly Native American who'd been roaming the streets, she invited him to stay with us. Because he'd lost his family in a house fire, he was overcome with grief and had resorted to drinking and living in the streets. Staying with us seemed to provide him the solace, connection, and safety he needed to process his grief.

Because of Papá, my mother and the rest of us had already endured the chaos, destruction, and sadness caused by addiction. So, for folks in need who had substance abuse problems, like Leonard and Jonathan, Miguel and Mamá enforced a strict no drinking or smoking policy. Many of our guests ended up giving up smoking cigarettes completely and experiencing their first dry period in years due to our house rules. Many guests freed themselves completely from substance addictions they'd been wrestling with for years.

Rosario, a 21-year-old woman from Mexico, carrying her three year-old daughter, Daniela, in her arms, had been wandering Phoenix's back alleys. For a few days they'd been taking shelter behind a mechanic's garage, but then they were told to leave.

When my mother met them, they'd been traveling for almost a month, wearing the same clothing all the while, which explained the discoloration and stench from days of repeated exposure to dust, mud, grease, and sweat. Their shoes were coming apart, and they wore no socks. Little Daniela's hair was short and spiky. It looked like steel wool, and she had droopy sad eyes, symptoms a doctor would have identified as a failure to thrive. Like her mother, the little girl's fingernails were long with dirt crusted in them. They were as sad and desperate as they were unkempt, grungy, and hungry.

Mamá's appearance made a stark contrast: a bright white and freshly ironed blouse, a neatly pressed skirt, glowing skin, shiny and tidy hair, clean hands, freshly cut and spotless fingernails, and an optimistic and open attitude.

When Rosario and Daniela came to our door, asking for a little food and water, Mamá ushered them inside and sat them at the table. She placed before them two tall glasses of milk as well as warm tortillas. Within ten minutes, she had ready for them pinto beans, rice, and a salsa made up of a tomatoes, onions, peppers, and cilantro.

Rosario thanked Mamá again and again. She and Daniela ate quietly, conscious of their bedraggled appearances in Mamá's orderly house.

"*Mas, mija.* You and Danielita must eat a little more," my mother encouraged.

When their hunger was satisfied, Mamá pulled up a chair to sit between the mother and daughter. She took their hands and promised them, "You can stay with us as long as you like. Do not be afraid. We will help you."

At these words Rosario burst into tears. Mamá turned to hug the young woman. Rosario hugged her back, cautiously, as if she didn't want to soil Mamá with her grimy clothing or hands.

"I am going to find you and Daniela some clean clothing. In the meantime, you two can take a bath or a shower," suggested my mother.

As the rest of us came back home over the course of the late afternoon and evening, we met Rosario and Daniela, who at this point had bathed and were wearing spotless clothes that Mamá had rounded up for them. We all did our best to make these two new guests feel welcome.

At dinner, we tried to engage Rosario in conversation. "Where are you from?" Miguel asked her.

"Monterrey, Mexico," she quietly replied. Then she continued, "And again, thank you for letting us stay here with you. God bless you and Nena for allowing us to stay with you in your beautiful home. And all your children, thank you." Then she burst out crying. The little girl smiled shyly at us.

Miguel gently explained to Rosario, "We have been through trying times ourselves, and it was only because other people helped us, that we made it. The only way we can repay our debt to those folks is to help other people in need, people like you. We'll do everything we can to make things good for you and your daughter."

Mamá further shared, "In 1960 two complete strangers in Nogales took in my son Edgar. They let him live with them for almost a year until he could get his documentation sorted for an American visa. Elvira and Javier are their names. Those two helped my family tremendously. Now that we are in a position to help others, that's what we are doing."

When asked to tell more about herself, Rosario explained that she and Daniela were on their way to California because they had a relative there. But, the truck dropped them off in Phoenix because they did not have enough money for full transport to California. In fact, the *polleros*, or smugglers, had actually tricked Rosario. Originally, they told her the fee was $100 USD to deliver her from Monterrey to Los Angeles, California. Once they reached the border, the *polleros* asked for another $100, which was all the money Rosario had. Once they reached Phoenix, they demanded more money from Rosario. Since she had no more, they left her in Phoenix.

Later Rosario confided in Mamá that her family in Mexico had disowned her when she had Daniela out of wedlock. Plus, Daniela's father abandoned her. She contacted a half-brother in Los Angeles who said he would help her out, and that's why she left Monterrey.

Miguel asked his colleagues at the jewelry store that if they had extra clothing that would fit a young woman and toddler, to please donate it. Also, he helped Rosario get a cleaning job at a nearby hotel. He knew the owner and told him the truth about Rosario's status—that she had no documents. The owner simply needed someone dependable to do cleaning, so he hired her. Because Rosario was such an excellent worker and good-natured person, the hotel owner wanted to sponsor her in the immigration process. While Rosario was grateful for this man's kindness, she preferred to concentrate on getting to California and once there she'd pursue legal immigration.

Mamá took care of Daniela while Rosario was at work. She found the little girl a real joy. Like Rosario, Daniela had a happy disposition and made a good playmate for Salvador. Mamá enjoyed the mother and daughter so much that she called them her *regalos de Dios*, gifts from God.

While Mamá occasionally allowed Rosario to contribute some groceries to the household, she refused any cash when Rosario tried to press it on her. Mamá knew how important it was that Rosario save her money in order to make her bigger goal happen.

Mamá desperately wanted to read and write, and Reyna, Lupe, Asunción, Jorge, Manny, and I had been giving her mini-lessons. Rosario couldn't read well, but she could read a little, so she joined in the reading and writing lessons too. Rosario and Mamá sat like eager schoolgirls with us as their teachers. The two ended up making tremendous progress over their months of studying with us and reading the Bible together.

Even though Rosario wasn't interested in pursuing legal immigration until she reached California, Mamá encouraged her to learn all she could about it now, so that when she reached Los Angeles, she would already have a good grasp of the complicated process.

Mamá described the fear and problems I had encountered when I was living in Phoenix illegally. She described the terrifying raids and how I'd almost got deported two times. "Please, *mija*, start gathering the necessary documents, so you don't have to live a life of fear in the United States," she urged.

Because Miguel and I had vast experience navigating the immigration process for ourselves and leading others through it, we gathered forms for Rosario and made an outline for her of all the steps in the process as well as all the documentation she'd be responsible for gathering. We helped her attain her and Daniela's official birth certificates from Monterrey, letters from her last employer, and letters from clergy. We even aided her in making contact with her half-brother in LA.

In discussing the interviews with the American Consulate that Rosario would eventually have to do to get a visa, Miguel advised, "Tell the truth. Tell them you came to the country illegally. Tell them everywhere you've been and what you've been doing as well. I think they'll likely be very understanding because telling these people the truth means a lot. It tells them you're trying to do things in a correct way, and you're trying to mend your wrongs for crossing illegally."

After almost a year, Rosario and Daniela were ready to go to Los Angeles. We got Greyhound tickets for them. We also made sure Rosario's relative would meet them when their bus arrived in the terminal in LA.

The night before their departure, we gathered with Rosario and Daniela for a special meal. It was reminiscent of the reunion dinner we'd had when Mamá and the rest of the children first arrived in Phoenix. Instead of Miguel, this time it was Mamá who spoke.

Mamá said, "First, we must thank God for so generously bringing Rosario and Daniela into our lives and for giving us the opportunity to enjoy their company. They made our lives better and made us appreciate life even more. They will be deep in our hearts and our minds, and we will never forget them. We wish them well on their journey to unite with their family in Los Angeles."

It wasn't a sad night or a sad departure. Really, it was a celebration of our unexpected friendship with Rosario and Daniela and of all the good wishes we had for them.

Mamá even confessed to Rosario, "You realize that some people think that Daniela is my granddaughter. You want to know something? That makes me extremely happy. I long to someday have a granddaughter like her."

At the bus station the next day, Miguel held Daniela, bouncing her up and down in his arms. She gave him a kiss. Mamá embraced Rosario. Rosario kissed Mamá several times. Mamá picked up Daniela, kissed her several times, caressed her hair, and patted her rosy cheeks. I hugged them both.

Shortly, they boarded the bus, and it disappeared from sight.

"*Adiós, y que Dios los proteja,*" Mamá whispered.

Chapter 9

Co-Conspirators

"Dr. Hernández, Dr. Hale wants to see all the chief residents immediately in the ER," Luisa, his secretary, informed me.

"What's going on?" I asked.

It was 1982. I was in my final year of residency at Maricopa County General Hospital. I was one of five chief residents, and Dr. Hale, the chief of surgery and one of the finest and most respected surgeons in America, was our director.

Luisa answered, "You know that Dr. Hale isn't a man of many words, so I can't tell you."

When I arrived in the ER, Dr. Hale was standing there, wearing his customary bolo tie, bifocals, and flat-topped haircut. He didn't say anything but instead peered at each of us with a grim expression.

Finally, he stated, "In the next room there's a man who apparently needs a Kwell bath because he has lice. I was told that one of you refused to touch and examine this man, who is a transient. Before each of you agreed to accept training here, I made it clear that at this hospital we care for many indigent and poor people, and if you could not do that, then you had an opportunity to exit out. You five agreed and stayed. Whoever it is among you that refused the man, I ask to step forward."

We stood. In silence. No one moved.

Dr. Hale scrutinized each of our faces. After a few minutes, he stated, "We have too much to do to stand here. I will find out which of you did this."

Soon after we were dismissed, Dr. Hale found me and pulled me aside. "Edgar, tell me—who is it? Who do I have to fire?" he pressed.

While I knew who it was—for that matter, everyone knew except Dr. Hale—I wasn't going to be the one to tell him. It was a tricky situation for all of us in the know.

In the end, Dr. Hale gathered all five of us in the room with the patient. He had all of us chief residents scrub the man down and apply the lice treatment. Dr. Hale did this with us as well.

This whole episode took me back to 1969, a few years after my mother and siblings started their new life in the USA. However, in the event that took place then, it was my family that was scorned as the filthy ones, and it was my mother who never flinched. Instead, similarly to Dr. Hale, she insisted on dignity, equality, and kindness to all. And, along with Mrs. Davis, our neighbor and her fellow "conspirator in kindness," so to speak, Mamá pulled it off—she took care of the problem and opened everyone's hearts. What a coup.

Miguel was at work when he received the phone call.

"Okay, we'll be there in 15 minutes," he responded.

Next, he called Mamá: "Nena, the school just called and said we need to pick up the girls. They have lice, and they can't be at school until they're treated."

Because Mamá didn't drive or own a car, she went over to our neighbors' house, the Davises, to see if Mrs. Davis would drive her to the school.

In her first two weeks in Phoenix, with a platter of enchiladas in her hands, Mamá was crossing the street to introduce herself to our neighbors, the Davises, when their door opened. A thin, attractive African-American woman, wearing a yellow dress dotted with pink roses, a blue hat, and red lipstick, stepped out the door. It was Mrs. Davis, and she was carrying a chocolate cake.

Miguel had been friends with the Davises since he'd bought the house in the neighborhood years earlier. I too had been friends with them for years. They were from Mississippi. Mr. Davis's father had worked for an aerial pesticide company, and after he died, Mr. and Mrs. Davis decided to move to Phoenix where they'd inherited a small home years earlier. Mr. Davis started his own termite and pesticide company in Phoenix, and it was very successful.

Because they lived in a neighborhood in which Spanish was the prevalent language and because Mr. Davis's company worked with the farming community in which Spanish was also the commonplace language, the Davises learned to speak Spanish really well.

Mamá and Mrs. Davis met on the sidewalk, both holding large plates of food.

"Hello. I'm Evelyn Davis, I was just coming over to your house to welcome you to the neighborhood," she greeted my mother.

"No English. Sorry," Mamá responded sheepishly.

"*Yo hablo Español*," Mrs. Davis shared.

My mother's face lit up.

"*Mi nombre es* Evelyn Davis *y soy tu vecina*." Mrs. Davis went on to point out that since they'd both decided to meet one another—and bring gifts of food—at the same time, that, as she observed, "*Estamos destinados a ser amigas*. It seems we're meant to be friends." They both laughed.

Indeed, they became great friends. Mrs. Davis introduced my mother to secondhand stores, and they regularly scoured these stores together hunting for treasures. They cooked together and played Bingo. After my mother sent us children off to school each day, she and Mrs. Davis met for half-hour Bible sessions. My mother would listen as Mrs. Davis read aloud scriptures in her exquisite ariose voice. The two always cited their faith as what had brought them together. They were God-loving ladies, true believers in giving to others and never asking for anything in return.

Mrs. Davis was happy to drive my mother to the school. She waited in the car while my mother went inside to fetch my sisters.

Upon examining Asunción, Lupe, and Reyna's scalps, my mother confirmed that, indeed, they had lice, "*Sí, es verdad. Tienen piojos.*"

Another mother, also retrieving her daughter, barked at Mamá, "It's your dirty kids that gave my daughter lice!" Asunción translated this woman's words to Mamá.

"Now I'm going to have to cut her hair and shave her head," the woman snidely added.

After Asunción translated this, Mamá told Asunción, "Please tell her not to do that. I will wash her daughter's hair myself. There's no reason to cut the girl's hair off. Please tell her I will help."

Asunción pointed out to Mamá that a lot of kids had lice, so it probably wasn't our fault, which meant we weren't obligated to take care of this woman's daughter.

"*Mija*, what you say may be true, but we need to help her and her daughter. She is very upset."

In the end, with Asunción as the translator, my mother made arrangements with the teacher and all the parents of the seven other children with lice that she would be the one to treat all the children at our house.

Not surprisingly, Mrs. Davis was eager to assist. Before driving home, they stopped at a pharmacy to buy Kwell, the special shampoo for treating lice, and very fine-toothed combs. Mrs. Davis brought over some towels and buckets, and hers combined with ours made enough for the ten children.

Early the next morning, all ten of the children, including Asunción, Lupe, and Reyna, met at our house. Mamá lined up ten empty garbage cans, each turned upside-down, for each child to sit on. First, the shampooing with Kwell: each child got shampooed twice and then sat for thirty minutes with their shampoo-covered hair wrapped in plastic. This was to allow the shampoo to kill the lice. Then Mamá and Mrs. Davis combed their hair to remove the lice. I combed my sisters' hair.

The following day, we did this same treatment to all the children a second time. During this final treatment, the children and their parents were more relaxed. They were smiling and laughing. By the conclusion of the treatment, Mamá had won them all over. They were thanking her for her kindness and warmly hugged her, Mrs. Davis, and even me before departing.

Mr. McCormick, the principal of Monroe Elementary, had a policy that when report cards came out, he wanted to personally meet with any parents who had three or more children at the school to discuss the report cards. Pedro, Jorge, and I had all gone to this elementary school at one point—it was where Mrs. Cane taught the eighth grade. During this time period, Lupe, Asunción, Reyna, and Manuel were students there. Because Mamá's English was just emerging, Mrs. Davis accompanied her to this meeting, as she would anytime Mamá might need translating help.

The two women, both in their early forties, walked the shiny floors of the school. Mrs. Davis wore a brown hat with a green flower on top. She was an expert at matching her hats and dresses, and today's outfit was particularly striking. She also wore her customary red lipstick, and her splendid song-like voice resonated throughout the halls. My mother wore a red and white dress and shiny white shoes. Their outfits were among their latest finds in their second-hand store treasure hunting.

A young lady stopped them to ask, "Are you the new teachers?"

Mrs. Davis chuckled with joy and replied, "No, my dear, but I wish I were a teacher! Don't you, Nena?"

"*Sí*, Evelyn, *eso sería un sueño hecho realidad*. At this time, the only hope is for me to live through my children's success, but someday I will learn how to read and write, *si Dios quiere*."

Once in the reception area, a good-looking lady, tall in stature with brown hair, welcomed them, "Please come in and have a seat. My name is Natalie, and I'm Mr. McCormick's secretary. He'll be ready to see you shortly"—she turned to my mother—"And you are Magdalena Hernández, the mother of Lupe, Asunción, Reyna, and Manuel?"

Mrs. Davis answered, "Yes, this is Mrs. Hernández. She prefers to be called Nena. I'm Evelyn Davis, Nena's good friend. Nena's English is getting better all the time, but I am here in case she needs any translation help." Then Mrs. Davis turned to Nena to translate all that was said.

My mother introduced herself to Natalie in slow and careful English, "I am Magdalena Hernández, Nena. I am the mother of Lupe, Asunción, Reyna, and Manuel," and held out her hand.

Upon shaking Mamá's hand, Natalie, speaking in excellent Spanish, told her, "Welcome, Nena. It is wonderful to finally meet you. We know many of your children very well—Edgar, Pedro, and Jorge, as well as Lupe, Asunción, Reyna, and Manuel. You have wonderful children, and you must be very proud."

"*Gracias*, Natlie, *tu eres muy amable*," my mother responded and then asked, "How is it you speak Spanish so well?"

Natalie explained to them, in Spanish, that she and her ex-husband had lived in South America for ten years.

Before she could say more, Mr. McCormick emerged from his office and greeted my mother and Mrs. Davis with warm handshakes. "Please come in," he welcomed them.

Once they were seated, Mrs. Davis explained to Mr. McCormick why she was present at the meeting.

Mr. McCormick thanked her for her assistance and then began the meeting, speaking slowly so that Mrs. Davis would have time to translate, "Presently you have Lupe, Asunción, Reyna, and Manuel here at our school. In the last week or two, I recall seeing Edgar here, visiting Mrs. Cane. Mrs. Cane is the best teacher I have ever known in my entire career—and she thinks a lot of Edgar and so do I. Edgar tells us he will be a surgeon someday, and all of us are certain he'll achieve his dream. You are an incredible mother who has raised great children."

"*Gracias, Señor McCormick*," Mamá responded.

"How is Miguel? We used to see him frequently, but not so much lately. How is he?" inquired Mr. McCormick.

"He is doing well, but he is working more than ever. Bringing us to the United States and renovating the house was expensive. He's working hard to pay off those expenses," Mamá answered in Spanish and then Mrs. Davis translated.

"He's a very unique man, very special." the principal commented.

Mrs. Davis agreed, "Yes, sir, indeed, he is," and then she translated his words to Mamá, who then thanked him for his kindness.

Mamá noticed that Mr. McCormick had a Bible on his desk with different-colored bookmarks in various places in it. Mrs. Davis, following Mamá's eyes, took notice of the Bible too.

Mrs. Davis remarked, "That must be one very busy Bible, Sir."

"*Si, un buen libro*, a very good book. Why do you have so many bookmarks in it?" my mother asked and Mrs. Davis translated.

He explained, "I have seven markers for seven different important passages I quote for students I meet with for disciplinary reasons."

"May I?" my mother asked, and Mr. McCormick handed the Bible to her.

She looked at the Bible, caressed it, carefully opened it, and scanned a few pages before slowly closing it. "*Gracias, esta muy bonita.*"

Mr. McCormick asked, "Do you have anything in particular that fascinates you about the Bible?"

My mother replied in Spanish, "It's sacred and a believable truth. All of it fascinates me."

Next, Mr. McCormick addressed the reason for the meeting: "All your children are doing very well. They are learning English quite rapidly; however, they need to read more at home. They are okay with their numbers, but reading is important. Does Edgar speak to them in English or Spanish?"

"Mostly English," my mother answered. "I speak to them in Spanish, but I am hoping they will talk to me in English, so I too can learn it fast."

"Yes, that's the message to take from our conversation. It's like sports. You have to practice a lot to become a good athlete. Do those heavy workouts. Same thing at home, you have to try hard to speak English at all times. Even if you stumble and they correct you, just try and try hard. I think you will be fluent in English one of these days."

My mother looked over at Mrs. Davis, smiled, and replied to him, "Oh, yes."

"Sir, is there anything else Nena should know about the children?" asked Mrs. Davis.

"That is all. Please say hello to Miguel and Edgar."

They stood, thanked Mr. McCormick for his time, and exited his office where they came upon Natalie sitting at her desk in the reception area.

Natalie stood and walked around her desk to say to them in Spanish, "There's something I'd like to speak to you about. A favor."

"*Por supuesto. Qué es?*" Mamá asked.

"My ex-husband and I have a daughter, Daisy. After we returned to the USA, we then got divorced. He moved to Boston and remarried, and Daisy ended up living with him. I only get to see her a few times a year. It's been really difficult."

"*Qué terrible. Lo siento.* I'm sorry," Mamá murmured.

"However, presently Daisy is spending an extended period of time living with me here in Phoenix. The sad part is that she was in an almost fatal automobile accident, so she's staying with me during her recovery. It is slow and painful, but I am just so grateful that Daisy is alive and we are together during this time."

Mrs. Davis and my mother looked at Natalie with sympathy.

"*Como podemos ayudarte?* How can we help you?" Mrs. Davis asked.

"I heard that Nena is a fantastic cook. And, only recently, for the first time in her life, Daisy had enchiladas, and she fell in love with them. I want to make a special lunch for her, and I was wondering, Nena, if you could come to my house and teach me how to make enchiladas, and then we all have lunch together. There will be ten of us—and Mrs. Davis, you are welcome to come too. My daughter would be so delighted, so pleased if you did this. What do you think?"

My mother smiled and replied, "I'll be very happy to do that for you."

"Oh, what fun!" Mrs. Davis interjected. "Do you have a cake for dessert?"

"No, we're going to have brownies and ice cream."

"Oh no, you must have a chocolate cake with ice cream! I insist."

"Nobody makes a cake as well as Evelyn," my mother added.

"It's a deal! Let's do it!" Natalie exclaimed.

A few weeks later, I helped them to load Mrs. Davis's car with special pans, spices, and supplies, for the lunch. Mrs. Davis ended up making a few chocolate cakes, one for Daisy, and others for me and my brothers and sisters to enjoy.

Mamá and Mrs. Davis were enchanted by Natalie's large and luxurious home. In the back garden, a table for ten was set up, complete with silver candlesticks, properly arranged silverware, flower arrangements, a tablecloth and matching napkins, and glasses and plates of various sizes. In the kitchen, Natalie took notes and also took part in Mamá's enchilada preparation.

My mother was careful to instruct Natalie on the importance of never using the oven when making enchiladas—only the stovetop—to keep the tortillas light and crispy (and not soggy and heavy, as happens with an oven).

Although my mother had hoped to practice English, Mrs. Davis pointed out, "I think the enchiladas will taste better if we speak in Spanish when preparing them." Natalie and Mamá laughed in response.

While they were cooking, a young lady on crutches entered the kitchen, asking, "What smells so good?"

Natalie answered in Spanish, "Daisy, meet Nena and Evelyn. They came in especially for you. Nena is teaching me how to make enchiladas"—to my mother and Mrs. Davis—"I'm trying to teach Daisy Spanish."

Once everything was ready, my mother quickly checked the table setup to make sure the silverware was placed properly, and the dishes, glasses, placemats, napkins, etc., were perfectly aligned, something that reflected back to her first job as a teenager at the military camp in Arteaga. After my mother declared, "*Todo está perfecto*," it was time to teach everyone how to assemble the enchiladas.

Natalie began by introducing my mother and Mrs. Davis to the guests, elegantly attired professionals, "This is Magdalena Hernández, everyone calls her Nena, and this is Evelyn Davis, Nena's friend. I met them at the school, and to make Daisy's day very special, I asked these wonderful ladies to come and teach us how to make enchiladas, Daisy's newfound favorite food. We are so very privileged to have Nena and Evelyn here." Natalie then read a passage from the Bible and thanked God for Daisy's life and her recovery.

The guests raised their glasses to my mother, Mrs. Davis, and Daisy. Next my mother and Mrs. Davis stood before the guests to explain how to assemble their enchiladas.

"First, everyone please take one of these lightly-fried tortillas and place it on your plate," my mother started and Mrs. Davis translated.

"Next, spoon a helping of this shredded chicken mixture onto the tortilla . . . Top it with some *salsa verde*, sliced lettuce and diced tomato as well as a sprinkle of this Mexican cheese. Remember, you'll be rolling this up, so don't put too much inside it."

"*Excelente*. Now, it's time to roll it up. Start from this end and roll it like this," my mother stated and then demonstrated.

"At this point, you can add more cheese, lettuce, and tomato on top if you want. That is your enchilada. Now, it is time to eat. *Buen provecho*."

My mother's enchiladas were a success. Mrs. Davis's chocolate cake and the ice cream were another big hit.

After dessert, Natalie delivered another thank you to Mamá and Mrs. Davis, hugged them, and presented them each with a Hallmark card and flowers. Mamá and Mrs. Davis were beaming. It was a delightful get-together.

Daisy stated to Mamá and Mrs. Davis from across the table, "You know, when Mom gives a card, she always writes a unique and beautiful poem in it. Won't you read us the poems she's written for you?"

"That would be delightful," a gentleman remarked.

Another lady chimed in, "Oh yes, I love Natalie's poetry. Daisy is right. Please read us the poems, it would be very special to hear them with your voices."

"Please, won't you?" Daisy asked a second time. Then she added for Mamá, "And she writes poems in Spanish. I imagine yours will be in Spanish, Nena."

Mrs. Davis, in effort to save my mother from feeling awkward or ashamed, answered, "Thank you for letting us join you today. Nena and I, actually, need to go."

"It will take two minutes total. Come on. Please," several guests insisted.

Others contributed, saying, "We insist, please read them. It'll be fast and very special to hear each of you read them aloud."

My mother looked at Evelyn and then said to the table, "*Gracias por todo*," and signaled to leave.

Daisy begged, "I'm very grateful for your kindness, the delicious meal, and your wonderful visit. You both are so special, and I think it would make a very warm memory for all of us here if you read the poems."

My mother, who had moved a few feet away from the table, quickly turned to everyone and stated in slow, careful, English, "I am Magdalena Hernández. The people say Nena. I am from La Mira, a pueblo in Mexico. I have ten children. I cook tortillas on a fire. No gas. No electricity. In the *Estados Unidos* I have the electricity. Refrigerator. Stove. *Una lavadora*. I do not go to school. I cannot read or write. I cannot read a poem. Daisy is *un milagro de Dios*. Special. In *el futuro* I read and write. I love the Bible. *Gracias por todo*."

Mrs. Davis took Mamá's hand, and they exited.

Everyone at the table was silent. Stunned and moved.

Years later, Mamá had to go to Monroe School's principal's office again, but for a very different reason. By this time, Mr. McCormick and Natalie no longer worked there, and Mrs. Davis didn't accompany her. It was a secret mission of sorts . . .

Jose Angel, our one sibling whom Pedro didn't bring to the USA with everyone else in 1966, ended up legally immigrating and joining us a few years later when he was eight years old. Like the rest of us, Jose Angel started school at Monroe School. Unlike the rest of us, he had a serious mischievous streak. For example, when he was in fifth grade, he set off a cherry bomb in the hallway of Monroe School. There was a lot of smoke as well as the sound of an explosion. This was the reason for Mamá's visit with the principal.

To his credit, Jose Angel admitted he was responsible for the cherry bomb and apologized, but—not surprisingly—he got suspended indefinitely with the possibility of getting expelled. The only possibility for him to get to return was if the principal, Mr. Craig, could meet with Mamá and Jose Angel, and discuss the incident together. Based on that discussion, Mr. Craig would make a decision about Jose Angel's future at Monroe School.

Jose Angel confessed the whole situation to Mamá but begged, "Please don't tell my siblings. They'll be so disappointed and angry at me, Mamá. Please don't tell."

Mamá agreed not to tell the rest of us.

It was a hot day in August, and they had a three-mile walk to get to the school. Jose Angel was riding his Stingray bicycle, a small, low-rider bike with a banana seat and wide ape-hanger handlebars. He encouraged Mamá to sit on the handlebars, and away they went.

After a mile, Jose Angel turned a corner, and my mother ended up falling off the handlebars and onto the sidewalk. She scraped both her knees and her hands in the fall. They were bleeding. Plus her hair got disheveled. She cleaned herself up in a gas station and got back on the handlebars. However, they had a second fall.

While a polished appearance was extremely important to Mamá, after the two falls, she couldn't help but arrive at school with a disheveled and disorderly appearance. Even still, she stayed composed and never got upset or frustrated about the two falls or with Jose Angel.

At the school she found a faucet outside the building to try to clean herself up some. As she didn't have a comb, she could only wipe her hair with water and rearrange it with her fingers to try to make it neat. As they didn't have any bandages or Band-Aids, it was difficult to stop the bleeding of her knees and hands.

Once they found the principal's office and entered for their meeting, Mr. Craig was alarmed about Mamá's obvious injuries. He asked, "Are you okay?" a question that Jose Angel had to translate. He translated the whole conversation.

She communicated to Jose Angel that he should tell Mr. Craig that she's fine.

Puzzled and still concerned, he attempted to continue the meeting as planned, "Son, does your mother know why you are here?"

"Yes," Jose Angel confirmed.

"Did you tell her what you did?"

"Yes."

Mr. Craig then led a conversation about Jose Angel's poor judgment and how scary and potentially very dangerous the cherry bomb was. Mamá indicated that Jose Angel had told her all about it, that they both talked about what a mistake it had been, and that Jose Angel understood and accepted the dire consequences for the act.

Mr. Craig was not happy with Jose Angel. "You may be expelled for good for what you did," he told them. He indicated that Jose Angel had really threatened everyone's sense of safety.

However, at the same time in this discussion, he was obviously very concerned by Mamá's apparent injuries. "Your mother has dirt and grass in her hair. Her hands and knees are raw. My secretary and I are concerned about her. What happened?" he asked Jose Angel.

"I brought Mamá to school on my bicycle. She sat on the handlebars, and we fell down twice."

Mr. Craig insisted that Mamá leave with the secretary and get cleaned up and receive Band-Aids for her hands and knees.

While waiting for our mother to return, Mr. Craig asked Jose Angel for more details of the two falls. He showed a lot of concern and told Jose Angel how sorry he was about what happened.

When Mamá returned, Mr. Craig asked Jose Angel to translate to her, "I'm sorry about her accident. Also tell her that normally we would expel you outright, but since you admitted to your mistake, we are going to let you come back to school. But don't ever do this again. If you do, I will expel you. Please tell your mother what I said."

When Jose Angel translated Mr. Craig's words, he added in an extra sentiment, "And Mr. Craig says that I'm a really good kid and everyone at school appreciates me."

Because Mamá understood more English than Jose Angel realized, she raised an eyebrow at the "poetic liberty" he took in translating. Then she turned to Mr. Craig to reply, "*Si, gracias, señor.* Thank you, sir."

 On the way out, she told Jose Angel, "I am so glad you are going to be okay. I'm so happy he gave you another chance," and smiled at him.

Next, she hugged him and then announced, "Jose Angel, your punishment for the day is that you'll be walking your bicycle. We are both walking home."

For years and years afterwards, Jose Angel and Mamá loved to recall this memory together.

Mamá and Mrs. Davis's friendship thrived on the "challenge" of finding ways to help others. Both truly believed in being so personally blessed that it was their duty to help others. They both had a deep love for all human beings, including the most destitute of the destitute.

Mrs. Davis told me on many occasions that without my mother, many people would have died or just vanished. But my mother would not let anything happen to those people.

Upon exiting a thrift store, Mrs. Davis leaned over to pick up her handbag that she'd dropped. Mamá paused, waiting for her, when a moaning sound, a noise of agony, reached their ears.

They peered down a side alley where they made out a bulge in a dark green sack. They cautiously approached.

There was movement in the sack. Mamá noted, "*Un pie*," when a foot appeared.

Mrs. Davis acknowledged, "*Si, es un señor.*"

At the sound of her voice, a disheveled head poked out, revealing a red-bearded face marred by cuts, scrapes, and scabby skin. His green eyes seemed disoriented.

Within moments, a window opened, and they heard a man call out, "You get away from here, you piece of trash!"

The disheveled man pushed the bag down and away from him to try to move himself upright. In doing so, he revealed his legs, ankles, and feet mangled by scabs that had blackened. It was evident to my mother and Mrs. Davis that the man was in severe pain and in need of serious medical help.

Mrs. Davis knocked on the door that led to the space where the person who'd shouted was staying. A man with an exasperated expression on his face answered the door.

Mrs. Davis asked him, "We want to call an ambulance or the police to help this man out here. Could you do it? Or could we use your phone?"

"The police already know him. He's been in and out of jail, the hospital. A worthless suck on the resources that the rest of us pay for with our hard-earned tax dollars. He won't change cuz he don't want to, and we're sick of taking care of his dirty ass. Piss off," he replied and shut the door.

Meanwhile Mamá was trying to talk to the man. She detected the familiar foul odor of alcohol and cigarettes. He seemed in a stupor, belligerent, fighting off some unseen enemy, and at the same time fighting off my mother's attempts at connection.

When Mamá and Mrs. Davis tried to solicit help from passers-by, they kept walking, speeding up their pace even.

One man explained, as he kept walking, "That's a nasty one. He might hurt you if you get too close. Best to keep a distance."

In a moment of real awareness, the indigent man stated, "Leave me alone. I want to die. Leave me alone."

Mrs. Davis said to him, "We want to help you. The police or the hospital—let's get you some help."

"No police! No hospital!" he hollered.

Mamá and Mrs. Davis realized he was too combative to stay in our back garage. He seemed feral and could get aggressive with our other guests, but they were determined not to leave him.

"What about the abandoned storage space off that alley that runs behind your house?" Mamá suggested.

"*Buena idea*," Mrs. Davis agreed.

A man in a pickup truck stopped outside the alley and called to Mamá and Mrs. Davis, "I walked by about ten minutes ago and heard you all asking folks to help you with that man. If you gotta place to take him, we can put him in my pickup, and I'll drive him there."

Twenty minutes later, after situating the man in the dilapidated storage shed, Mrs. Davis and Mamá agreed to gather some items for him and meet there thirty minutes later.

At the determined time, Mamá approached with a tray in her hands. On the tray sat a big glass of *horchata* [rice water] and a large bowl of *cosida* [beef soup]. Mrs. Davis was already there helping the man situate himself on a pillow. She also brought a blanket and aspirin.

The man never said a word. He didn't fight them. He had the soup and *horchata*. He took some aspirin. He seemed to be in a daze and very sleepy.

While she didn't know if he was in a state to comprehend her, Mrs. Davis told him, "You can stay here for a while, or you can leave anytime you want. We aren't holding you here. But know that you are very sick, so we want you to stay. We will care for you until you are better."

Back at Mrs. Davis's house, the two women discussed the man—his family, background, present state, future—what could it be? Mamá placed her hand firmly atop Mrs. Davis's Bible.

Mrs. Davis stated, "*Nena, espero que Dios lo proteja.*"

"*Si, es verdad,*" my mother responded.

The next morning, after we children left to school, Mamá checked in on the man. Not wanting him to feel threatened, she didn't enter the old shed he was housed in. Instead she stood a short distance from it and called, "*Señor! Señor! Estas adentro?* Are you there? *Señor!*"

At that, he appeared, standing in the shed's opening. "What's your name?" he muttered.

Because it was a familiar English question, Mamá answered, "Nena."

"Don't call the police," he told her.

"*Entiendo, no policía. Podría conseguirte algo de comida?*"

"No Spanish." he answered.

"*Dame un momento,*" Mamá told him and left to retrieve Mrs. Davis.

When they returned, they stood in the small lot but at a distance. Two rusted refrigerators separated them from the man.

"My name is Spencer Holloway. I've been up and down in life, moving from place to place for a while now. I had a son who died of testicular cancer when he was 7. Since then, I have been trying to find him," he shared.

Mrs. Davis rapidly translated this to Mamá, who uttered in response, "*Qué terrible. Qué triste.*"

Mrs. Davis then asked, " 'Find him'? What do you mean?"

"When I drink, that's when I can see him. So I drink . . . I don't have a home. I don't have money, but I'm not a criminal. I have a drinking problem . . . You two are the nicest people I ever met."

"*Tienes familia?*" Mamá asked.

"Do you have a family?" Mrs. Davis translated.

"No. Once I had a wife, back in Oklahoma. She was an alcoholic but left when our son was only two. I cared for him after that."

Mrs. Davis and Mamá conferred. Then Mrs. Davis said to Spencer, "We want to help you. We want to help you, so you can get better. But we aren't going to give you alcohol or cigarettes."

"Just no police," he responded.

"And no liquor or cigarettes," Mrs. Davis repeated.

"Where are you from?" Spencer asked.

Mrs. Davis answered, "My name is Evelyn, and she is Nena. She was born in Mexico, and her English is limited. I was born in Mississippi and live nearby with my husband, Glen. Nena lives with her children close-by."

Spencer commented, "The food was good, haven't had a meal like that in a long time."

My mother left him a tube of antibiotic ointment for his skin scabs on the ground between the two old refrigerators. Mrs. Davis explained to him what it was for.

Before they left Mamá asked Mrs. Davis to tell him that they would pray for him to change his life.

Spencer's response: "Won't do much good."

Because they knew that people in their neighborhood might not agree with their helping Spencer and that it could be dangerous for him, they didn't discuss him with anyone. Several times a day, they brought him food, water, other drinks, and aspirin. They prayed for him, both together and individually, as well.

One afternoon Asunción remarked to our mother, "I saw one of our cups in that little lot in the back alley behind the Davises."

"*No digas nada*"—don't say anything—Mamá answered.

Not understanding, Asunción began to cry. She asked between sobs, "Is it one of our guests? Are they hurt? What's happening?"

"No, *mija*. Nothing like that. It is a man that you don't know that Mrs. Davis and I are helping. He's very sick and too scared to stay with us. He feels safer there. We bring him food, drinks, and medicine, so he can get back on his feet."

As the weeks passed, Mrs. Davis and Mamá wondered about Spencer, what he was going to do, how he was handling going off the drinking and smoking, and what would happen to him. They wondered, worried, hoped, and prayed for him.

One morning with a tray of breakfast in hand, Mamá stepped into the lot, calling, "Señor Spencer! Señor Spencer!" but she got no reply. She walked nearer to the shed and called his name again, but still no response. She then walked to the doorway of the shed and spoke his name. When he still didn't respond, she walked inside. He was no longer there.

Carrying the tray, she went to Mrs. Davis's backdoor. Balancing the tray in her right hand and on the railing, Mamá managed to free her left hand, so she could knock.

Mrs. Davis opened the door, saying, "*Buenos dias, Nena. Que esta pasando?*"

"It's Spencer. *Él no ésta allí.*"

"I'm on my way," Mrs. Davis told her.

At the lot, Mrs. Davis pointed out a note tacked to one of the rusted refrigerators. It read:

Angels,

I lost total trust in people until I met the both of you. I did not think anyone on Earth cared.

I wonder if you all are thinking, "Spencer left so he could start drinking and smoking again." The answer is no. When Evelyn described to me how Nena's husband died from his addiction to drinking and smoking, I couldn't believe it. I couldn't get over how he threw his life away and left such an angel behind.

Thank you, angels.

After Mamá heard the note's translation, she and Mrs. Davis looked at each other and then back at the note, in silence.

Finally, Mrs. Davis murmured, "Miracles happen. Who are we to question such miracles? A miracle we will never know."

"*Sólo Dios sabe,*" my mother added and continued, "*Oramos para que Dios lo proteja.* God, we beseech you to protect this man."

"Amen," Mrs. Davis said.

They returned to our house and sat together on the sofa for a Bible reading. Mrs. Davis opened the Bible and began reading aloud in her song-like voice. Mamá leaned back and fell into a state of deep listening, all the while dreaming of a time in the future when she too could read the Bible so fluently.

Chapter 10

AMIGO O ENEMIGO

"Edgar, having you here is always a special occasion for me. Sit down and tell me what you've been doing. What lives have you saved today?" asked Mamá as she sat beside me, opened the Bible, turned several pages, closed it, and smiled.

"Mamá, tell me, how are you doing today?"

"I feel great as long as you are here, *mijo*. As long as you are healthy, I am very happy."

I stood up from the table to get some sweet tea, and Mamá unexpectedly stood at the same time and gave me a hug. It was almost like she took the opportunity to stand at the same time as I did, so she could steal a hug from me. My mother was spontaneous about hugging. She loved a warm hug. She would tell me that each hug filled her day and provided, at the same time, everlasting energy.

"Mamá, do you remember La Cantina de Michoacán, that restaurant on Central Avenue?"

"Yes, Edgar. You took me there for dinner a few months ago. The food was wonderful."

"Last night, when one of the musicians refused to play anymore because he felt sick and wanted to go home—a brawl erupted. A couple of guys called him a *joto*, not a very nice name, as you know. The musician tried to avoid a confrontation, but suddenly an eruption of blows began. He had a guitar with him, and that was his only defense—it actually saved his life."

"How is that?"

"One of the two guys who'd been drinking a lot took a swing at the guitarist, but that guy fell to the ground. Then a second guy came at him with a knife. Instead of stabbing him, he stabbed the guitar, and his hand got tangled in the frets and strings. The attacker ended up cutting his hand severely. The knife did penetrate the guitarist's abdomen, but not with the force it could have."

"What happened to the guitarist? The men? Are they okay?" she asked cautiously. My mother was always concerned about everyone. She never wanted anyone to be hurt, even if she didn't know them. She always thought that everyone was related—we're all a massive, extended family—and she did not want anyone to suffer in life.

"I operated on the guitarist. He had only a slight injury to his internal stomach, and he will be fine. It was the guitarist who told me the whole story after the surgery," I explained. "The other man had major surgery on his hand to repair neurological and tendon injuries. He will probably be out of commission for at least a year while his hand heals and the function comes back to normal. Unfortunately, he will have a permanent disability."

"*Oh Dios mío* . . . Edgar, do you remember when we took in a guest who was also a musician?"

"Yes. Romero—his name was Romero. That was about fifteen years ago, around 1970. I was a student at Arizona State University."

"Do you remember how he came to us?"

"Yes, he was playing in a local band at a wedding we went to."

"He was such a talented, kind man."

"Yes, Mamá, he was," I agreed.

After the wedding, one of the musicians approached Mamá and quietly introduced himself, "*Hola, señora, mi nombre es Romero.* My name is Romero."

"*Mucho gusto, Romero. Soy Magdalena,* but I go by Nena. You are a wonderful singer and musician."

Mamá noticed that even though he had great charisma and presence on stage, this young man, probably about 28, was quite soft-spoken, perhaps even shy.

"Nena, *mucho gusto.* You are very kind. I was told that you sometimes allow people to live with you . . . If this is true, I'd like to talk to you about it," Romero said to her in a low voice.

Mamá could tell he wasn't accustomed to asking for help so directly, so she did all she could to make it easier for him, replying, "*Si, es verdad. Dime,* what do you need? We'd love to help you."

Romero went on to explain that he was working at a restaurant helping the cook. Also, he did work cleaning hotel rooms. At night, he would freelance at another restaurant playing the guitar. Currently he was living in the back of one of the restaurants, but he'd love to stay with us until he saved money for his own accommodations. He promised he'd be out of the house for most hours of the day and that he would contribute to our household as much as possible.

"It would be a pleasure to have you stay with us, Romero," my mother assured him.

Romero ended up staying with us for about four months. In those months, all of us came to know and appreciate this young man, especially Mamá, who developed a close friendship with him. Though he typically left early in the morning and arrived back at the house late at night, on the occasions when he was in the house, he played the guitar for us. Although he confessed that he didn't have much education, as a child, he'd learned to read and write a little, so he and Mamá would work on reading the Bible together. He was an excellent baker, and he taught her how to make incredible *empanadas* and other Mexican pastries—*conchas, orejas, cuernos de azucar*, and *campechanas*. He even manicured Mamá's nails.

He told us that he had a twin brother in Guadalajara who was also a musician and performed in a theater. Then Romero went on to confide, "I don't have my papers. I'm actually waiting for my twin brother to send me some official documents and certificates, so I can begin the immigration process. My greatest wish is to live in the United States with papers and to perform in theaters in the San Francisco area. But, *verdaderamente*, I find the process confusing."

"*No te preocupes*, Romero. Miguel is an expert on immigration, and Edgar knows quite a lot as to how to obtain proper documents. They will help you," Mamá told him.

Miguel and I were happy to help Romero. He was one of the kindest, most sincere people we'd ever met, plus his baking was exceptional.

Two of my sisters were watching television as my mother went about doing some housework. She was preparing sauces for lunch and dinner, and also folding laundry when she heard a knock on the door.

She opened the door to find standing there a tall man, professional-looking in a blue suit and tie adorned with a tie clip. He had a medium-build and a blond crew cut. He was well shaven. Bushy blond eyebrows protruded prominently above his thick, black-rimmed Clark Kent style glasses. He was 30 years old at the most. Probably younger. He likely was someone who frequented the neighborhood, but this was the first time he'd knocked on our door.

She began, "*Buenos días*. Good morning."

Unwavering, the man demanded, "*Quien vive aquí*?" which translates to "Who lives here?"

"*Quién eres tú, señor*?" my mother replied with a questioning look. This translates to "Who are you?"

"*Papeles*, do you have papers?" he asked next. (Their conversation proceeded in Spanish.)

"Yes, we have papers. *Todos temenos papeles*, we all have papers," she answered.

At this point, Mamá worried that I might show up at the house. All my documents were in order, and I was even a US citizen at this point, but she was concerned that I might get agitated by this document check. She didn't want me to relive the times I witnessed the many deportation raids when I'd been a child living in Phoenix without documents for those several months in 1959. I'd had two very close calls myself, and it was traumatizing. Mamá silently prayed to God that I would not show up while the officer was there. She deeply felt that this would bother me greatly.

Even still, she figured he wouldn't leave until he saw some papers, so it was best to be open, friendly, and hospitable.

"*Por favor, señor, entre.* Come in and have a seat at the dining room table. Let me show you my green card. May I offer you something to drink?"

Once he was seated, Mamá handed him her green card, explaining, "Here it is, *señor*. As you can see, in my photo I'm holding a baby, my son Salvador. The Consulate in Nogales said that it made more sense for him to share his green card with me because he was just a baby and his features would change so much over the years. When he's between 12 and 14, they said that's when he should get his own green card."

The man quickly glanced at the green card and was ready to return it to her before she'd completed her explanation.

"Let me get you something to drink," Mamá offered. As she stepped into the kitchen, she called back to him, "I'm sure you already know everyone who lives here, yes?"

"Yes," he confirmed, "there's Miguel, Pedro, Jorge, Edgar, Lupe, Asunción, Reyna, Manuel, Salvador, and Olivia."

"Yes, you are correct, *señor*, although Olivia now lives somewhere else. She took a job, and she has to live within that vicinity."

He nodded, "True, I actually have that in my notes."

Then, softening a bit, he remarked, "There's a lovely smell in your house. What is it?"

At this, Mamá realized he must mean the scent of cinnamon. Then it hit her—cinnamon, *empanadas*—Romero! She did her best to maintain her cool.

"*Es canela*, cinnamon. We have *empanadas*. Let me get you one with that cold drink," she suggested.

It was a Saturday, which meant that Romero was at the restaurant helping the cook, but Mamá knew that sometimes, not always but sometimes, on the weekends he had an hour or two to spare between the restaurant and the hotel, depending on how busy either place was.

In the kitchen, Mamá placed an *empanada* on a plate and filled a glass with cold *agua de tamarindo* from the fridge.

As the man waited for her, he made small talk, commenting, "I see you have a Bible. Good book, isn't it?"

"*Sí*," Mama agreed, noticing that she was beginning to feel more relaxed with the man.

When she returned to the dining room with his food and drink, he asked, "Do you know why I'm here?"

"*Sí, señor*. I do. I know you have a very important job and that you are a very important man," she answered sincerely.

She saw him relax at her response. Plus, he seemed to be enjoying the *empanada* as well as the *agua de tamarindo*. She noticed too that his hands were clean and his nails well kept, something she was very particular about. His shirt was nicely pressed, and there was no lint on his suit. He wore a nice watch with a fresh, honey-colored leather band, leather that we in my family call *cuero*. He had very nice manners.

"How are you enjoying the *empanada*?" she inquired.

"It's particularly good. Thank you."

"Its secret is tons of cinnamon. Did you know cinnamon is very good for you? It mobilizes a lot of the chemicals in the body to make you function better," she remarked. Her comfort level with this man was getting better as time went on.

"Is that so?" he replied.

"*Sí*. Tell me, what's your mother's name?" Mamá asked.

"My mother? You asked, 'What's my mother's name?'?" he asked. Upon seeing her nod, he answered, "Her name is Margaret, but people call her Maggie."

"She must be beautiful because the sound of her name is very precious."

He answered, "Yes, she is beautiful."

My mother told him, "My name is Magdalena, but everyone calls me Nena."

"I knew you were Magdalena," he admitted, "But Nena, I didn't know you went by Nena. The name fits you very well."

"*Gracias*," she said. "Do you have a picture of your mother?"

"Yes, I do." He pulled out his wallet and showed her a photo.

"Oh, she is very beautiful. Such lovely eyes. You resemble her 100 percent," Mamá observed.

"*Muchas gracias*, Nena," he told her with a small smile.

"Do you have any sisters or brothers?" she asked.

"Yes, I do. They're all in Colorado."

"Colorado?"

"Yes, it's a state very close to us. It's very cold there. It snows a lot. I was born there," he explained.

"Snow, I've never seen snow," she said. "What does your mother do? Does she work?"

"Yes, she's a teacher part-time, and the rest of her time she takes care of the children."

"Can I see her picture again?" she asked.

"Yes," he said and pulled out the picture again, showing it to her. This time Mamá noticed the badge attached to his wallet as well.

"What's her mother's name? *Tu abuela*?"

"Shirley," he answered. "*Mi abuela* is quite ill and probably will not live very long," he confided.

"*Dios mío!* What's wrong?" my mother asked.

"She had cancer, and the cancer has come back."

My mother grabbed the Bible, opened it briefly, turned a few pages, and closed it.

"A good book," he commented again.

"Yes, a very good book that I like to read very much," she explained. "Do you have family of your own?"

"No, I don't. I'm not ready to settle down. I'm too busy at work right now and have not thought much about that."

"Do you have a girlfriend?"

"No, not really."

My mother offered, "That's too bad. A good-looking man like you is bound to find a wonderful wife one of these days."

"Yes, that will come with time. Right now, I'm trying to move up the ladder at work, and I want to move up in rank. That's going to take some time. Once I accomplish what I want to do, then I'll start seeking someone to marry in the future since it's something my mother really wants me to do. She wants to have grandchildren."

"I think that's very nice. That's very wonderful! Excuse me, *señor*, I'm going to get some *empanadas* for the children, so they'll have something to eat. I'll be right back." She then went to the kitchen to retrieve some more *empanadas* and glasses of milk for my two sisters.

When my mother returned to the dining room, he asked, "Do you have anyone else living here with you?"

"We have occasional guests who visit and stay with us. I don't let them leave when they're tired, so they stay here and rest for a few days. They are nice, decent people."

"But do they have papers?"

"I don't know, but I make sure they are good, loving Christian people and love the Lord. I'm sure your mother loves Christians and loves the Lord."

"Oh, yes, she does, very much," he agreed.

"You see, I could tell by looking at her picture that she is a good, loving Christian. She is beautiful and has a very nice smile. Does she read the Bible?" my mother asked.

"Yes, she takes it to church every Sunday."

"How about reading it at home? Does she read the Bible at home with her children?"

"That too," he answered.

As they were talking, Mamá moved back into the kitchen and called out to him, "As I prepare lunch, we can talk a little more. I'd like to know more about your mother. You see, I'm always interested to see what mothers do for their children and what their children do for them. I've always loved to see parents and their children together. I hate when children are separated from their mothers. It's something very hurtful, something I know much about. So, tell me more about your mother."

He moved into the kitchen to continue the conversation. As he sat down in a chair at our tiny two-person kitchen table, my mother took a couple of pans and put them on the stove.

This man did not know that my mother was not going to turn him loose until he had lunch and they would talk and talk in a long conversation. She thoroughly enjoyed talking with friends and family, and with my mother there was no time limit for completing a conversation. Her conversations were thorough and detailed, and afterward, she could recount that conversation verbatim.

"I don't think Miguel and Pedro will be here for lunch today. Edgar probably won't be able to make it either. You know, Edgar's going to be a surgeon someday."

"Oh, is that so?" he asked.

"Oh, yes, he's at ASU right now, earning two degrees, actually in a short amount of time. And he'll be a surgeon in a matter of a few years. Now, tell me, what type of meals does your mother make?"

"They are not hot and spicy like Mexican food. I can smell that hot chili you are cutting, and my mother does not make food like that. She makes great mashed potatoes. Do you know those red potatoes?"

"No, I have not seen red potatoes."

"She makes both white and red mashed potatoes, gravy, and a fantastic meatloaf. She makes the meatloaf, piles on mashed potatoes, and covers it all with gravy. She puts gravy on just about anything."

He then described what meatloaf was all about, but my mother kind of knew what it was. She'd had it once before at a small diner. She had liked the taste of it.

She noted, "Excuse me for a minute. I need to retrieve the children's plates and give them more to eat. They're watching cartoons and won't even know I've taken anything from them. They're glued to the TV, and I'll try not to disturb them."

Upon returning to the kitchen, she said, "Mashed potatoes—white and red potatoes. That's wonderful."

"Yes, and wonderful fried chicken. She is an excellent cook, like you."

By this time about two hours had passed, and he was tangled up with a master of conversation. My mother could entertain almost anyone, and for certain, they would never be bored. One conversation would lead to another topic and thus would sprout to a very lengthy conversation. My mother could lead you into a lengthy discussion whether you liked it or not. It could be a discussion that would develop into many categories—stories captivating—and this man was a captive. He just didn't know it.

"Do you like enchiladas? You are going to be having enchiladas for lunch with us. And tell me, what is your name?"

"Stevenson, Officer Stevenson."

"Do you have a first name? Your mother does not call you 'Stevenson,' does she?"

They both smiled.

"No, she calls me Roger. I was named after my grandfather."

"That is a wonderful name. How long has it been since you saw your mother? Do you visit her?"

"Yes, but it has been some time since I last saw her. I've been very busy. As I said before, I've been trying very hard to move up the ladder in my rank. See, we officers are like the military. We have different ranks, and I want to be a high-ranking officer, so that I can give orders instead of taking them."

"Your ambition and dreams are commendable, but I think it would be a good idea to visit your mother more frequently. Did you know my Surama left home when she was 12, Pedro at 9, Jorge at 7½ , and Edgar at 9½? Each time, it was devastating. I became disabled, like I'd lost a part of my body. Mothers make these kinds of sacrifices, so their children can have the best lives, but it is still so difficult. I reunited with all of my children here in Phoenix just a few years ago after being separated for many years. You must visit and call your mother often. I know she misses you."

"Nena, I know all of you have your papers in order, but only Pedro, Edgar, Miguel, and Olivia are US citizens. It does, however, take time, but it is certainly something to be very proud of."

"Yes, you are correct. Soon, though, God willing, we will all be citizens, something to be very proud of."

Several hours had passed, and Officer Roger Stevenson was becoming very comfortable with my mother, enjoying their lengthy and warm conversation as well as her enchiladas.

My mother did not think he was a threat to her or even to our guests if they were to come home. In fact, she was no longer worried about Romero. She felt very comfortable that no harm would come to him, so she showed no anxiety. She showed total tranquility. Mr. Stevenson had no idea how possessive my mother was and how very convincing at the same time.

"Do you own a farm in Colorado?" she asked.

"Yes," he confirmed, "how did you know?"

"I saw the barn in the background of your mother's picture. I come from the small town of La Mira, Michoacán."

Officer Stevenson smiled. "I know. I know all about you," he explained.

"Do you see that stove? Look at it, it's beautiful. Look at this refrigerator. We even have a special machine that whips cool wind throughout the house. I never had these things before. This all is a gift from God, from the hard work of Miguel and the rest of the family. It is something I wish more people would have. I left many people behind in La Mira, and I wish they could have the things I have. Bathrooms in the house—those don't exist in La Mira—did you know that? Did you know that in La Mira, like all the women, I did my cooking over a fire from coals that I made myself by burning wood pieces? I made tortillas, by hand, three times a day, and beans and occasionally some eggs—all over the fire. I did this for my whole life until I came here. I am grateful to be here."

My mother knew this young man had a good upbringing and a good heart. My mother wished he could know how kind and hard-working all of our guests were who stayed with us.

"Did you know it took Miguel seven years to remodel this house, so we could all live here together? It has been tough, but we manage well, thanks to God and thanks to the Good Book," she said. "Mr. Stevenson, God has been good to you. You are an important man with huge responsibilities."

"Yes," he agreed, "my responsibilities are huge."

"Do you talk to your mother about what you do for a living?"

"Sort of. I guess she knows I am an immigration inspector, but she doesn't ask me much about what I do every day at work."

After he finished his additional helping of enchiladas, he noted, "You are a very good cook, Nena."

Mamá admitted, "Actually it was my step-son Miguel who taught me how to cook. I have cooked for my children for years and years. Once I came here to the United States, Miguel taught me other things I didn't know because there are many ingredients, foods, and kitchen machines here that are new to me. I'm very grateful for his lessons."

"Is that right—Miguel actually taught you how to cook? That's incredible! Tell me, Nena, do you know people in this community who do not have papers?"

"I'm sure I do, but I don't always see them because they are always working," she responded.

"I see. Where do they work?"

"Oh, everywhere. Here, there, any place they can find a job to keep busy. They work in bakeries, restaurants, and they do just about anything to earn a living. They are very hard workers," she said.

"Do you know anyone in particular?"

"No, not really," she answered. "How about some more *agua de tamarindo*, Mr. Stevenson? You know I make it myself. Have you ever seen a *tamarindo*? Let me show you"—she retrieved a container of tamarinds from the refrigerator—"This is one of the most interesting fruits. Sometimes this fruit has two seeds. Sometimes they're joined together and covered by a fruit layer and then the whole thing is covered by a brown shell. You see?"

"Weird. I've never seen one before though I've enjoyed the drink for years. It's tangy, yet sweet. So, do you like it here in the United States?"

"Oh, yes, it is a wonderful life. It is a miracle from God. The life, the facilities, and opportunities are plentiful and wonderful. When I tell people here how I used to make tortillas every morning, mid-day, and evening, starting with grinding the soft, boiled corn to make the dough, hand-patting it into disc shapes, and then placing them on a hot griddle to cook them over a fire, people don't believe it. Also, they can't imagine no electricity, no refrigerator, no gas. And dirt floors. Sometimes when I talk to people, they think my life before in Mexico is a made-up story because all they have ever seen is what they have here, wonderful facilities. And thank God they have them, and thank God I have them now too. It seems people don't understand since they have never lived any differently."

She opened the Bible, turned a few pages, and ran her finger from the top to the bottom as if she were reading.

Officer Stevenson looked at her and remarked, "You love the Good Book, don't you? Do you read it a lot?'

"Yes, I do love it, and I read it always."

Mr. Stevenson had no idea my mother could neither read nor write because her gentle touch on the Bible was quite convincing as well as her deep yearning and enthusiasm to become a strong reader of the Bible.

She smiled at him and told him that he too should sometimes read it. He said that his mother often read the Bible, but he paid little attention to it.

"Maybe I should," he conceded.

"Yes, you should," my mother encouraged.

"So, have you had people living here in your house who had no papers?" Officer Stevenson asked. "Or do you know anyone else who has people living with them who have no papers?"

Suddenly, there was a knock at the door. My mother excused herself and went to answer it.

"Evelyn, please come in," Mamá greeted Mrs. Davis.

"Nena, I'm just dropping by this chocolate cake, so all of you can enjoy it for dinner," Mrs. Davis told her.

"Thank you. Come in, come in, and meet Mr. Stevenson. He's a friend of the family. He knows Miguel and all of the family."

"Why that is very nice," Mrs. Davis answered. She walked inside to where Mr. Stevenson was sitting at the table.

Upon her entrance, Mr. Stevenson stood and said, "Call me Roger."

"I'm Evelyn Davis, a neighbor and good friend of the family," she replied.

They shook hands.

Mrs. Davis, wearing a red-flowered dress and bright red lipstick, sat down by my mother, and my mother told her in broken English, "Mr. Stevenson speaks excellent Spanish. I do not get to practice English with him."

My mother continued, this time in Spanish, "Mr. Stevenson knows us very well."

"*Bueno*," Mrs. Davis replied and to Mr. Stevenson, "The Hernández family is wonderful. They are hardworking and God-loving people."

Upon seeing Mamá's Bible, Mrs. Davis pulled it to her and remarked, "Nena, do you know that the Bible brings us together?"

"Very much so. Mr. Stevenson's mother loves it too. He calls it the Good Book."

"Amen, indeed, it is," Mrs. Davis agreed.

Mrs. Davis asked, "How is it that you two know each other?"

Mamá answered, "Mr. Stevenson knows Miguel and the rest of the family. He has an important job helping people with their immigration papers."

Mrs. Davis turned to Mr. Stevenson, "Where do you work?"

"I'm an officer with the United States Customs Office. I make sure I know where people live."

At this, Mrs. Davis looked at him and said, "Your mother should be very proud of you, young man."

He smiled and then stood to leave, remarking, "I should be leaving. My visit has been way too long."

"No, Mr. Stevenson. Please stay and have dinner with all of us. We will be having dinner in a few hours."

Mrs. Davis stood up also, noting, "I need to be getting home myself, starting some dinner preparation before Glen comes homes."

The three of them walked to the front door and then stood on the front porch to finish their conversation.

"Will you be making your delicious fried chicken?" Mamá asked her.

"Actually, yes."

"Mr. Stevenson, Evelyn makes the best fried chicken ever. I'm sure your mother would love it, especially with those mashed potatoes and gravy your mother makes"—and to Mrs. Davis—"His mother cooks mashed red potatoes with gravy."

"Oh, how delicious," Mrs. Davis commented, "I must make some for Glen. Mr. Stevenson, when you come back, you must stop and say hello."

He smiled and said, "Yes, I will."

Suddenly Romero appeared. He was carrying two dresses on hangers.

As he walked up the porch steps, Mrs. Davis asked him, "Romero, how are you doing, darling? *Cómo estás?*"

A total silence ensued.

After a moment, Mrs. Davis hugged Romero. Mamá hugged him as Mr. Stevenson looked on.

Mrs. Davis noted, "Those dresses are beautiful, Romero."

"They are for Nena," Romero said shyly.

"For me?" my mother continued to gently hug him.

"I cleaned a room at the hotel, and the people that had stayed there left these dresses in the closet. The owner called them, but they said to keep the dresses. The owner didn't want them, so I asked him if I could have them to bring them to you."

"For me?"

"Yes," said Romero.

Mamá turned to Mr. Stevenson to explain, "This is Romero. He is a friend of the family. We read the Bible together, and we pray for his mother and his twin brother, so they can be safe. Romero made the delicious *empanadas* we just ate."

Mr. Stevenson reached out and shook Romero's hand, saying, "Those are fine *empanadas*."

Mr. Stevenson then turned to look at my mother, Mrs. Davis, and then over at Romero.

My mother stepped forward to him, saying, "Thank you for visiting. We'll tell Miguel that you stopped by, and please say hello to your mother, Maggie. Please come again and visit us." Then she gave him a hug.

"Yes, I will. Thank you, Nena," he told her and then walked to his car.

Once inside the house, Romero broke down in tears. As he sobbed, he uttered, "*La Migra, sí*? That was an immigration officer, wasn't it?"

My mother and Mrs. Davis embraced him.

"Do not worry, Romero. Now he's a friend. *Un amigo*," Mamá assured him.

Chapter 11

GOD'S HANDS

"Edgar, I have so many tortillas that I decided to make us *chi-laquiles* for lunch."

"Mamá, you know I love them."

Our mother taught us that when we've got a lot of tortillas, so many we know we won't be able to eat them in time, that's when it's time to make *chilaquiles*.

This is how Mamá made *chilaquiles*: you cut the tortillas into small pieces and lightly fry them in a large, wide pan, like you're making nacho chips. In the same pan you scramble four or five eggs and mix them with the nacho chips, so they stick. Then you cover all that with a chili sauce of your choice and let it simmer for five minutes. In the meantime, you dice some onions and add to them a bit of oregano and a touch of vinegar. You then add this onion mix to the pan and sprinkle Mexican cheese on top. Done. It's quite easy to prepare and it makes a delicious meal.

I was so looking forward to having lunch with my mother—not just because of her *chilaquiles ricos*, but also because I had some surprising news from work that I knew she'd enjoy hearing.

As I'd expected, while she was preparing the *chilaquiles*, Mamá asked, "*Digame*, Edgar, how are you doing? What's going on at the hospital—anything interesting?"

Because I wanted to surprise her, I played it cool, saying, "Let me see . . . Since it was a holiday yesterday, the ER was quite busy. I had to perform several surgeries, but that's to be expected."

"Did you meet anyone who stood out to you?" she inquired as she dropped tortilla pieces into the hot oil.

"Lots of fighting-related surgeries. Someone came in with a knife in him, buried right in his chest area. I had to remind the staff not to remove the knife under any circumstances."

"Edgar, how terrible! Tell me, what happened to this person?"

"It was a man about my age. I managed to remove the knife and repair the vessel in the middle of his right upper lung that it had penetrated. The man will recover."

"*Gracias a Dios,*" I heard Mamá say.

"Mamá, there's more to it than that. You see, the man was Lonny Ramirez—"

"*No lo creo!* How can this be? How could you handle it, *mijo*? I am shocked!" Mamá interjected.

About 14 years earlier, when I was at Phoenix Union High School along with Jorge, Lonny Ramirez was also a student at the school. He was an active gang member too. Along with some other gang members he led vicious attacks on teachers and students, including me and Jorge. He led an assault against me after school at my locker, bashing up my face and almost worse until another student, Danny Carbajal, who later in my life became a good friend, stopped it. He was also in a group that jumped me and Jorge in our neighborhood. His violence—and his ever-lurking potential for violence—terrorized me and my family. It was a difficult time. This violence and fear made up our reality for several years.

"Mamá, I'm not bringing him up to make you remember those bad years. I've got some good news for you."

"Please tell me because right now I feel afraid," she admitted.

"For one thing, the police were there at the hospital, and they informed us that Lonny was the victim; they'd arrested the perpetrator."

"*Verdaderamente?*" Mamá murmured in response.

"And, Mamá, Lonny recognized me. He grabbed my hand and told me he knew I was Edgar, but he was calling me 'Dr. Hernández' because I worked so hard for the title. He showed me respect and appreciation. He regretted his past. Mamá, it was incredibly touching."

Mamá started weeping. "*Dios es grande.* Miracles happen," she solemnly stated.

"When I think back to all we went through with Lonny Ramirez and the gang violence, Mamá, I can't help but think of Joey—and how compassionate and kindhearted you were to him. To me, that was another miracle playing out, the way your kindness ended up changing him and his life—and all those other people's lives too."

It was the late '60s, and there was great political and social unrest. The Vietnam War had started, and male students at Phoenix Union High School were getting drafted all the time to serve. However, it wasn't the draft that my family and I were most concerned with—riots, assaults, and gang violence, both at school and in our neighborhood, were the greatest threats.

On our high school campus there were numerous marches organized for various causes, including peace, improved schools, better jobs, and equality. Students who were gang members would take advantage of these gatherings to jump other students—and then total chaos would ensue. The organized marches sometimes turned into riots that could go on for a few hours until the administration, that hadn't wanted to draw attention from the outside to the fact that the school was suffering from a serious disturbance, reluctantly would call the police. The attacks were sometimes so nasty that ambulances were called. It was scary.

In the course of a regular school day—riots aside—the number one fear of every student and teacher was getting assaulted by vigilante students, who typically were members of gangs. "Light" attacks included getting kicked, punched, or slapped, possessions or money getting stolen, or getting verbally abused.

I witnessed at least a half a dozen assaults and beatings of teachers. These occurred in the classroom. A student or students, usually gang members, would hit a teacher in the head, push the teacher in the chest, or stand over the teacher and berate them to the point of total humiliation. Those teachers would leave the school and get replaced by other teachers—and it would happen all over again. At one time, I had five different teachers in one year for the same class.

The rest of us in the class witnessed the assaults occurring but felt helpless to stop them because we were afraid for our own safety. Gangs retaliated violently against anyone who interfered with gang members in any way.

I'd already gotten assaulted once by some gang members. They wanted my lunch money, approximately $2, which I gave them, but then they decided to attack me anyway. I ended up having to go to the hospital for stitches in my head. I actually felt lucky it wasn't worse. Another student, Danny Carbajal, intervened and managed to stop them before they could successfully kick me in my torso.

When Jorge and I were walking home from school, we both got assaulted in the parking lot of a convenience store. We recognized some of the gang members assaulting us as students from our high school. Jorge ended up getting the brunt of the violence. They fiercely banged his head into the store's outer cement wall. On top of the physical head trauma, Jorge's whole emotional well-being got shattered into fragments for the following year.

My mother nursed Jorge. He had headaches, as well as violent panic attacks, almost like nightmares. Mamá would give him aspirin and scalp massages. He never went to see a doctor. We had no money. We simply weathered the storm and prayed to God for recovery.

Mamá did a lot of praying during those years, praying for all of us and our safety, praying for everyone in our neighborhood, even praying for the boys choosing the gang life.

One Sunday Miguel emerged from the grocery store to find a very short, very chubby man standing there. Atop his head he wore a small, worn-out round black hat. He was poorly shaven, but you could make out a thin mustache on his face. His skin was dark, and his hands thick and chubby. He looked like a tramp, a very fat tramp.

"Can I help you carry those groceries?" the man asked in Spanish.

"Yes, thank you," Miguel replied.

At that moment, the owner of the grocery stepped out and called to Miguel, "Miguel, I was hoping to talk to you!"

The owner explained to Miguel that the large man had been living behind the grocery store near the dumpsters for the last week. He wondered if Miguel, Mamá, and our family could help the guy. During this conversation the man stood near the two of them, waiting to see what Miguel would decide.

"Yes, I'm sure Nena will be fine with it. We are happy to help," Miguel told the owner and the man.

"*Gracias a ti y a Nena también,*" the owner stated.

"What's your name?" Miguel asked the man.

The man removed his tiny hat and answered "*Mi nombre es Roberto,*" all the while tugging on his belt. "Is Nena your wife?" he went on to ask Miguel.

"No, Nena is, well, she's my step-mother even though I'm a few years older than her. Basically, she's more like my sister. Anyway, let's get in the car and go to the house and talk with Nena about how we can help you."

Because of Roberto's striking appearance, we children were quite intrigued to make his acquaintance when he arrived at the house.

Roberto told Mamá, "My name is Roberto, and I'm from a small village in Veracruz, Mexico."

Miguel interjected, "I have a brother in Veracruz. His name is Alberto, and he's a professor of anthropology there."

Jorge added, "I lived in Veracruz for several years with Alberto."

As the rest of us unloaded the groceries from the car and began unpacking them, Mamá continued to speak with Roberto, "Where are you planning on going, or is Arizona your final stop?"

Roberto simply looked at her. He didn't respond. It seemed like he was in a daze.

"Are you hungry, Roberto?" Mamá gently asked him.

To this, he admitted, "Yes, I haven't eaten since yesterday. But, as you can see, I have plenty of reserve, so maybe I could last a week without eating." He smiled slightly at this attempt at lightness.

At this point my younger brothers and sisters surrounded Roberto. To them, this barrel-shaped, peculiar-looking man seemed to be a tramp from another world. They examined him from top to bottom.

Roberto shifted his lazy gaze their way. Sluggishly moving only his eyes, he took each of them in. After this mutual reviewing, the children scampered away.

"Do you have any luggage?" Mamá asked him.

"No, none."

She assured him, "Roberto, you can stay as long as you like with us"—motioning to him—"Come on into the kitchen and let me get you something to eat."

After giving Roberto a big plate of rice, pinto beans, tortillas, and salsa, my mother found me to ask, "Edgar, do you know anyone real big like Roberto who might have some clothes they can spare?"

"I will try to find someone," I promised. Then I recalled, "I do know someone. Sam, one of the silversmiths, wears suspender pants. Sam is also a very large man, and he is very nice. I think I may be able to get something for Roberto. I'll find Sam today."

"Ask Sam also," Mamá went on to say, "if he can spare anything else—shoes, shirts, anything really. It looks to me like Roberto has been wearing the same clothes for quite some time."

My mother made a list of things she thought would help. Then she told me, "Edgar, also get him a toothbrush."

With his hunger and thirst satisfied, Mamá returned to her previous question, the one he'd been unable to answer earlier: "Tell me, do you have any plan? Any idea of what you're going to do?"

Roberto explained, "I was supposed to be working at a farm in rural Chandler, but the owner of the farm didn't show up to get me, as planned. He was supposed to meet me at a gas station where I was dropped off, but he didn't show. So, I've been going from one place to another."

"How did you get here?"

"I was working on a farm in Yuma for the last two months, but there just wasn't a lot of work for me. So, that farmer in Yuma called his brother, Jimmy, also a farmer, and arranged for me to work on Jimmy's farm in Queen Creek. Jimmy is the guy I was waiting for at the gas station, but I guess Jimmy changed his mind or got mixed up about where to meet me because he was nowhere to be found. I stayed by the gas station for about twelve hours. I didn't want to move at all because I was afraid I'd miss him. I didn't know what he looked like or what kind of car he would be driving. All I knew was they gave him my description, and I'm sure I'm unmistakable if anyone is looking for me."

"*Qué lastima.* How did you get to Yuma?"

"When I made it to the border, I paid $75 that I'd been saving for quite a long time to a man to bring me across. He hid me underneath the trunk of his car, and one evening, when it was really busy, the man and his wife drove across the border. I could hear the American guard ask for documents. The man and his wife showed their documents. I could hear all the conversation. Once I came across, I ended up at the farm in Yuma, and that's where I was for the last couple of months. I don't have any immigration papers . . . Nena, is it going to be okay with you if I stay here? Do you think we can find Jimmy and his farm in the Queen Creek area?"

Mamá thought for a moment. Then she asked, "Do you have any more information about the brother in Yuma? Do you have the name of the farm or any addresses or phone numbers?"

Moving slowly, he pulled up his pants, tightened his belt, reached into his pocket, and withdrew a few pieces of wrinkled papers with some writing and numbers on them.

My mother took them, so she could give them to me for review later on.

Roberto softly admitted, "I have difficulty reading."

She smiled at him and replied, "Guess what? I too have that problem."

Roberto smiled.

Mamá continued, "However, it's only a matter of time. Soon we will all learn to read and write. The Bible I have here will teach us both."

Again, Roberto smiled.

Later that afternoon when I returned with two large pants, suspenders, and two shirts Sam had given me, Mamá smiled and said to Roberto, "See, I prayed for clothing for you. Now you have it."

He smiled wider and longer than before as he thanked my mother and me.

She went on to say, "Roberto, you don't have documents. What is your plan? Sooner or later you'll be confronted and perhaps deported."

"I know, Nena, but I had to do something. We had no money. We were barely making it in Veracruz. My two sisters and their children don't have enough, and one day I overheard one of my sisters say, 'If only Roberto didn't eat so much, perhaps we could do much better.' So, I decided to leave and see if somehow I could do something to repay them."

Mamá replied, "You know that we have two experts in the family who may be able to help you. Edgar and Miguel will help you with the immigration process, but we need to find Jimmy. Do you know why we have to find him?"

"Because I can't stay here forever," he answered.

"More than that, Jimmy could be an important person to sponsor you and get your legal papers. Do you understand what I'm trying to say?"

Roberto gave a nod of understanding. Next, he went on to say, "I don't want to be a burden to you."

"I think it's essential that we find Jimmy or his brother," Mama explained. "Somehow, we need to do that."

He told her, "My life now is in your hands."

"No," Mamá corrected, "we're all in God's hands."

After Roberto finished his meal, I took him to the garage, which would be his home for the next few months. I gave him his clothes and a toothbrush, and told him I would bring him towels, soap, and a razor. I showed him the private area where he could shower.

Roberto was indeed *gordito*, a fat guy, and he was also very charismatic. Once he cleaned up, he looked good, like a shiny penny, like an Oliver Hardy replica.

I knew we were not in the best financial shape, yet somehow we tended to ignore it and always hoped for the best, not just for ourselves but also in terms of the guests we took in. It was a spirit of living, unity, and love that my family shared. It's what kept us together and kept us blessed. We never talked about our fears that our guests could be deported although we knew deportation was active in our community, and anything could happen in an instant. My mother always said it was divine action that saved our guests: "If God wants them deported, then they'll be gone."

"Edgar, could you make out anything from those wrinkled papers Roberto gave us?" asked Mamá.

"It looks like the farm in Yuma is called something like 'Dateland Farms.' There's a lot of numbers, but they don't make sense. It's too short to be a phone number. Maybe it's a zip code. The other farm could be 'Queen Creek Farm.' Roberto kept saying something about Queen Creek and Chandler, so I think the farm where he was going to be working with Mr. Jimmy must be in Queen Creek, Arizona."

"Edgar, let's keep trying to find this contact."

"Yes, Mamá, I will . . . There's a kid at school, well—when he bothers to show up—and he's from Yuma. The problem is I know he's gang-affiliated. He's threatened me twice, stole money from me, and he's close with those guys that jumped me and Jorge."

My mother told me, "I pray every day for the boys in gangs. I pray that their minds and spirits will be moved by God, and they will change their pattern of life and learn to love one another. Perhaps, Edgar, if you speak to this boy, then somehow he will open up and change for the good. We know that God performs in mysterious ways."

It was one of the things about my mother. She would always think the best of people. It was true of Miguel as well. He would give all people the benefit of the doubt. Even if they were labeled "bad," "violent," or "prejudiced" in some way, he would always look for every bit of goodness in each one of them.

Miguel and Mamá prayed that something would happen and the gang members would change their lifestyles for the good of themselves and everyone around us, including the children they were harming in our neighborhood. My mother remained concerned about the well-being of these boys in gangs, despite the fact that they had been cruel many times, not just to us but to many in the community.

"Edgar, what's this boy's name?" she asked.

"Joey," I answered.

"Edgar, please talk to this Joey and don't be afraid. Let him know how important this information is, so we can help Roberto. I don't think he will harm you if you explain to him the purpose at hand. Tell him the whole story—even if he walks away from you, if he ignores you, tell him. Please, we have a gentleman we need to help. I am certain Joey will help us."

Because of my previous run-ins with Joey, even though Mamá was assured that talking to him would be fruitful, I felt afraid, not just that he wouldn't help us but that just talking to him would trigger him to do violence against me or the family. So, I decided to get Miguel's opinion on the situation.

Miguel told me, "I agree with Nena, talk to him. Show no fear, but show kindness. Smile and touch him. Let him know this is very important and that you're trying to help someone and would love for him to help Roberto. I think you will be fine."

In the meantime, my mother consulted with Mr. and Mrs. Davis about Roberto. She told them Roberto's story. Mr. Davis offered to help us find Jimmy and to reach out to find information about the farm in Yuma.

As Mr. Davis owned a termite and pesticide company, Mamá asked whether he could give Roberto some work. Mr. Davis was concerned about giving him work when he didn't have his papers, but he agreed to give Roberto some odd jobs.

On Monday morning, I arrived at school early and went to the library to study before class, as usual. I hoped to see Joey, but he wasn't there. I even dared to go outside during lunch, which most students didn't do for fear of getting assaulted, but I still couldn't locate Joey.

Several days passed and when I never found Joey, I decided to approach one of his friends.

Orlando told me, "Joey's at home. He's real sick."

"Really?" I replied, surprised, "What happened to him? What's wrong with him?"

"I don't know, but he's pretty sick. His mother is taking care of him, and she took him to a doctor."

"Do you know where he lives?"

Orlando ended up giving me Joey's address.

Later that day, after I told Mamá all I'd learned, she decided, "We should go visit him, Edgar. Maybe we can talk to him and perhaps meet his parents."

Mamá decided to visit the Davises to see if Mrs. Davis would join us in making a call at Joey's. I accompanied her, carrying the large dish of *chilaquiles* she'd prepared. It was her custom to always bring a dish of food, no matter whom she visited. She took a great deal of pride in preparing and bringing enough food so there would be plenty for unexpected guests and leftovers for all to enjoy later.

"Come in, Nena!" Mrs. Davis called out upon hearing Mamá's knock.

"It smells like chocolate in here," Mamá remarked upon entering the house.

"Oh, yes, I'm baking chocolate cakes for a party, and guess what? One is for you. And where is Edgar? I thought I heard his voice."

"I'm here, Mrs. Davis." I was carrying the wonderful smelling dish of *chilaquiles* my mother had prepared.

Upon seeing me, Mrs. Davis asked, "What do we have in this nice dish you're carrying? Nena, you shouldn't have! It smells great! *Chilaquiles*—my favorite!"

Before we all sat together to eat, Mrs. Davis called Mr. Davis to the table and also invited Roberto, who was working in the back yard. Roberto had been cleaning the hoses used for fumigating. They all had to be flushed, air-dried, and ready for the next day. Roberto had been in the process of wrapping them in newspaper and packing them.

When he saw us all sitting at the table together, Roberto seemed reluctant to join, but Mamá pulled out a chair and told him to sit and enjoy a meal. That's one thing about my mother. She always liked to have guests sit by her, so they could talk. A conversation while having a meal was the most delightful pastime for my mother.

Over the meal Mamá told everyone about the latest news in our attempt to locate Roberto's farm employers. Mamá explained, "Edgar has been on the lookout for a school friend who may still have family in the Yuma area because that family may have information on the farm there where Roberto worked. This school friend, Joey, has been absent from school all this week, and only today did Edgar learn that he's very sick and at home. We have his address, and we'd be very grateful if one of you would join us in making a visit."

Mrs. Davis was thrilled to help. The plan was to make the house call on Saturday morning. Also we decided to try to find Joey's family's phone number to avoid showing up unannounced. However, we ended up having no luck in that area.

On Saturday morning Mamá, Mrs. Davis, and I piled into Mrs. Davis's car with a large platter of enchiladas and a chocolate cake that we were bringing along. We didn't know anything about Joey's illness or how we'd be received, so we hoped that some tasty food would soften our unannounced visit. Also, my mother's theory was the best and most productive conversations take place while enjoying a meal with someone. Especially when the food is good, the conversation is quite marvelous and enjoyable. She hoped that if we could enjoy a meal with Joey and his family, they would be more inclined to help us find the farmers connected to Roberto.

Once we found his house and Mrs. Davis parked the car, I was slammed with apprehension. After all, Joey was a gang member. He'd forced me to hand over my lunch money on one occasion. He was affiliated with the gang members who'd attacked me and Jorge. A spike of panic cut into me, reminiscent of what I felt in 1959 when I deceived the American guard and crossed the border.

Mrs. Davis knew all this about Joey too because my mother insisted she understand the full picture before joining us. Even still, both she and my mother seemed calm and positive—not worried at all.

Feeling their calm, my own anxiety subsided. After all, I was with two guardian angels. I was protected.

Joey's house and yard were poorly kept. The grass was overgrown. The few trees and flowers were withering. Trash littered the yard. The house was in dire need of a paint job. It looked gray with old paint withering from the boards. The screens covering the windows were torn. The screen door itself had a section of screen missing from the lower third. Coming from the back yard of the house we could make out sounds of dogs barking and slamming themselves against chain-link fencing. Once we knocked on the wooden panels of the screen door, the barking became louder and more frenzied.

We knocked and knocked, but no one answered. Before departing, we decided to do another round of knocking. This time someone answered.

A thin woman with slightly dark skin and curly black hair opened the house's main door but remained behind the closed and locked screen door.

Before she could say anything, I immediately spoke, in Spanish, "Good morning. My name is Edgar, and I'm a friend of Joey's. I haven't seen him at school. This is my mother, Nena Hernández, and this is our neighbor, Mrs. Davis."

At this, the woman opened the screen door. We could see her dark eyes and long eyelashes as well as a 1½-inch scar that ran vertically down the mid-right of her forehead. She remained standing in the doorway. She inquired, somewhat suspiciously, "*Quiénes son ustedes?* Who are you?" in Spanish. (Our conversation was mostly in Spanish.)

I repeated, "I am Edgar, and this is my mother and Mrs. Davis. Is Joey in?'

"Yes," she revealed, "but he is very sick."

"That's why we're here. I haven't seen him at school, and I wondered how he was doing," I told her again.

My mother then joined, saying, "I am Nena, Edgar's mother. What's your name?"

"Elizabeth," she answered and went on to share, "I'm Joey's mother, and I'm very sick also."

"What's wrong? *Que pasa?*" my mother inquired.

"My son is very sick, and I've become sick with worry for him," she quietly explained, pulling some strands of hair across forehead.

"Can we come in? We brought Joey some food, but there's plenty for you too."

Mrs. Davis then spoke, "I'm Evelyn Davis, friend and neighbor of Nena. We are here to visit with you, and hopefully you can enjoy something to eat with us."

My mother added, "Please."

I looked at this lady once again and asked, "Is Joey here? Is he all right?'

At this she looked beyond us. Next, she looked at each of us, then in between us. Finally, she pushed the screen door open. The barking stopped.

We entered the house, finding that its inside did not match the outside. Inside it was clean and smelled fresh.

"My house is very messy. Please excuse me. I wasn't expecting guests," Elizabeth

apologized, again rearranging the hair on her forehead so that it swept across the right-hand side, presumably in an attempt at hiding the scar there. She ended up arranging it in such a way that it covered her right eye as well.

My mother countered, "Please don't apologize. Your home is beautiful and smells lovely."

"Where's Joey?" I asked. It was disconcerting speaking to her when half of her face was covered by her hair. It was like speaking to someone who was sort of in hiding.

"He's sleeping. He has been sleeping on and off for several days. We took him to the doctor, and the doctor said it was going to take time for him to get better."

"Is he any better?" my mother softly inquired.

"Maybe—but not really. Oh, I don't know. He got hit real hard. Plus, he needs to go to the city court real soon. I'm sick over this whole thing," uttered Elizabeth. Again, she lifted her hand to feel her hair, making sure that it swept across her forehead. My mother hugged her.

Mrs. Davis said, "Poor thing."

Holding Elizabeth's hand, Mamá told her, "We're worried about Joey and hope he is going to be okay."

Elizabeth then invited us to take a seat at the table, telling us, "Please sit down. I'll get some glasses and plates."

On her way to retrieve these items she stopped in front of a mirror, pulled a bobby pin from her pocket and arranged some of her hair so that it dip down in front the right side of forehead and stay in place there.

By this point, I decided not to say much. I felt that Mamá was the best to talk to Elizabeth. Mrs. Davis was very attentive and showed concern, yet she didn't speak either.

Still I found it troubling that we were enjoying this fine meal together with Elizabeth complimenting my mother's enchiladas when Joey was lying in a room just fourteen feet from us, and we had no idea what exactly had happened to him or how he was doing—or anything. It was very puzzling to me.

"These are the best enchiladas I've ever had," Elizabeth remarked, "I'm sure Joey will enjoy them as well."

Mrs. Davis agreed, "I am sure he will."

My mother asked, "How many children do you have?"

"Only Joey. I lost one baby, and the other child died of leukemia when he was eight years old. Losing his brother was very hard on Joey. I don't think he's ever gotten over it."

My mother told Elizabeth, "I too lost one child at age two. It is so very hurtful. I am very sorry for your loss."

Spotting a Bible in a nearby cabinet, Mamá asked, "May I look at your Bible?"

"Of course," Elizabeth answered and got up to hand it to her.

My mother picked up the Bible and placed her right hand on the cover.

Mrs. Davis commented, "Oh, the Good Book," and touched it too.

I continued to wonder in silence when they were going to talk about why we were here. I hesitated to interrupt their conversation, but I wanted to intervene to find out more about Joey and get to the point of our visit. I was reluctant to do so, so I kept waiting, trying to remain courteous and attentive.

Over a piece of Mrs. Davis's amazing chocolate cake, Mamá asked Elizabeth, "Is there a husband in the house?"

First, she quickly felt with her hand to make sure her hair in the bobby pin was secure, and then she explained, "No, only Joey and me. My husband went crazy after our son's death, and he could not take living with us anymore. Suddenly he left, like a light switched off never to shine again. He was a good man, but I think he developed severe depression, so he just left. We've never heard or seen anything from him since, and I think this has affected Joey significantly. We have no knowledge of him. I started working in a hospital janitorial service after my husband left. We are doing okay. At least he left us the house. It's neglected outside, but at some point, we'll clean it up."

"How about your parents, sister, brothers?" my mother inquired.

"My husband was born in Yuma. Joey was born in Yuma, and I'm from Mexico. However, my parents are in Yuma. They've been living there for some time now. They are struggling somewhat with medical problems. They're getting older, and bothering them just causes a lot of stress. I hate to call them for anything unless I really have to."

"So, do you know people in Yuma?" my mother asked.

"I know Yuma very well. We moved to Phoenix because of my son who needed treatment for leukemia, but we still keep in touch with friends and family in Yuma."

As Elizabeth was talking, the telephone rang. She stood and said, "Excuse me. I must take this call."

At this point we had already been there about ninety minutes. As already mentioned, my mother was notorious for very lengthy, thorough, and extensive conversations. She was a great listener and had amazing patience. When she and I had conversations, she would listen intently, interject with brief comments, and then turn me loose in the conversation. This was exactly what she was doing while talking with Elizabeth. She always told me, "Edgar, this is how you learn about people. You get to know people—their family, what they do for a living, their soul, their spirit—this is what you need to do to know and appreciate people more. This is what a good doctor should do. A doctor should listen and speak only a few words." I agreed with her. She was trying to tell me that listening was more powerful than talking.

We could hear Elizabeth talking on the phone, "He's coming along slowly. Probably doing better than me, I should say."

In her responses to the caller, Elizabeth seemed very caring toward Joey, but my curiosity about what was going on with Joey was piqued. Also, why, by now, hadn't he come out to see us? It was almost as if he didn't exist. There was no noise in the other room. I wondered whether he was even there. But Elizabeth gave us no reason to doubt her honesty about his being sick and in the house. Still it was quite mind-boggling to think that he was sick and in his room for the almost two hours we'd been there.

Into the phone, Elizabeth said, "He is still having severe headaches, but his wounds are healing slowly. The bruises on his back and arms and legs are healing although they hurt quite a lot. He was given medication for his headaches and pain, as well as some sleeping pills, so he has been sleeping quite a lot. The doctor says time will heal everything."

My mother and I exchanged looks. We both were reminded of Jorge's awful headaches when he was beaten up by gang members from Joey's very own gang. Maybe something similar had happened to Joey.

Elizabeth's phone conversation continued, "He has to go to court in three weeks, and I'm hoping all goes well. I think it's going to be okay; however, he's had two marks on his juvenile record. I'm scared about that, and I'm scared about his future."

It seemed that this visit—whose original purpose was to gather information about Yuma to help Roberto—was morphing. It wasn't just Roberto's life and future on the line. Joey too was at a crossroads and in need of lots of help, compassion, and direction.

Suddenly, we heard her say into the phone, "Mom, thank you for calling. I'll call you tomorrow and let you know how Joey is doing . . . Please don't worry . . . I'll call you, and if you like, you can come over and see him. I just don't want to bother you. I don't want you to worry . . . You know how your blood pressure is, how it can get out of hand. I don't want to worry you, but you're welcome to come over and see us if you want . . . I have company and can't talk more at this time. Yes, Joey has a friend and his mother and her friend visiting. They want to know how Joey is doing . . . Yes, I'll tell them that you appreciate that they are here visiting . . . Yes, Mom, I promise I will call."

When Elizabeth returned to the table, Mamá then explained to her about Roberto and his situation. She said, "We now understand that you are from Yuma and your mother may still live there now. We hoped you might help us find the farm where Roberto worked."

Elizabeth responded, "This is incredible that all of you would take the time and interest in helping this man who isn't related to you and who is probably here illegally. I'm shocked."

"This is very personal to me. We all owe much to strangers and acquaintances, and we are way behind in payments to them," Mamá explained.

Elizabeth asked, "You owe what? I don't understand."

"Edgar's immigration process was complicated and did not go well. In 1960 he had to stay in Nogales until his papers were ready. It was total strangers who took him in for almost a year. Total strangers and help from the Lord are the reasons Edgar is here. Total strangers helped my son, so we are indebted to strangers and must pay something back. We need to help Roberto."

Elizabeth's demeanor changed as time passed by. "I understand now. Wow . . . And Joey and Edgar are good friends, right?"

Mamá answered, "I think so, right, Edgar?"

I replied, "Yes, Joey is a nice guy, and I hope to know him much better when he recovers. I hope we can be better friends."

Elizabeth turned and smiled at me to acknowledge what I had just said. Then after a quick pat of her hair held by the bobby pin, she told us, "We know all the farmers in Yuma. My father will find out where Roberto worked. Can you tell me about Roberto?"

Mrs. Davis answered, "Roberto is unique, an unmistakable character. Have you ever seen Laurel and Hardy? He looks like Oliver Hardy. He's very fat, has a chubby face, wears a tiny hat much smaller than his head, and has a very thin mustache. If anyone has seen him, they will not forget him."

"I think we can find helpful information for you and perhaps help Roberto find this Jimmy fellow," Elizabeth offered.

Then she went on to say, "We have to go to court in three weeks, and we're hoping nothing happens to Joey."

"What happened to Joey? Why is he sick?" Mamá ventured to inquire.

As she asked this question, I moved in close, hoping to find out more about what was going on with him.

Elizabeth explained, "Joey has been involved with bad people for about three years. He has two citations and a record with the police and juvenile court. He's gotten several warnings that if anything happened again, he'd be incarcerated. About seven days ago, when Joey told me he was staying with a friend, the police called me at 1:00 a.m. They told me I need to come right away"—she started weeping—"He's missed so many school days that at this point, it's not possible to make it all up. It's like there's no point for him to go back and finish the year . . . Three weeks from now his fate will be decided for him."

"Being a mother, I know how difficult it must be to see your son hurt," Mamá told her, "Just care for him. Tell him we came by, and hopefully you'll be able to help us find some information, so we can help Roberto."

With tears dripping from her eyes, Elizabeth told us, "I was born in Mexico, and I immigrated at the age of three. Both my parents also are immigrants. My ex-husband and Joey were born here. They are lucky to have been born here and not have to deal with the problem of immigration. I feel for these people—Edgar, maybe sometime you can talk to Joey about school and becoming something?"

"Yes, ma'am, we shall talk again after he recovers. I hope he's better soon and is able to return to school."

Elizabeth quickly smoothed down her hair, felt the bobby pinned bit of it to make sure it was in place, then picked up the Bible from the table and held it to her chest as we walked to the door.

My mother asked her, "You never heard anything from your husband, did you?"

"No, he left to Los Angeles and has never communicated with us. Personally, I think this is the reason Joey has turned to gangs," she answered, and then she burst out crying again.

My mother stroked her hand, as Elizabeth grasped the Bible tightly to her chest. Then my mother and Mrs. Davis gave her a hug.

Mamá assured her, "I understand how this would be a problem."

Mrs. Davis added, "Please take care of yourself and may God bless you."

I also gave her a hug and handed her a note with our address and phone number on it.

Five days later my mother received a phone call from Elizabeth. They talked for an hour. Elizabeth thanked her for the kind visit. She wanted Mamá to pass on thanks to Mrs. Davis as well.

She had information concerning Roberto. Apparently, it was at Dateland Farms that Roberto had been working in Yuma. Her father knew the farmer, Ronald Preston, and considered him to be honest and a good boss. They surmised the problem to be with the brother, Mr. Jimmy, and not the owner of Dateland Farms. Elizabeth went on to give us Ronald Preston's address and phone number.

"*Muchas gracias* for the information. Tell me more about Joey. How is he? And what about Joey's father?" Mamá asked her.

Elizabeth began, "First of all, let me say that when I told Joey of your all's visit, he was surprised. He confessed that he hadn't treated Edgar very well at school. All he wants to do now is make up for it."

Next she shared, "My parents told me my ex-husband is back in Yuma. He's heard about Joey and wants to accompany us to the hearing as well."

Upon revealing this, Elizabeth burst out crying and my mother also wept.

"What will happen with my boy?" she asked. "All I want is for his father to see him and truly understand what Joey went through. Joey's on probation, and because of the latest incident, the judge will be deciding about incarceration. Joey needs his father on his side right now. It's all I want . . . But I'm afraid. I'm afraid it could be harder having his father there. What if he doesn't support Joey?"

"Elizabeth, be hopeful. I think you should be happy. He will once again be with his son and you. What happened to Joey? Tell me what happened."

"Joey hasn't talked to me about it, not at all. But yesterday an investigator came by the house. He told me that it wasn't Joey's fault.

He said that Joey was at the bus station when a fight broke out. Some kids in a gang were trying to steal a purse from an elderly passenger. One of them was beating her up. Another beating up her husband. Joey intervened, trying to help the elderly lady. That's when he got hit in the head with a broken bottle, but he managed to scare off the attackers."

"Oh my," mother said.

"The elderly couple plus two outside witnesses are the ones who explained all this to the investigator, so this seems good for Joey and the hearing. But still, I get so overwhelmed."

Before ending the call, Mamá told her, "I will pray for all of you and hope for the best. We must stay in touch."

With Mr. Davis at the wheel and Mrs. Davis, Roberto, my mother, and me as passengers, the car pulled into the gravel road marked Queen Creek Farm. A succession of palm trees, all the same height and growing in even intervals, lined the driveway. As we proceeded farther along, we found orchards of peach trees as well as tall, healthy pecan trees. When we reached the farmhouse with its open yard dotted with more large pecan trees, the car came to a stop and we got out. Roberto actually stayed in the car, and I stood just outside it.

Sighting numerous workers, all of whom appeared to be Latinos, Mamá and the Davises approached one of them.

"*Buenos días. Estamos buscando al Señor Jimmy*. We're looking for Mr. Jimmy," Mamá stated.

"*Está en la casa*," the man told her, pointing towards the farmhouse.

At that time a medium-sized, blonde-haired, and blue-eyed lady wearing boots and jeans emerged from the house.

In perfect Spanish she asked, "What can we do for you?"

Mrs. Davis told her, also in Spanish, "We are looking for Mr. Jimmy."

"Yes," my mother interjected, "*Está aqui, Señor Jimmy*?"

"How are you today? My name is Betty Jo, and you are?"

"My name is Nena Hernández, and this is Glen and Evelyn Davis, my neighbors. My son Edgar is standing at the car."

At the mention of my name I walked to them, and at the same time a tall, blue-eyed man emerged from the house and approached the group.

"I'm James Preston. People call me Jimmy," he said introducing himself.

We all shook hands. I noted that their hands were rough like my grandfather's.

Mr. Jimmy's skin was tanned like my grandfather's as well. His face was thick, rough, and leathery, a testament to his years of hard work outside in the sun.

The two seemed puzzled about the visit. Puzzled and intrigued.

Mr. Jimmy asked in beautiful Spanish, "Are you looking to buy peaches or oranges?"

"We came to talk with you, sir," Mamá answered him.

I noticed Roberto would stick his head out the car window from time to time, resembling a turtle, sticking its head out of its shell to smell nature.

"Would you all like some lemonade? We just made some," Betty Jo told everyone. Then she led the Davises and my mother to the porch where they took a seat. I went back to stand next to the car to be with Roberto.

Once settled in on the porch, my mother began, "I am very sorry to disturb you, but we have spoken to your brother Ronald in Yuma. He's a very nice man and very polite."

"Okay," Mr. Jimmy said.

"You see, we are concerned about Roberto, the man in the car."

"Who is he?" Betty Jo asked, puzzled.

A lady emerged from the house with a pitcher of lemonade. She began serving everyone.

Jimmy and Betty Jo said to her, "*Gracias*, Estela."

By this point, the Davises started their own conversation with Mr. Jimmy, discussing how Mr. Davis's father used to air spray farms in Mississippi. That immediately sparked a conversation that went on for the duration of my mother and Betty Jo's conversation. So, there were two simultaneous conversations, one about spraying bugs on farms and the other about Roberto's future.

"So, Jimmy's brother made arrangements for this man to be picked up by my husband and we didn't do it, is this correct?" Betty Jo summarized to my mother.

From where I was standing at the car, this was quite a sight to see—my mother having a deep conversation with this lady. I will never forget this event. My mother couldn't read or write, but she could sell a conversation to anyone!

"Yes, as I understood it from my son Edgar's conversation with Ronald Preston in Yuma. Edgar talked to him over the phone yesterday, and he's the one who told us how to get here."

Betty Jo asked, "How is it that you know this man, Roberto? And what do the Davises have to do with this?"

Roberto had very slowly squeezed out of the car and was approaching the porch.

Looking at him, Betty Jo noted, "He is a big man, a very unique-looking man."

"Yes, even Mr. Preston in Yuma said the same thing. He knew exactly who we were talking to him about on the phone," Mamá told her. Then she went on to explain, "Since Mr. Jimmy did not pick him up as per arrangements made with his brother, Roberto roamed the streets and landed in our house. He is now our guest, and we are trying to get him here where he was supposed to end up. We took him in and now he has been living with us for a couple of months. He is illegal, no documents. He was told he would have a sponsor here. Mr. and Mrs. Davis are dear friends and neighbors. The Davises offered to help us with Roberto."

"Jimmy never said anything to me about any of this. We have twenty excellent workers here. Actually, Nena, if you look over there behind those pecan trees, you will see several cottages. Our workers and their families actually live on the farm with us. We know them well, and Jimmy and I have helped them all with immigration. We're all one big family here on the farm," Betty Jo explained.

"You're a wonderful and beautiful person, Betty Jo," Mamá told her.

"Thank you, I guess I need to be honest with you. I told Jim that we were going to give up on helping anymore workers because we don't need more help. We have all we need." She paused to stare at Roberto, then asked, "Is he a good worker?"

"He is really good, very honest and respectable, never complains. He's been doing a little work for Mr. Davis who has already sponsored three people. However, Mr. Davis's business is too small to take on more workers."

"I still don't understand why Jim would make a promise, knowing he could not keep it," she remarked, looking over at Jimmy a couple of times. Mr. Jimmy, noticing her looks, shot a curious gaze in her direction.

Roberto had been standing near my mother. He then moved to serve himself a lemonade. He said, "*Gracias, señora,*" and walked away to allow them to continue their conversation.

Betty Jo said again, "Boy, he is a big man."

Mamá replied, "Yes, he is, but very honest and hardworking. He is very good with children, I have five little ones at home, and they all love him. He's a real gentleman."

"We have five kids also. We trust all our workers. Some have families here living with us."

"That is wonderful, Betty Jo," Mamá said in response.

Mrs. Davis then pulled her chair over to join them, saying, "Your husband gave me a box of your all's peaches, and I want to thank you for them. I will make peach pies, and you are invited to visit me and Nena anytime." She handed her a piece of paper with her name, address, and phone number on it.

Betty Jo was not ready to end the conversation about Roberto. She asked Mamá, "Nena, why are you doing all this for this man? He has no papers, you also said he does not read or write, and he is not even related to you."

"All of us in our family immigrated and have legal papers. Let's just say we owe much to people who helped us along the way, and we want to pay back. Roberto is just one of a few debts we have."

"I see, I understand," Betty Jo replied, looking intently at my mother. "You are a good Christian. My mother said the Lord moves us all into the right places in life. Do you have a Bible?"

"Oh, yes, I do. I visit it every day," Mamá answered.

Mrs. Davis added, "Nena and I love reading the Good Book, don't we, Nena?"

My mother looked down at her feet and replied, "Yes, Mrs. Davis is a good reader, and I love listening to her read the Bible. It's so soothing to hear her read it, sounds like a symphony."

"I'm sorry about what happened with this man, and I will see what I can do," Betty Jo told her.

My mother looked up at her, declaring, "Thank you. I don't mean to be insulting to you or your husband by coming here. It's that I hate to see something like this happening to this good human being."

"Yes, I understand," Betty Jo told her. Then she hugged my mother and Mrs. Davis, saying, "You two are a rarity, some type of angels."

"As are you, Betty Jo," my mother replied.

Six weeks passed. Joey did not end up getting incarcerated or sent to a juvenile home. He was taken off probation for what the judge called his valor and good behavior. His father was visiting him quite often. Joey was a changed young man with a desire to restart school.

Jimmy and Betty Jo showed up at our house unannounced. They'd come into Phoenix to go shopping and decided to visit my mother and Mrs. Davis—both of whom were delighted by the visit. Betty Jo left a Bible for my mother and cases of fruit for her and Mrs. Davis.

When I got home, Roberto was no longer there. The Prestons had been in a rush. Roberto had been all smiles when he got into their car.

We were all smiles ourselves at the positive, life-affirming turn of events.

Chapter 12

Two Laws

When I'd first seen the name "G. Davis" on the day's list of patients, I hadn't thought much of it. It was only later in the morning that I wondered if it could be Glen Davis. As I hadn't seen the Davises in the waiting room, I figured it probably wasn't, but still, there was a possibility.

When I opened the door to the consultation room, I was delighted. Indeed, it was my Mr. and Mrs. Davis. Though they remained great friends with my mother, after I got married and moved away, I hadn't seen them often enough in the past fifteen years. They were true-to-the-heart people, and such good friends with my mother, especially in her first years in the USA when she needed a lot of support.

As I exchanged warm hugs with each of them, Mrs. Davis, wearing a small black hat with purple flowers on it and her usual red lipstick, said, "Edgar, you have no idea how wonderful it is to see you. How are you?"

It was moving for me to hear Mrs. Davis's strikingly melodic voice.

"I'm doing really well. It is so good to see you both. How are you all?" I asked in reply.

That's when I found out the reason for their visit to my office: Mr. Davis had thyroid cancer.

After examining Mr. Davis, I told him he'd need to have surgery to remove the tumor in his thyroid, something that I would do for him. I assured him that he would be fine and the cancer eradicated.

In describing the surgery, I told them, "I make an incision at the base of the neck. There's a huge freeway of veins, arteries, and nerves, in that area. I will then remove the thyroid gland, a gland that sits on top of the windpipe. The thyroid gland is butterfly-shaped. It produces chemicals that regulate and balance all the chemical activities of the body. You can then take pills that do the same work as the thyroid once did. Sometimes after this surgery, patients develop slight temporary hoarseness. So, that's the side effect. I've performed this surgery many, many times, and I am confident that it will be a success. I want you both to be confident as well."

"Your mother would tell people all the time how her son was going to become a surgeon. She said it all the time, Edgar. When we would go shopping and meet people at stores, she would say this to folks," Mrs. Davis told me.

"And thank God," Mr. Davis added.

"Amen," said Mrs. Davis.

Mrs. Davis hugged me again, saying, "I always knew your mother was right when she told people that you would be a surgeon."

I answered their additional questions, and we made plans to schedule the surgery. After that, our consultation concluded.

Right before exiting, Mrs. Davis started crying. Amidst her tears she asked, "Will Glen be okay? Tell me, Edgar."

I said all I could to assure her he would be great, something I believed with all my heart.

"Edgar, I know I should have no doubts that he will be fine because the Lord made you who you are, and He will guide your hands. He has guided your hands and your intelligence throughout the years, and I feel very comfortable that He has brought us back together for a reason."

Mr. Davis added, "Amen."

So I asked her, "Why are you crying, Mrs. Davis? Mr. Davis is going to be fine."

Mrs. Davis said in almost a whisper, "It's because I remember something, something I know your mother never told you that happened in 1969 when she and I went shopping."

"My mother tells me just about everything, so this must be something that I don't know."

Mrs. Davis continued, "I can assure you that you don't know this story because I promised Nena I would never discuss it, but I think now is an opportune time to tell you . . ."

And so she told me. Admittedly, I agreed that I was glad they had spared telling me and everyone in the family about the incident at the time it occurred. It was amazing and scary.

But before going into the incident, I want to say that Mr. Davis's surgery was, indeed, a success.

After the surgery, I found Mrs. Davis and my mother sitting together in the waiting room. I could just make out Mrs. Davis's musical voice softly reading the Bible as my mother listened intently.

"It's all done, and he is fine," I told them.

"Thank God, and thank you, Edgar," Mrs. Davis told me.

Mr. Davis did well post-operatively. He beat the cancer.

Here's what Mrs. Davis told me happened in 1969.

Mrs. Davis and Mamá were off together, with Mrs. Davis driving, going to explore a secondhand store. Mrs. Davis was always in search of old-fashioned hats as well as boldly colored floral dresses. My mother was hoping to buy some clothes for the girls and for the younger boys.

"What ever happened with that couple from Mexico who were staying with you? Did you ever hear from them?" Mrs. Davis asked.

For seven weeks a young couple from Mexico, Alberta and Oscar, had been staying with us. For the past several years, they'd come to do the seasonal harvest in Utah, Oregon, and Washington. They'd work for three months and then return home to Mexico. The reason they worked was to earn money to pay for their schooling to become teachers.

However, this year things turned out badly. The man providing their transportation robbed them point blank, taking all their belongings and their small savings. Stuck in Phoenix, they eventually found their way to our house where they stayed while they worked to earn the money to make it back home (they were too late for the seasonal harvest).

My mother told Mrs. Davis, "Reyna and Asunción got very attached to them. They were such lovely people. Apparently, there was a raid on the restaurant where they were working. When Alberta and Oscar could not produce any documents, they were deported. They had already planned on returning to Mexico two weeks later, but still—the raid and deportation must have been frightening. *Un gran temor.* Plus, they were so kind and shy. I imagine it was very unpleasant for them. *Muy desagradable.*"

"*Qué terrible*! I hope they are okay, Nena. They worked so hard and were such considerate young people."

"Yes, I agree. They actually sent us a very kind letter that Edgar read to me. In the letter they thanked me and the family for helping them. They told us about the raid. They explained that they had to stay in a detention building for a while. Then they were released out in the streets of Nogales. Although officers asked them where they'd been staying in Arizona, they did not confess anything about our family," Mamá confided.

"Poor Oscar and Alberta. No documents. Too bad. Such sweet people," Mrs. Davis commented.

Once in the secondhand store, Mrs. Davis explained, "Nena, you'd be surprised at the bargains you can find! Rich people from North Phoenix buy beautiful clothes when they're in fashion, and later when the fashion is over, they donate those clothes and buy more. And, of course, we are the beneficiaries of those donations—shoes, clothes, hats. Expensive stuff once bought at expensive stores at an expensive price."

"Yes," my mother agreed, "I have seen the beautiful dresses you have found. Let's look at dresses first."

One of the other ten or so shoppers approached them, saying, "Some of these expensive clothes can be destroyed if you don't properly clean them with special chemicals rather than water and soap. Let me give you the name of my sister's dry cleaning business. She will give you a discount. Just let them know her brother Simon sent you."

Mrs. Davis and Mamá thanked the man, but Mamá later commented, "These are good quality jackets and pants, but I don't think I have to use that man's sister. I can wash them by hand. You know, Evelyn, I used to hand wash clothes by a river. Only later did I have a faucet at home and I could hand wash clothes at home in the *pila*. That's when our village got running water."

Mamá and Mrs. Davis continued chatting and browsing. They scooped up two shirts and some pants that were high quality and also the right size for the children.

While Mrs. Davis was trying on a hat, she noticed two well-dressed men enter the store. One went to the front of the store, the other to the back. She didn't make anything of it but was aware of them and wondered what they were doing in the store. She continued to sort through more hats, occasionally looking around. She made note that most people in the store were Latinos. Then she saw Jack, the owner, talking to the men.

Mrs. Davis turned to my mother and inquired, "Nena, *los hombres quien son?* Who are those men?"

My mother looked around and put her items on a nearby table. She replied, "They're probably looking to buy ties or something. Maybe shoes."

Mrs. Davis uttered, "I'm not so sure. I think something's going on."

As they sorted through more items, they noticed that other customers were starting to spread out and leave.

One of the men remained inside while the other stood just outside the door to the store. The man inside started to approach people individually to talk to them, almost like giving them a test. If someone didn't know the answer, they got escorted outside.

A lady got close to my mother and Mrs. Davis and began to explain to them in Spanish that it was a raid that was happening. But then they were interrupted by the man working the inside.

"Good morning," he greeted Mrs. Davis and my mother.

Mrs. Davis answered with a smile, saying, "Good morning to you, sir."

My mother likewise wished him a good morning.

"Do you have identification?" he asked.

"Oh, yes, sir. My name is Evelyn Davis, and this is my friend Magdalena Hernández."

"Do you have ID?"

Mrs. Davis pulled out her wallet from her purse and showed him her driver's license while my mother searched for her green card. That's when she realized that she'd brought cash with her, but she'd accidentally left her purse back at the house.

Mamá whispered to Mrs. Davis, "*Se quedo en la casa.* It's at home."

When the man started interrogating my mother, Mrs. Davis interjected, "We are simply doing some shopping. Nena is my neighbor, and she left her ID at home.

"*Papeles, señora?*" he pressed my mother.

"*Estan en la casa.* They're at home in the house," she answered. She told him her address as well.

"Yes," Mrs. Davis, "and my house is just across the street."

He turned to Mrs. Davis to say, "You can go, but she stays with us."

"No, sir, that's not possible. She can't stay with you; she is my dear friend. Why are you doing this?" Mrs. Davis argued.

"Because she is illegal. She has no documents."

Mrs. Davis protested, "That's incorrect, sir. She has documents, but she just doesn't have them at hand. She is legal. I know her and her family very well. Please, sir, let me go and get her documents. It won't take very long. She is a fine, honest lady, and I know her very well." She pleaded with him, touching his shoulder and repeating, "Please, please, do not take her."

"No, that's not possible," the man maintained.

My mother asserted, "*No soy ilegal.* I am not illegal. I have a green card. *La tengo en la casa.* Señora Davis can get it."

"You'll have to accompany us to the detention office," he directed Mamá. Then to Mrs. Davis he said, "You can do whatever you want. You can come with her, or you can go get the documents and bring them to the center. Here's the address. The bus will leave for the border at 4 p.m. If you or whoever isn't back by then, she'll be deported."

Again, Mrs. Davis pleaded, "Please don't do that. You have to give us more time. She is here legally. I promise I'll bring the documents before 4 p.m."

"I wouldn't waste any more time then if I were you," he recommended.

My mother looked somewhat concerned, but she wasn't upset. She told the man, "*Lo entiendo.* I understand."

Mrs. Davis told her, "I need to call Miguel."

"No, please don't do that. It will only upset everyone and frighten them. If you could just bring my green card, everything will be cleared up. I have faith in this man. I've been honest, and he's just trying to do his job. Calling will upset them way too much. Evelyn, please bring my green card to the center, and everything will be fine."

Mrs. Davis, still quite shaken, made to give Mamá a hug, as Mamá assured her, "They are only doing their job. Evelyn, they don't know I have my papers, but we will prove them wrong. You'll find my purse on top of my Bible on our long, thin kitchen table. Once you bring the green card, we'll show it to the officials. It will be fine."

They gently yet firmly directed Mamá into the line of detainees. The line of people trudged to a bus that had been waiting in the store's lot. Mamá smiled at the other folks in line with her, thinking how they reminded her of many of the guests who had stayed at our house. They were just normal people looking for work who ended up at the wrong place at the wrong time.

Mamá found a seat on the bus and closed her eyes for a moment. When she opened her eyes, she glanced at the empty seat next to her. She longed for her Bible, but it too was at home with her purse. Imagining the Bible by her side, she made to reach out for it, but there was nothing there. She was not afraid, mostly stunned by what had happened.

Now more than ever, she was taken back to 1959 when, as a child, I too came very close to deportation on two separate occasions, something none of us like to talk about. It was way too painful to discuss with anyone, even family. She imagined me running, trying to escape an immigration officer, all the while imagining how painful it would have been for me if I'd gotten separated from my brother, never to reunite again. Once she allowed her imagination to wander like this, she became agitated and started to cry.

Suddenly a lady near her tapped her on the shoulder and offered, "We are now in God's hands, and there's nothing we can do about it. Truly, if you think about it, we broke the law and are here illegally."

My mother looked at her and softly replied, "*Tienes razón.* You are right."

Then she looked around the bus, noticing about thirteen people in total, all displaying wooden facial expressions. Not a hint of a smile. My mother described it like sitting at a funeral.

The twenty-minute bus ride to the detention center seemed like 24 hours. My mother spent that time considering each person on the bus. "Where will they go? What will they do? How will they do it? Who are they leaving behind? Are they leaving children behind? Perhaps their parents? Their sisters and brothers? Who will care for those people? Will they even survive?" All these questions flooded her mind.

She thought of how last night and this morning, she had been hugging her young ones and making them breakfast, lunch, and dinner, and now she could be deported.

While on the bus Mamá noticed the people outside walking on the sidewalks, sidewalks she too had walked freely on, holding hands with the young ones and talking about a movie everyone had just enjoyed together. She remembered all of us walking home together, eating ice cream cones and laughing.

Then she began to worry that Mrs. Davis would not be able to find her purse, that perhaps she had placed it elsewhere. "But, no, it's surely on top of my Bible," she thought. A torment of negative possibilities cycled around her mind. All the thoughts were full of fear, which was contrary to her customary attitude of optimism, faith, and hope.

When the bus stopped, everyone exited. Men walked single file in one line. Women and a few children of various ages walked in another line. Everyone moved as if bearing heavy burdens— bowed heads, stooped backs, and slow, slow steps.

They were all very quiet, looking down at their feet as they entered a large room. An additional twenty to thirty people were already in the large room. Mamá sat by a couple in their early thirties who had two children, about 6 and 10. The children were playing as if nothing was going on. Something was about to happen to them, but the children did not know that.

Suddenly, my mother felt immobile, frozen, and began to wonder once again what would happen to these children and their parents. Would they stay or go? Certainly, she knew the answer, but she hoped for a miracle. Throughout the rest of her life, Mamá would raise the topic about the destiny of these people in this large room. She would forever worry about what would happen to all these people. It was like they had become her own flesh and blood.

Mrs. Davis drove away from the secondhand store at the same time as the bus of detainees and Mamá left it. For the first time in her life, Mrs. Davis exceeded the speed limit. She drove fast with her heart pounding in her chest and her hands sweating profusely, so much so the steering wheel seemed to be slipping from her hands. She cried and worried all the way to our house: "I should have fought more vigorously. I didn't do enough for Nena!" Then she changed to a prayer, "Lord, I did all I could. It was unpreventable. Nothing would have changed their minds. As Nena said, they were only doing their job."

Once she arrived at our house, Mrs. Davis kept repeating to herself, "Evelyn, get control of yourself. Nothing will happen to Nena .. . But what if they take her away before I get there? Perhaps they lied to me?" she wondered. Then she worried that the purse would not be there, that maybe the green card would not be in it.

When she tried our front door, she found it locked. Then she tried the back door—it was locked as well. All the windows she discovered to be closed and locked. She tried to calm her mounting panic.

Desperate, Mrs. Davis found a rock, broke a window, slipped her hand inside, and pulled the window open. As she was climbing inside, she cut her hand. As she later explained to me, "I felt a stinging sensation. My hand bled and bled, but I managed to climb inside. I ran to the bathroom and grabbed some toilet paper, and I wrapped it around my hand." For the rest of her life, she'd have an apparent scar on that hand.

Later on, she made a plan with Mr. Davis for him to repair the window when no one in the family was around to ask him what he was doing.

Once inside, Mrs. Davis immediately sprinted to the kitchen to grab Mamá's purse on top of the table—but it wasn't there. She went to Mamá's bedroom but couldn't find it. In fear she searched the whole house over, all the while imagining Mamá being handcuffed like a criminal and put on a bus for the border.

She was very tempted to phone Miguel, but she managed to resist. She returned to the bathroom to get more toilet paper to stop the bleeding of her hand. In the bathroom she yelled aloud several times, "Where's the purse? Where's the purse?"

Upon exiting the bathroom, she spied a small table in the hallway—Mamá's purse was sitting on it along with her Bible. Mrs. Davis grabbed it and started searching its contents. She immediately became frustrated because there was so much stuff in the purse. She even thought of her husband complaining when she, herself, couldn't find something in her own purse because it was so full of stuff.

Finally, Mrs. Davis found the green card. Before leaving the house, she wrapped clean toilet paper around her hand. Then she grabbed Mamá's Bible, kissed it, and she left.

Once she got to the car, she leaned against it and prayed that God would help her regain her composure, so she could drive safely. Checking her watch, she realized it was getting late. She started talking to herself, asking, "Did the man say 4 or 2 or 3 p.m.? Wait—he said 4."

Mrs. Davis did all she could to find patience when she was driving to the detention center. At stoplights, waiting for people to cross the street, waiting for the light to turn green—it all seemed to take a long, long time. Finally, she arrived at the detention center. There was only one other car there and no bus.

A military guard approached, asking, "Can I help you, ma'am?"

"Yes, I'm looking for the detainees. One of my friends is with them, and I've brought her green card," Mrs. Davis explained.

"You must be talking about the people who came in earlier," he said. "They put them in a different building. See the one down the street? She will be there."

Mrs. Davis then drove to the other building. Looking in the rearview mirror, she adjusted her hat and then cleaned the mascara that had run down her face with some of the toilet paper around her hand. Finally, she stepped out of the car and entered the building.

After Mrs. Davis located Mamá, she ran over to hug her. They embraced with Mrs. Davis assuring her, "I have it. I have it, Nena." They were crying and giggling as if they had just won a bingo game.

A guard approached, asking, "Ma'am, what are you doing here?"

Mrs. Davis replied, "I've brought Magdalena Hernández her green card. She is my friend."

The guard ordered, "Bring her over here, and we'll tell you what needs to be done next."

My mother asked, "Evelyn, what happened to your hand?"

"I had to break a window to get in. I cut my hand on some glass, but it isn't anything. I had trouble finding your purse, but I'm here now and everything will be all right."

"Oh, Evelyn, your hand," Mamá lamented.

Together they walked over to a guard who took them to a small office where Mamá was asked to come inside. An agent told Mrs. Davis she had to wait outside.

Once inside, a man took Mamá's green card and, speaking in Spanish, asked, "So, your name is Magdalena Hernández?"

"*Sí, señor.*"

"And who's the lady outside?"

"She is Evelyn Davis. She and I were shopping together at a thrift store."

"Yes," he said, "I know all about that. So, who is Mrs. Davis?"

"She is my neighbor and was with me at the store. She went to my house to get my green card and bring it to me here because I didn't have it with me."

"She had to go to your house to get your documents?" he asked.

"Yes, and she had to break a window to get in, so she could find my purse and identification. You see her hand? It's bleeding. She cut her hand when she broke the window."

He could see Mrs. Davis's hand wrapped in blood-stained toilet paper.

After looking at the green card again, he continued, "Yes, that's definitely you. Where's the baby?"

Confused, my mother asked, "What baby?"

He pointed to the picture on her green card, asserting, "This baby."

"That is my son Salvador. He was only two when we immigrated, so the Consulate in Nogales told us it was best that he get his green card picture taken with me. They said if they took the picture of him as an infant, he would be unrecognizable when he was older. They told me that when he's 14, I could take him in for his own card."

"Sounds like nonsense to me," he commented, "and where is the baby now?"

"Salvador is now five, and he's at a Christian retreat with his sister, Olivia. They are in Prescott and won't be back for several days."

"Who is Olivia?"

"Miguel's sister."

"Miguel who?"

"I live with him."

"We will need more information on Miguel as well."

"Yes, sir."

"We have to have the baby here to do the verification. We need to see if he matches this picture."

"But, sir, this detention is not about the baby. It's about me, and that is my green card. That's me, so I'm in the United States legally. I'm a legal resident of the United States."

"That may be the case, but we need to verify that, indeed, the baby is with you."

"But the baby is not with me. He's in Prescott."

Then another gentleman walked in and asked, "What's going on here?"

At this moment, my mother noticed a Bible on a table in the room. She reached for it and took it in her hands. The man interrogating her silently watched her. Calmly she opened the Bible, looked at a page, and then turned several pages. Then the two men started talking.

The second man asked, "So, what's the problem?"

The first man responded, "This is Magdalena Hernández, and this is her green card. But the problem is the baby."

"What baby?"

"The baby who's in the picture on the card here."

He then explained what Mamá had told him about why the picture was taken with Salvador in her arms.

The second man kind of rolled his eyes and then told the first, "Let me talk to her." To Mamá he asked, "You live here in the United States, right?"

Before replying, she placed the Bible back on top of the table.

"Yes," she confirmed and then gave her address, adding, "The lady waiting outside, Evelyn Davis, is the neighbor who brought me my green card. She is my dear friend."

"Yes, I know. Something's just not right here, and legally we have to detain you here until the baby is brought over, so we can verify the authenticity of your card and the whereabouts of the baby. We need to know if he is okay."

"But I don't understand why that needs to be done. Plus, I need to get home, so I can feed my children. They'll be back from school at 4:30 p.m., and I need to be there."

"That may be the case, but we may need to hold you."

Now, a third man entered and looked at my mother. He asked, "What's going on? We need to get moving."

One of the men explained, "This is her green card, and we just want to make sure the baby is okay. She said the Consulate recommended a single picture of the both of them and told her the baby could get his green card when he turned 14 years old. Kind of odd? Right?"

"No, that's the way it's done," the third man answered.

Finally, my mother spoke up, "I have a very good friend who works with you here and knows me and my family very well. He is an immigration officer, a very important man."

"What's his name?"

Mamá answered, "Roger Stevenson. He's a friend of the family." She was referring to Roger Stevenson who had met her about a year earlier when he was making the rounds of homes looking for people who had no papers. He ended up sitting, eating with my mother, and talking for around four hours.

"Call him, and he'll tell you that he knows me," Mamá added.

Again, she picked up the Bible and looked at it, saying, "This is the Good Book of the Lord."

All three of the men looked at her and then at each other, puzzled yet sympathetic. She smiled at them.

The third man finally decided, "Let's see if we can find this Mr. Stevenson." He dialed a number, then asked into the phone, "Is there a Roger Stevenson there or at another office in Phoenix? . . . Do you know where we can find him? . . . Casa Grande or Tucson? . . . What's that number?"

He dialed another number and glanced over to see my mother as she stroked the Bible again. Then he said into the phone, "Do you have a Roger Stevenson working there? . . . Is he in? . . . Would you please give him a message? Tell him to call this number. Let him know we have one of his friends here, and we need to talk to him as soon as possible." As he made the comment, he looked at the other two men and then at my mother. He gave her a millisecond smile and then winked at the two men.

After setting the phone back down, he asked Mamá, "Do you enjoy reading the Bible?"

"Yes, very much, señor," she answered.

"This Roger Stevenson, who is he?" he went on to inquire.

My mother answered, "He is a very important man. He holds a high position, and soon he is going to be running one of the divisions. In fact, he may even be your boss, either currently or else very soon."

All three men's expressions became skeptical, suggesting they doubted that Roger Stevenson was her friend or that he had much importance. My mother simply smiled at them.

As they were talking, the phone rang.

The third man answered, "Hello . . . You're Roger Stevenson? . . . We have a person here who claims you are a friend of the family

and a very good friend of hers. Her name is Magdalena Hernández
. . . So, you know her well? . . . Okay, sure . . . Of course . . . Thank
you—"

My mother raised her hand and told the man, "Please tell Mr.
Stevenson that I would like to meet his mother one of these days.
I'm hoping she is okay and that he has visited her and that he should
visit her more frequently."

Though he was puzzled about her message, the man repeated
her words into the phone. He added too that Mamá was holding
the Bible.

"Yes, okay, I'll tell her . . . That's good enough for me . . . We'll
catch you later." Then he hung up the phone.

The man turned to her and asked, "You don't know Mr.
Stevenson's mother, do you?"

"No," she replied, "she lives in Colorado, but maybe one of these
days we will meet. Maybe at a different time and place. Maybe not
even in this world, but I'm certain I will meet her."

"Mr. Stevenson said he is a field officer, not a supervisor. How
did you meet him?"

"He visited us at our home a while back, and we got to know
him well. I also got to know his mother although I never met her.
She reads the Good Book and is a very good cook. He told me about
all the great meals she cooked and that she took the Bible with her
to church every Sunday."

The man leaned over and said, "Can I tell you something? You're
a very interesting and kind person, and you're lucky to have a friend
like Roger Stevenson. I believe you are right, someday he will be a
much more important person in our office than he is now. I also
want you to know that I will try to meet him one of these days. He
is the type of man we need in this line of work."

My mother agreed, "Yes, he is very good."

At this time my mother had a positive feeling. She truly felt she'd turned the interrogators into warmer, kinder people.

The man returned her card to her and let her know she was free to go. Everyone exited the room.

Upon seeing Mrs. Davis, that third man told my mother, "This is a fine friend you have here. I'm sure you know what she has been through to get your card."

"Yes, I do. Sir, can I ask what is going to happen to these people here?" Mamá ventured to ask.

"Sadly, every single one of them will be on the bus at 4:00 p.m. and be at the border by 7:00 p.m. where they will all be set loose. I have no idea what will happen to them after that."

Mrs. Davis asked, "What will happen to their relatives here?"

"That we will never know," he answered, "because none of them will tell us anything. They won't tell us where they lived, who they will leave behind—brothers, sisters, parents. They are totally afraid to tell us because they want to protect those people."

"I feel sorry for them," my mother admitted.

The man confided, "It is an event people in this department must deal with every day. It is a very difficult thing to do. We're human beings. We care more about these people than you might think; however, the law is the law. We have to respect it and enforce it."

My mother looked at him, saying, "*Si, lo sé. Lo entiendo muy bien.*"

Mrs. Davis went over to hold my mother's hand, as she told the man, "Thank you so much for your kindness, sir."

Mamá told him she'd like to give him a hug for his kindness.

Although his hesitancy indicated he wasn't used to it, he agreed with a shy "Okay."

When she and Mrs. Davis left, they could see the people walking single file through a white door. Outside was a bus waiting for them.

My mother and Mrs. Davis began to cry as if they had just lost a member of the family or a loved one. It was a quiet ride back home.

While I didn't learn about my mother's close call with deportation in 1969 until decades later, I was with her in 1970 when we had our own run-in with an immigration officer.

In 1970, when Roberto was staying with us while we were working to help him find the farm he was supposed to get to, my mother asked me, "Edgar, can you go to the immigration office and get an application for Roberto?"

Seeing as I'd gone to this office at least nine times before to retrieve applications, it was a task I was accustomed to. My mother decided to accompany me since she also needed to go to the grocery store.

At the office, I asked the man working the reception, "Can I please have a green card application?"

A female guard who'd been watching approached the man at the desk and asked him to speak to her in private.

Mamá, who'd accompanied me inside, wondered, "We're only asking for an application. What's the problem?"

"I don't know, Mamá. I've been here many times before, and this has never happened. I'm curious too."

When the man and the female guard returned, the guard said to us, "Can you two please come to the back for a moment? I'd like to speak with you."

We followed her, and she directed us into a small room where we were told to sit and wait. Puzzled and somewhat concerned, my mother and I did as we were instructed.

A few minutes later, the female guard returned. She was a very heavy-set lady, about 5'9," middle-aged, with green eyes, and some gray in her hair. She had chubby cheeks and broad shoulders. She wore a stern expression on her face. Her nametag indicated her name was Officer Graves.

Reaching her hand out to us and waving it around quite close, she said with some impatience, "I'm going to need to see your IDs."

I handed over my driver's license, and my mother gave her green card. Officer Graves snapped them into her possession and left.

About ten minutes later, she returned. With that same stony face, she inquired, "Who wants this application? Who is it for? A family member? A person living with you? What's the purpose of this application? Do you have a green card, young man?"

I answered, "No, I don't because I'm a US citizen, ma'am."

"Where is your passport?"

"I have it at home."

"Why do you have it at home? Why don't you have it with you?" she asked.

Though she was quite pushy and doing her best to intimidate us, I answered as politely as possible, "Like many people, I only use it when I'm traveling abroad. My driver's license tends to serve as sufficient ID when I'm in country."

She then took a seat next to me with Mamá sitting across from her. Turning to face me and leaning towards me, she continued the interrogation, asking in a low voice, "When did you become a citizen?"

"In 1969 I came to this office for my exam and had a beautiful ceremony in the courthouse on Washington Street."

"Is that so?" she asked slowly, increasing her volume of voice with each word.

"Yes, ma'am," I confirmed.

"Who's the application for?" she persisted.

I told her, "It's for an acquaintance who wants to immigrate legally."

"Why didn't this person come in for the application?" she pressed.

I answered truthfully, "I would say, they are afraid."

My mother then reached across the table to touch my hand. She quietly asked, "*Está bien todo*? Everything all right, Edgar?

"*Si*, Mamá. The officer wants to know who the application is for," I explained.

"Let me ask her in Spanish," the officer told me, meaning she wanted to interrogate Mamá. With both hands on the table and eyebrows furrowed, she asked Mamá, "*Para quien es esta solicitud*? Who's the application for?"

"It's for a good person. *Es para una buena persona*," replied Mamá.

At this, the officer stood slightly from her chair and leaned across the table to solemnly demand, "How good can this person— who is here illegally—even be? This 'good person' broke the law, right? *Dónde está esta persona*? Where is this person?" The volume of her voice heightened when she asked again where the person was.

My mother's response to this scolding was simply, "Señora, what's wrong with asking for an application?"

Officer Graves answered, shaking her hand in front of Mamá's face, "The problem is that your son has come here for applications in the past on many, many occasions."

My mother responded, "Yes, my son. He's an amazing person. Do you know that someday he will become a surgeon?" My mother then smiled gently.

The officer sat back in her seat but didn't soften. She didn't let up. With narrowed eyes, she inquired, "Who's the child in the picture with you on your green card?"

"That's my son Salvador."

"Why doesn't he have his own green card?" she questioned, as if she'd caught us in a snare.

"Well, that seems to be a topic of some controversy. What happened is that the wonderful American Consulate in Nogales told me that because Salvador's features and appearance will change so much, it is better that he wait to get his own green card when he is around 14 years old. He advised me to have Salvador and me share the same green card until then. That was the recommendation," Mamá explained.

"So, where's the child?" the officer interrogated accusingly.

"He is in kindergarten at Monroe School," answered Mamá.

The officer turned and leaned in quite close to question, "Where do you go to school? Where did you go to elementary school?"

I told her, "I too went to Monroe School. Now I'm at Phoenix Union High School, and I'm finishing my junior year."

"What is the name of your teachers?"

"Mrs. Tudor was my fifth grade teacher."

"When?"

"That would be . . . 1959. My eighth grade teacher was Mrs. Francis Cane. I have many different teachers in high school."

"And what are you going to do after high school?"

"I am going to go to Arizona State University, then to medical school, and then I will train to become a surgeon."

My mother placed her hand on mine and smiled, but the officer showed no reaction. Her facial expressions were either stony or agitated from accusations.

Twisting her face into a small smile, she asked—as if she'd struck gold—"You got your green card in 1960, so how is it that you were in the fifth grade in 1959?"

I looked at my mother and then back at the officer, who was still wearing that snide grimace. I took a breath and answered, "Ma'am, I was here illegally in Phoenix for 7½ months. Then I went back to Nogales to immigrate legally."

My mother started to cry.

I told her, "It's okay, Mamá. It's the truth and we have no reason to lie. She knows everything about us."

My mother looked at the officer and asked, "*Algo mas quiere saber?* Is there anything else you need?"

The officer's only reaction was a soured look of disgust. She interrogated, "Do these people live here in the USA or in Mexico who you are and have been picking up applications for?"

My mother replied, "These people are afraid to come in for an application for fear of deportation. Since they are afraid to come in for an application, I don't see anything wrong for us to come here and retrieve one for them.

Despite the officer's stone face, relentless questioning, and multiple attempts at intimidation, my mother maintained gentleness and a polite manner. She even reached out and touched the woman gently on her hand. The lady didn't move or show any reaction.

My mother went on to explain, "We sent applications on a couple of occasions to some people in Mexico, so they could apply for immigration as per their desire, very much the way we did ourselves. Also, we've helped people already here that want to immigrate legally while they are living here illegally. This also is a good thing. Don't you think so?"

With narrowed eyes and a furrowed brow, she simply looked at my mother and asked, "Who are these people? *Quienes son?*"

So the duel continued. On one side: an educated woman with many credentials and some security clearance. On the other side: a woman with no education, no credentials, and a huge heart filled with love for everyone around her. I was proud of how softly and innocently my mother communicated.

My mother responded, "We are here only to help these people by obtaining applications for them, not to be informers."

Mamá continued, "I know several people who are here illegally and have been here working for some time, but this is sacred information. I can't tell you anything about them other than they are really good, decent, loving, and hardworking people."

"If they are so decent, why are they here illegally, breaking the law?" the officer huffed, waving her pointed index finger around the table at both of us.

"That only God can answer," my mother replied, "It's what's in their hearts that I know. All they want is a better life. Look, my son Edgar was here illegally, and he went back to Nogales and immigrated legally. Who are we to think these people can't someday do the same? My son will become a productive citizen who will make us proud. He will save lives someday"—Mamá paused to touch the officer's hand—"You are a very important person and lucky to be here in our most wonderful country."

Like a robot, the officer inquired, "Can someone verify as to the honesty of both you and your mother?"

"What do you mean?" I asked.

Slamming both hands down on the table, she uttered, "You know it's against the law to harbor illegals in your home. Did you know that?"

Mamá told her, "Our home is open to our friends and friends of our friends. We don't ask people for documents, so it's likely we have had people without documents in our home, both visiting and perhaps living with us. For many years we have had guests in our little home who needed a place to stay in times of dire need."

Officer Graves dryly stated, "That may be the case, but it's still illegal."

Mamá then remarked, "It seems then we are talking about two laws. Apparently, the law I keep in our home is different. That's the duty to help people in need by offering a temporary stay until they are back on their feet. I call it a Christian law. The Good Book has that law written all over it. Additionally, we have had several people living with us who are citizens of our great country."

Her response: "We don't agree with harboring illegals whatsoever."

The officer redirected her attention to me, twisting her body in my direction and turning up her lips into a condescending smile, to share, "Becoming a doctor or a surgeon entails years and years of study. Plus, it's very expensive. Did you know that?"

I replied, "Yes, ma'am."

My mother interjected, "He will get it done with the help of the good Lord."

At this point, a gentleman, tall, blond, with blue eyes and wearing a suit, entered the room. He had a warm smile on his face as he asked us, "How is Miguel doing?"

My mother and I looked at each other. Then she asked him, "How is it that you know Miguel?"

He explained, "I know him well. He's an incredible person. I used to work out of the Nogales Customs Office. Last time I saw him was, I believe, when you came across with your young children and a baby in your arms."

My mother held up her card and pointed to the photo of Salvador, saying, "Yes, this baby."

As they were speaking, I noticed his badge read Rex "Will" Thompson. Also, it was quite shiny and slightly different than that of Officer Graves. When I looked at her, she was sitting back in her chair with her hands in her lap and her gaze directed at the table. Her previous confidence and sense of command had seriously decreased.

Rex "Will" Thompson continued, "I understand you are asking for applications for people who want to apply for immigration, right?"

"*Sí, señor*," Mamá answered.

"And these people are both here and in Mexico, yes?"

Mamá confirmed, "Yes, sir. Miguel and Edgar help many people prepare their documents as they go on their way."

He said, "I think this act is a novelty and speaks well of you two. You understand that we know pretty much about everyone who crosses the border legally."

"Yes, sir."

"It is our understanding that Miguel has immigrated over ten members of his family as well as many others. You understand the efforts, don't you?"

"Yes, sir," Mamá and I responded.

"We feel many can't accomplish what Miguel did, and we always hope to help as many folks as we can."

My mother added, "Sir, these people are God-loving human beings who want to better their lives and their families the best that they can. Unfortunately, some can't even read or write, but their intentions are good. Some came in desperation. I am sure most regret it and wish that it could have been done differently. Also, I very much recognize there are a lot of not-so-honest people. We try hard to also love them and help them the best that we can."

Mr. Thompson told us, "I have been in the immigration department for 29 years, and I think what you are doing may be defiant, but at the same time, it may very well be an act of kindness. Perhaps these people may be luckier than they can imagine to have a friend in desperate times."

My mother smiled.

Officer Graves seemed to fade into the surroundings, as if her presence and will had been reduced.

Mr. Thompson directed Officer Graves, "Please get them the applications they've requested."

I looked at my mother as she smiled at me. "Honesty is good for the soul," I stated. Those were the very words the American Consulate told Miguel in 1960 when Miguel confessed to him that I'd been in Phoenix illegally for 7½ months and that he was sorry we'd broken the law.

My mother asked the gentleman, "Mr. Thompson, what's your mother's name?"

He was taken back by her question. Then he responded, "Catherine, but everyone called her Cathy. She died two years ago but lived a great life. She was a lady who had faith, loved her children, and loved everyone around her. She believed in the Scriptures."

"I too believe in the Good Book," my mother commented. Then she asked the officer, "And you, Officer Graves, what's your mother's name?"

She too was surprised by my mother's question. She softly answered, "Her name is Bonnie, and she lives in Oregon."

"Thank you and I hope you visit her very frequently," Mamá stated.

They gave us some applications, and we walked out and down a hall.

As we walked away, my mother turned around at the same time as Officer Graves turned to look in our direction. My mother smiled at her, and she smiled shyly at my mother.

My mother continued to host guests at our house and to assist many people in gathering papers and filling out applications for immigration. As she stated, the law governing our house was its own. It was the Christian law.

Chapter 13

Mind and Heart

In 2002 when Mamá was eighty years old, she and my sister Surama were talking over breakfast. Suddenly Surama noticed Mamá was not responding. She looked confused and dazed as if she wanted to say something but couldn't get the words out. Then Surama noticed that one side of her face was drooping. She appeared obtunded, quiet, and almost immobile.

Surama then noticed Mamá was struggling with her face and lips, as if attempting to speak. She moved a hand as if trying to signal something. Then she didn't respond anymore. My sister saw her leaning to one side and noticed her mouth was slightly crooked with some saliva dripping from that side.

Mamá couldn't walk, but with difficulty Surama managed to get her to the couch. She called Asunción to take Mamá to the hospital. By the time they got there, Mamá had almost completely recovered with the exception of a slightly drooping eyelid and lip. I was notified when they were in the emergency room.

When the doctors reviewed Mamá's neurological workup, they discovered she'd had a stroke. They recommended a surgery for a carotid endarterectomy. This type of surgery is used to reduce the risk of stroke by correcting stenosis, or narrowing, in the carotid artery or removing plaques from it, a major artery in the neck that supplies blood to the brain.

A doctor discussed with us all the risks and options for treatment going further. When I considered her risk for a future stroke as well as the potential risks of the surgery, I felt we should leave her alone and do no surgery. In arriving at this conclusion, I tried to put myself in the position of a surgeon listening to the options, both surgical and non-surgical, keeping in mind that at this time surgery was not the only option.

In the end, Mamá elected to take blood thinners and medications to control her blood pressure.

When she returned home, her body and mind returned to normal functioning, which was a great relief to all of us. She could proceed with her daily activities as if no stroke had occurred. All my sisters noted how quickly she recovered and how well she was able to care for herself, her home, as well as her many grandchildren and even great-grandchildren.

Mamá was instrumental in helping me, my siblings, and our spouses (and later even our children) adjust to the many aspects of parenthood. She gave numerous newborn babies their first baths. On a regular basis and on any given day, she would find herself feeding and caring for any number of grandchildren and eventually great-grandchildren. It was quite endearing to see her holding the newborn babies, grandchildren, or great-grandchildren. Sometimes even friends and neighbors would seek her help.

Two years later, when Mamá and Surama were drinking coffee together, suddenly Mamá became unable to speak, and her eyelid also drooped. Surama, recognizing the signs, quickly got Mamá to the hospital where she had the same tests, examinations, and CT scan as before. Everything was normal with the exception of the ultrasound, which showed the carotid artery was narrowing, as in 2002. As before, I was notified.

While again surgery was recommended, Mamá declined. She was going to leave it to the good Lord, something she'd said in regard to her first stroke too: "My life is in the hands of the Lord, and I won't do anything." She felt very good and again had no residual deficits. She proceeded with her daily life, mobile and with sound mind.

However, Mamá did reveal to me, "I'm afraid, Edgar. I don't want to end up like that nice man in Los Coyotes." For decades now, this had been a fear of hers.

Mamá had her third stroke in 2007. She was watching television when she felt numb on one side of her face. Then she could feel it drooping. Also, she felt nauseated.

Luckily, at the hospital the same neurologist who had treated her the previous two times attended her. Again, all her studies were normal except for the narrowed carotid artery. And again, the recommendation was surgery. Within 24 hours of admittance to the hospital, she fully recovered. Once again, she returned home where she prayed for health and read the Bible for strength, peace, and solace. After years of painstaking lessons and attempts at reading, in her old age Mamá finally learned to read.

The neurologist told us that it was amazing that our mother, who had had three stokes, was able to recover completely within 24 hours and that she suffered no residual deficits. He said we were lucky because many patients like my mother ended up needing full-time care.

At home, Mamá cooked and functioned fully. No one could tell she'd had a stroke. Her attention to detail at home and her support and care with the grandchildren and great-grandchildren were no different than prior to her strokes.

In 2009, when she was 88, she suffered her fourth stroke. She had the same symptoms and recovered in 48 hours with no residual effects.

In 2010, at age ninety, she had a fifth stroke. This one was extremely difficult for her. Unlike with her previous strokes, this time she was in the hospital for a week, during which time she had some episodes of confusion, which led to poor recognition of all of us. She had to be restrained, which was difficult to endure. Once she was released she had residual effects, but within four weeks, she made a full recovery. She had a drooping face and eyelid, but her mind remained sharp and she was able to communicate fairly well.

Overall, we in the family were amazed and impressed by how she overcame this fifth stroke. She fully recovered, despite her age.

Her neurologist said, "For having five stokes at the age of ninety, her full recovery is actually a miracle of life." From that point on until her death a few years later, she had no residual problems.

In this decade, with these strokes—and really, in the years before as well—Mamá had two big worries. She always worried about ending up like the man in Los Coyotes, which I'll describe shortly, and her second worry was about Salvador, my little brother, who came to the United States in my mother's arms. Remember, her green card showed a picture of her holding baby Salvador in her arms, a photo that caused confusion for officers at various times.

The unfortunate case of my brother Salvador is that he developed a serious chronic depression that required medications for survival. My brother went from doctor to doctor, from clinic to clinic, but he could never be stabilized, no matter what medications he took nor which practitioner he saw. The medications had side effects—bloating, constipation, urine retention, and dry mouth—and also additional, more troubling side effects—surreal floating feelings and nightmares that resulted in sleep deficits. This lack of adequate sleep would then cause him paranoia and anxiety in his waking life. Because of these side effects, Salvador would often quit taking his medications after three to six weeks. After quitting, he would develop severe depression and even delusions, sometimes delusions of suicide.

My mother never forgot Salvador's talents. She described him as a brilliant contractor. He could build a home himself, from scratch. However, his depressive condition often would cripple him. Nobody could pinpoint a clear diagnosis, so doctors did not seem to know how to treat his condition.

Salvador went through turmoil on several occasions. One afternoon after another, he would show up in my office when he needed to be by me. When he felt scared, he would call me, and I would tell him to come to the office where I would keep an eye on him. He clung to me because he was afraid he would commit suicide. He felt safe by my side.

Meanwhile, I would keep in touch with Mamá about how he was doing. It was something that was agonizing to her. When Salvador was enduring particularly difficult episodes, I could tell she would suffer as well: sleepless nights and weight loss, similar to Salvador himself, actually. Her beautiful eyes would become sunken because she wouldn't drink enough liquids and wasn't feeding herself well enough.

Finally, it occurred to me that Salvador needed to allow his body a longer period of time—beyond three to six weeks—to adjust to the medications. Once his body adjusted, I determined that those very troubling side effects would mostly subside. I worked with him and one of his doctors to find an effective medication and to support him very closely during those first months on it. Finally, Salvador has been able to enjoy a relative reprieve from the roller coaster, relative in that even though he found a good medication, depression will always be a part of his life. A constant miserable companion who makes appearances every now and then.

Salvador moved to Rocky Point, Mexico, to take on challenging contracting jobs, something he's gifted at and greatly enjoys. Even still, chronic depression, even when treated, entails a life of ups and downs.

For this reason, Mamá beseeched me, "Of course, I don't want him to sidetrack you from your career and your own family, but please, *mijo*, leave a little space for Salvador in your mind and heart."

I promised her, "No matter where Salvador is, I'll be there to help him. There will never be a shortage of attention to him, whether I speak to him on the phone or meet up with him."

About the nice man in Los Coyotes and Mamá's other looming fear. When she saw him those few times, it left a pronounced imprint on her psyche. Even before she suffered a stroke, she feared a demise like his, and with every stroke she suffered this fear only grew. The man in Los Coyotes was someone that many of us in the family became acquainted with, but at different times, as I'll soon explain.

I first met the man in 1959 when I was 9½ years old. It was a few weeks after my father died and Miguel returned to La Mira to visit Papá's grave and then take me back with him to the USA.

After traversing the curtain of dust along that 50-mile craggy dirt road, the pickup we were riding in stopped in Los Coyotes, a village even smaller than La Mira. Los Coyotes featured a gas station and a small cantina-type restaurant. The "nice man" that my mother was talking about ran that little restaurant.

Miguel and I first met his daughter who worked as a waitress in the cantina. She was the one who informed us, "My father thinks he knows you."

That's when we met him. He had a great-looking Emiliano Zapata-like mustache and big, bushy hair. He'd known Papá and offered us his condolences.

Miguel later confided that our father was responsible for this man making a big change in his life. As Miguel explained it to me,

"Many years ago, Papá accompanied me on this same trip up to the border, and like we did today, he and I stopped in Los Coyotes. When we were there, that man came to Papá asking for medical help. The man's hand was severely infected. Apparently, the man had beaten his wife—punched her in the mouth and landed his knuckles into her teeth. Not only did he mess up his wife's mouth, he also hurt his hand. Our father agreed to help him—and also his wife—on the condition that the man swear he'd get his act together and stop hitting his wife. Apparently, the man has lived up to his word. He stopped the domestic violence and changed his whole life."

In 1966, Pedro, Mamá, and the children also stopped in Los Coyotes after slowly and carefully traveling that dusty road out of La Mira. Pedro was filling up his Mustang with gas when an older man approached, saying, "Your orange car is amazing. *Qué bonito.*"

The man went on to inquire, "Where are you all coming from? Where are you going?"

Pedro answered, "I'm with my mother and sisters and brothers. We are going to the United States of America. We're coming from La Mira."

The man then asked, "Did you know Miguel Hernández Cabrera?"

"Yes, very well. He was my father," Pedro replied.

"My God, how can this be?" the man asked with emotion. "I knew your father too. He changed my life. I also met Miguel, who must be your brother. He and a little boy came through here in 1959. I believe they were traveling to the United States too."

"Yes, you are correct, señor," Pedro confirmed, "That was my older brother Miguel and my younger brother Edgar."

"I remember them well. When you get back to the USA, ask Miguel about me. He will remember me, no doubt. My goodness. Praise the Lord."

Mamá approached and heard the latter part of the conversation. She was very moved.

The man turned to her, asking, "You are Magdalena?"

"Yes, sir, please call me Nena," she told him.

"And you all are going to the USA to be with Miguel and the little boy?" he asked.

"Yes, you are correct," Mamá told him.

"Is there anyone in your family left in La Mira?" he asked.

"My mother, my two sisters, and some cousins," answered Mamá and then added, "Plus the memories, going back to 1949 when we moved there."

"Please come inside. I welcome you and your family to sit and enjoy a meal."

So they had a meal together. When Pedro offered to pay him, the man refused.

When everyone loaded back into the Mustang, the man bade them farewell, saying, "May God be with you and keep you safe."

That was the first time my mother met this nice man in Los Coyotes.

In 1972, Mamá desperately wanted to return to La Mira to see her own mother for the last time. At eighty-nine, my grandmother was ailing and had very few days to live. So we pooled our money to finance Mamá's trip to La Mira.

In the six years since Mamá had left, La Mira had been undergoing big changes. A large company acquired the mines, and substantial roads were being built. Plus, a large seaport for international ships was to be built in Lázaro Cárdenas. This international venture would eventually change La Mira, morphing it, along with nearby villages, into a large city. The whole area would change drastically since our time there.

Mamá was blessed to get to see her mother again for the last time. She also visited her sisters, her cousins, Chucho, his twin daughters, and other friends. It was a special trip for Mamá.

When her bus departed from La Mira, it stopped at this same Los Coyotes gas station and cantina. Mamá was delighted, eager to greet the owner whom she met with Pedro and the children in 1966.

With a smile on her face, Mamá pushed open the door to the little restaurant. She quickly located him. Although she recognized him, he didn't respond to her, or to anyone. He'd suffered a stroke and was largely incapacitated. A woman was feeding him with a spoon.

When Mamá neared them, the lady asked, "Do you know my father?"

"Yes, I do and so does most of my family," Mamá told her. Then my mother went on to tell her how she and the children had met him in 1966 and how Miguel and I had met him in 1959—and how kind he'd been to all of us.

At mention of the 1959 visit, the lady responded, "Oh, yes. I'm his daughter, and I remember well when your young son stopped in here with his older brother. They were traveling to the United States. Miguel was good-looking and polite. I remember them both."

My mother noticed there was a Bible to the right of the man. She leaned over to greet him and to caress the Bible. The man did not respond. Saliva slowly dripped down from the side of his mouth. Occasionally his shoulders and arms would ripple from spasms.

It was seeing this man in this incapacitated, tragic state, being cared for by his grown daughter, that haunted my mother for decades to come. She described this scene to me and my siblings multiple times and expressed her fear of having a stroke. Her greatest fear was to have a stroke. What's amazing is that Mamá ended up not only having a stroke—she had five of them! However, her fear was misplaced because her strokes never incapacitated her as they had this man in Los Coyotes.

This wasn't Mamá's last time in Los Coyotes. In 1977, when I was in medical school, Mamá insisted upon returning to La Mira another time. Although my siblings and I weren't keen on it and we ended up worrying a lot, we knew we couldn't stop her. Mamá and Leticia, one of her cousins who was living in California, went together to La Mira by bus.

Their time in La Mira was brief. Chucho had died in 1975. Mamá did get to visit with his twin daughters.

On the return trip, the bus stopped at Los Coyotes. As Mamá had been so deeply moved and haunted by the nice restaurant owner, she was determined to see how he was doing. She felt apprehensive, and it showed in the sudden paleness of her face and her rapid breathing and noticeable perspiration.

As they were disembarking from the bus, Leticia, concerned about Mamá, inquired, "Nena, are you feeling okay? You don't look well."

"Leticia, I'm fine. I'm recalling an earlier visit to this cantina and wondering how it may have changed," Mamá answered.

Once inside, Mamá anxiously scanned the room, searching for the man and his daughter. When she couldn't locate them, she felt a bit panicked wondering where they were or if something had happened to them.

While Leticia was in the restroom, Mamá approached the man working behind the counter, asking, "In the past I've always seen the owner and his daughter, but I don't see them today. Where is the owner? What about his daughter?"

"*Él murió*. He died," the guy told her.

My mother froze for a moment, then ventured to ask, "And his daughter?"

"She isn't here."

"Where is she? What happened? *Que pasó?*"

The man explained, "When her father died, about two months ago, she left. Apparently, she's been sick."

"*Qué triste,*" Mamá uttered.

"It was a scary thing, her father's death. He had a stroke a few years earlier, and she'd been taking care of him. While she was feeding him, he suddenly started choking. There were all these people in the restaurant, and he started choking. He could not breathe and fell to the floor and went into convulsions. His daughter as well as others tried to help him, but nothing worked."

"That's so upsetting. Terrible. Poor girl. Where is she now?"

"She's probably at the cemetery," he answered.

Then Mamá sat there on the bar stool, silent. Almost statue-like.

The guy asked her, "Can I get you something to drink, ma'am?"

"*No gracias.* What was his name? I knew him and his daughter, but for some reason I never knew their names."

"Benjamin Contreras and his daughter's name is Marta."

"His wife?"

"Sandra was her name. Who are you?" he asked.

"My name is Nena, Magdalena Hernández, and you?"

"Margarito," he answered.

Mamá asked him, "Do you know the Contreras family?"

"Yes, very well, all my family knows them. Do you want me to give Marta a message?" Margarito asked.

"Yes, tell Marta that the Hernández Cabrera family loves her and will always pray for her and her parents who are now in a better place. Tell her that we are the ones who came by here in '66 in the orange Mustang."

When Leticia returned from the restroom, she noted to Mamá, "You look like you're feeling better. Let's get back on the bus."

Later on, somewhere near Culiacán, as the bus turned a corner and started down a curvy road, it came to an abrupt stop. Several men and a woman approached it.

The passengers, including my mother and Leticia, asked the driver what was happening, and he explained, "It's an assault. A robbery."

The bandits ordered everyone off the bus, including women and children. Next everyone was ordered to empty their pockets. The female bandit proceeded to check all the women and children, searching for anything of value they may be hiding on their person.

Mamá and Leticia were most concerned about losing their green cards. They didn't have much money, just the bus ticket to Nogales.

While everyone was feeling scared and anxious, one woman, who was holding a baby, really lost control. The lady seemed to go into a rage or a fit. She was thrashing around, all the while swinging her baby in wild arcs.

Mamá instructed the convulsing woman, "Give me your baby." The woman allowed Mamá to take the baby. In the meantime, other passengers got more agitated. Others became more silent.

Holding the child tight to her chest, Mamá asked the bandits, "How can you do this to your brothers and sisters?" She repeated this several times only to deaf ears. The driver looked on, showing no emotion or concern.

The disturbed woman only got worse. She went into a seizure-like state, biting her tongue as she thrashed.

The driver kept to himself and just watched this woman tiring herself out.

My mother, who was holding the baby, was never searched. Leticia lost her money but not her green card.

Eventually the woman's seizure stopped. Leticia helped clean her up. The bandits finished their robbery and departed. The driver called everyone back onto the bus.

Mamá and Leticia helped the lady onto the bus and gave her water.

"My pills, give me one of my pills," the woman begged.

Leticia searched the woman's purse. When she found a pill bottle, she got one out and gave it to the lady.

My mother was still holding the baby and looking on.

"*Mi hija*, my daughter!" the lady cried out.

My mother took the baby and placed it on the woman's lap. After a few miles, the lady's composure returned.

My mother asked, "Are you okay now?"

"Yes, thank you. *Estoy bien*," the woman responded.

Though the woman was better, the incident wasn't over for my mother. She sat up tall to look at the driver. She could see him furtively peeking up at the rearview mirror, surveying her and the other passengers from time to time. Once he noticed Mamá directing a firm gaze at him, he simply stared straight ahead. After they arrived at the city bus terminal, everyone got off to change buses. Before walking to the next bus, my mother told Leticia, "Give me a moment."

Mamá then sought out their driver. He was busy talking to another man. After noticing Mamá, he continued talking as if not wanting to give her time to speak to him, hoping she'd go away.

Once his conversation ended and before he could flee, Mamá said to him, "Señor, my brother, you may think no one noticed your lack of concern and total silence during the robbery, but you are wrong. Let it be in your conscience that all your brothers and sisters saw you, and you will forever continue to see them looking at you."

He wouldn't look her in the eye. There he was, a large, pot-bellied man afraid to meet the piercing eyes of a 50-plus-year-old lady only 5 feet 2 inches tall.

Before she left him, she gently told him, "I still love you, brother. My name is Nena Hernández. *Que Dios te perdone.*"

When he finally looked at her, he had tears in his eyes and a look of fear and guilt.

When my mother returned to Leticia, Leticia asked, "You feel okay?"

She answered, "Yes, much better now."

Chapter 14

LEGACY

It was a cold day with heavy rain during the middle of December. I was the surgeon on call and had just arrived at the ER. Inside the exam room I found a very sick patient, a man bundled up in an old, filthy blanket. The stench of dead tissue filled the room.

A nurse walked in, wearing a mask, and remarked, "Isn't this awful, Dr. Hernández?"

Silently I approached the man. I pulled back the blanket to discover around ten dark black necrotic patches dotting the skin of his legs. Also, there were some on his elbows. This dead tissue was the reason for the foul, carcass-like odor in the room.

"Sylvia, this man needs to be warmed up and have tissue debridement immediately," I informed the nurse.

Sylvia responded, "Tell me what I need to do, Dr. Hernández."

We got blood studies and placed an IV in him for fluids. Later I took him to surgery and peeled off 16 two-by-four-inch dead spots of skin. I placed cadaver skin on these areas to patch it until the man recovered. The plan was to graft him with his own skin at a later time.

That afternoon when I was visiting my mother, I told her about this patient.

Mamá responded, "I will pray that he finds rapid salvage and recovery, and I will pray for all of you who are taking care of him."

"Mamá, he reminded me of Spencer Halloway. Remember how you and Mrs. Davis cared for him when I was in high school? I was brought back to those years and how you were helping so many people even though you were just getting to know this new country."

"Edgar, I couldn't have done it without the help of Evelyn. Did you know that Evelyn is probably an angel?"

"I'm sorry?"

"Yes, an angel. I mean, an earth angel. Well, an angel here with us."

I was stunned by her comment and her delivery of it, for she did not smile. She was very matter-of-fact.

"I know she is a wonderful lady with a heart of gold," I remarked.

In the meantime, there was a knock on the door—and it was Mrs. Davis. As Mamá approached to open the door she called back to me, "Is this man going to be okay?"

"Yes, poor man. He has no place to go and no family. Yes, he will survive his injuries. I think so."

Mrs. Davis walked in, greeting my mother and then me with that fine musical voice of hers that was enough to make you smile or cry. "Edgar, how are you?" she inquired.

"Fine, thank you, Mrs. Davis."

"I'm so proud of you. I knew you had it in you. You always said you would achieve your dream." She hugged my mother and gave her a red rose, red like her customary red lipstick.

As my mother placed it into a cup of water, she looked at me, and I noted, "An angel, huh?"

"Yes, Edgar, an angel," my mother affirmed.

"Well," I added, "It's actually two angels, okay?"

Mamá smiled.

"I have to return to work, but I hope to see you both again soon."

Mrs. Davis told me, "Your patients will live."

I turned to her and said, "*Gracias*," then departed.

The image of those two ladies has stayed with me forever.

Mr. Davis died of a heart condition in 2008. Mrs. Davis died in 2010, also of a heart condition. My mother passed in 2013 at the age of 93.

Six months prior to Mamá's death, Surama—who'd dedicated her life to caring for our mother—prepared incredible chicken tacos with a special salsa for Mamá and me to enjoy over a long lunch together. It was over this meal that Mamá and I had a very special, very long conversation. It's a conversation that is everlasting for me. I return to it again and again.

"Edgar, I want to talk to you about my thoughts about my whole life because I am going to die soon."

"Mamá, after each stroke you've had, you were convinced you'd die soon. But that's not been the case. You've recovered beautifully. I'd love to talk to you about your whole life, but I believe you'll be alive for years to come," I responded.

It was true—Mamá had recovered beautifully from every stroke. Even at this point, though she explained that her body ached, she continued to be mobile. Her mind was totally clear as well.

"*Gracias, mijo*. But this time is different. I know it," she explained—and she ended up being correct. Similarly in my career I've encountered patients who have told me when they were going to die though I clinically couldn't discern it—and they ended up being right. It was almost like they had a sixth sense.

"Mamá, tell me about Papá. What stood out most to you when you met him?"

"He was such a contradictory mix of charisma and brains, on the one hand—and that constant smoking and drinking on the other. He was brilliant in the way he helped people, but so destructive in the way he dismissed himself," Mamá told me.

She recalled the wrenching pain she endured when sending Surama, Pedro, Jorge, and me away as young children: "While I was totally secure with the family members you were leaving with, your half-brothers and half-sisters, I never worried about that—but it was so personally awful. As I always described it, that moment of parting was like one of my limbs was torn off, leaving me disabled. Of course, I healed with the clear understanding that all of you would be well taken care of, but still—it was so hard."

"Mamá, both in your years in Mexico and in the USA, there must be over 250 people that without your help, probably would have died or suffered extremely due to disease and illness. Plus, you nurtured so many undocumented people, providing them food, shelter, love, and even arranging help with their papers, so they could immigrate. Who stands out to you when you think back on all these people?" I asked her.

After thinking for only a brief moment, she responded, "Roberto. Roberto stands out to me for two big reasons. First, because we were able to help him find a future as well as good employers, Betty Jo and Jimmy, who would help him get his legal papers. Number two, in the process of locating Betty Jo and Jimmy, we were able to mend a lot of things with the gang that was hurting Jorge, you, and the family. For that matter, we helped mend Joey and Elizabeth's family too."

When I asked her about her most memorable moment since she'd been in the USA—and there were many—without hesitation, she responded, "When I almost got deported when shopping with Evelyn at that secondhand store. I'd been helping so many of our guests avoid deportation, and finally, on that day I was living in their shoes. Evelyn saved me. Sure, if I'd gotten deported and released in Nogales, we probably would have been able to correct it; even still, it was still tremendously frightening. I am so grateful to Evelyn," and then she remarked, "And Glen and Evelyn's deaths have been hard. That's a big sadness for me."

I told my mother, "Isn't it interesting that throughout the years, you always touched the Bible, you looked at the Bible, you caressed it, yet you couldn't read or write. You'd have lessons here and there, but you really couldn't read or write. How is it that after so many years, you learned to read?"

"Edgar, I know why, but the how is more mysterious. It was my strong desire to know the God of the Bible that motivated me to put in all the effort over the decades to learn to read. For me, going from seeing marks on a page to seeing those marks as distinct words and sentences seemed to happen in an instant—but really it took years of hard work and lessons for that instant to occur. Reyna explains it saying that it was when I learned to blend letters that all those years of trying—particularly with her and Asunción's guidance—came to fruition.

"Something I've come to understand, Edgar, is that there are people who are educated, who have degrees, who can read the Bible perfectly well, but who have difficulty understanding it. I am grateful to the Lord each day for giving me the gift of reading; however, reading the Bible is one thing—and understanding the meaning of it is totally different."

I told her, "Something that gives me and my brothers and sisters so much happiness is coming to visit you and finding you sitting under that tall olive tree in your garden and reading the Bible. You make such a beautiful picture sitting under the olive tree and focused on the Bible in your hands."

At the end of our conversation, my mother told me, "Soon I will no longer be here physically. But spiritually, I will live within you, *mijo.* I guarantee that my name will come up throughout your life in many forms. I am a hundred percent sure that you and the family will talk about me—really, talk about all of us and the events in our life."

"Yes, Mamá, we will be talking about you. You're right. I think that's called a legacy," I said.

She responded, "When people do something great, you see it on TV, read it in the paper, or hear about it somehow that they have done something good. They saved a life. They've done something good for humanity. Those are usually called heroes. But people who do countless good things, not just once, but many times over the course of their lives, they become legends. Edgar, you will be a legend."

"On the contrary, Mamá, you are the legend. Never could I match what you have done."

"*Mijo*, you are always so generous," she replied then paused before saying, "Soon, I will be shopping with Evelyn Davis, an angel in heaven."

I responded, "Mamá, I don't want you to leave—but I understand better than anyone else that death happens to us all. As a surgeon, I've seen miracles, but one thing I do know is that the end for all of us is unavoidable. That, we know for a fact. So, I understand fully, but I don't want you to go."

During this special conversation, she never took the Bible from her lap. It was always with her. She never took her hands off it. As she elevated her arm to make a point, one hand was always on the Bible.

About six months later, at the age of 93, Mamá died. We were all with her when she passed—her many children, grandchildren, great-grandchildren, and friends.

Mamá's grave at the cemetery sits under a tall olive tree. All of us are filled with a bittersweet happiness when we visit her grave, imagining her peacefully reading her Bible under that tree for years and years to come.

Mamá's home—what we in the family call "Abuelita's house"—with its special landscaping and gardens designed for her enjoyment has stayed in the family. Her house still sits alone in Tempe, Arizona only to be used by all of us for uniting on special occasions, such as Christmas, Easter, Thanksgiving, or birthdays.

Chapter 15

NENA'S CHILDREN

Surama worked tirelessly in the USA from the time she immigrated in 1964. All of us in the family are forever grateful to her for
devoting years of her life to caring for our mother until Mamá's
death. Surama is now retired. She is a mother, grandmother, and
great-grandmother. She lives with her family in Phoenix, Arizona.

Pedro was described by Mrs. Crawford and Mrs. Smith, teachers
at Monroe School, as a student with great talent and intelligence.
He'd wanted to become a dentist; however, to help raise the money
to bring Mamá and our other siblings to the USA legally, he decided not to go to college and instead became a jeweler. Because of
his incredible talent, his skills and jewelry were revered. He came
to own his own jewelry store and pawnshop. While all of us were
very hard workers, Pedro was known as the hardest worker of all.
He even preferred to wait until the family and Mamá were better
settled economically before he would marry—which he eventually
did in 1973.
Pedro has retired as a jeweler. He is a proud husband, father, grandfather, and great-grandfather.

Jorge was a great student but was shackled by the fact that the gangs
were like a magnet to him. Jorge is quiet, gentleman-like, and with

a heart of gold. Perhaps because females chased him and sought his attention, gang members became angry and jealous and that's why they targeted him.

After he endured many assaults and fights, he felt that our mother could no longer cope with it all, so he told her, "You have sacrificed yourself for us. Now I will do the same." He then left school and became a top jeweler, which made all of us proud, especially Miguel and Pedro. He often brought precious gifts to our mother as well.

He married in 1971. He and his children owned a jewelry store and a pawnshop. He's a proud husband, father, grandfather, and great-grandfather.

Edgar—I am a proud husband and father, and I'm a happy grandfather of six granddaughters and one grandson named Miguel.
I achieved my childhood dream of becoming a surgeon, and for over 20 years now, I've practiced general surgery. In the last ten years, I've dedicated myself to the field of breast surgery, caring for women with minimal to devastating breast cancers.

Lupe always wanted to be home and by our mother's side. Our mother was her priority. She wanted more than anything else in the world to ease Mamá's constant work at home with the young children. Lupe became a star cook like our mother and sacrificed her education for the love of our mother. She married a teacher and now lives in Yuma, Arizona. They have two children and grandbabies as well.

Asunción earned a teaching degree at Arizona State University but never taught. She stayed close to our mother and helped ease her work and obligations. She married a jeweler. She is a proud mother and grandmother.

Reyna earned a teaching degree at Arizona State University and became a teacher in Oregon. She wanted more than anything to become a teacher. Reyna's husband, a juvenile diabetic, sadly died at a very young age. They had four boys. One is a doctor and the other three are still in college.

Here's something Reyna wanted to say about our mother:

Mom had never-ending, unconditional love, and devotion for all her children. Her greatest desire in life was that we would love and respect each other. She was happiest when she saw us gather together, when there was harmony between us, when we talked, laughed, and shared memories. She, in an almost unrealistic way, wanted only happiness for us.

I consider myself to be a fairly average person. Mom gave me a gift that has helped me accomplish better-than-average things—a wonderful work ethic. Mom despised laziness. She did not understand how anyone could not find joy in working. She labored joyfully all her life. She never stopped to rest for very long. I remember as a young girl being annoyed at her when she would sit down for what seemed like seconds, only to jump up to clean the kitchen, fold the laundry, or sweep the porch. She always invited us girls to go with her to join her in the work. She liked to clean, cook, and—as crazy as it sounds—wash dishes. Today, like my mother, I am happiest when I am working. As a teacher, I have put my efforts to help people learn, one thing our mother always desperately wanted to do.

I iron the outfit that I am going to wear to work the night before. When I iron, I remember Mom. Mom often apologized for not being able to provide financially for our needs. We lacked many needs, and she felt responsible. She became acquainted with a man and his wife, who owned a Mexican restaurant in Phoenix, and they offered her a job. She ironed shirts for them—it was ten cents a shirt. Over the course of years, she must have ironed many hundreds of shirts only to make a few dollars. She would tell me, "All work is honorable. Only thieves need be ashamed." She made many sacrifices for each of us. This is one of the many ways in which she manifested her love for each of her children. The money she earned was mostly used to buy clothes for us children, clothing that she likely had to alter, so it would fit us well.

Probably my most important memory of my mother is watching her read the Bible all by herself under a tall olive tree Edgar planted for her.

Manuel, or Manny, quit school early and became a jeweler, working with Pedro and Jorge. He lives in Tempe and now is retired. Manny does many other things outside jewelry. He married early and has children and grandchildren. His wife sadly died of ovarian cancer.

Jose Angel made it to the USA and the family via Los Angeles. He is a fine jeweler and runs a pawnshop at the same time. He has one daughter.

Salvador went into the residential and commercial contracting business. He was a very successful builder in the USA and now in Rocky Point, Mexico. Salvador "Chava" can build a house from scratch. He has one daughter.

Chapter 16

Nena's Recipes

These recipes were used and perfected by Magdalena "Nena" Hernandez over 60 years. All of the children, including the author, are experts at making these treasured meals taught by master chef "Nena".

NENA'S HUEVOS RACHEROS
Prepare diced tomatoes, slivers of onion, and ring size segments of Ortega chilis (remove the seeds). In an open pan, fry these items, add garlic and a pinch of salt. After this is done, add a generous amount of salsa (see next).

Fresh Salsa
Take 4-6 tomatoes, add one serrano chili, boil, then peel and place in blender then add garlic salt to taste and one cup of tomato sauce.

Fry a corn tortilla (1-2) in a pan with olive oil. Then place onto a plate, then add one over-medium or over-easy egg on top of each tortilla. Add generous salsa above on top of eggs. Always have a warm tortilla on your left hand or right (if left-handed) as this allows your tortilla to serve as a spoon as you cut and enjoy the Huevos Rancheros and beans. Enjoy portions with a side of homemade or commercially bought refried beans. Great breakfast!

NENA'S CHILAQUILES
1. Start with dry corn tortillas (commercial grocery store tortillas are fine), open package and lay out tortillas to dry, as this makes them firm. Cut into pieces like nacho chips.
2. Prepare diced onions mixed with one spoonful of oregano and a tinge of vinegar. (1/2 cup of total mixture)
3. One half cup cotija powder Mexican cheese (from local grocery)
4. Prepare salsa (see above). Set salsa aside

In a pan with olive oil or grape seed oil, fry the dry tortilla segments until brown. Mix 3 or 4 battered eggs onto hot chips and allow eggs to stick to chips. Then place entire salsa onto chips, simmer for a few minutes. Turn heat off and spread the cotija cheese on top of sauce, then spread the diced onions all over cheese. Use a large serving spoon to secure segments of chilaquiles and serve with a side of refried beans. Enjoy a fine breakfast!

NENA'S SHREDDED BEEF OR CHICKEN TACOS
1. Start with commercially bought thin corn tortillas
2. Dice tomatoes, thinly slice cabbage or lettuce
3. Boil chicken and shred, add diced onions, oregano and a pinch of vinegar to moist chicken.
4. Boil beef (any kind of beef) and shred (no onion or oregano or vinegar)
5. Cotija Mexican powder cheese

Take a corn tortilla and fill with either chicken or beef as above, fold and grasp with tong to keep closed. Place onto hot open pan with olive oil or grape seed oil and fry until brown, then place onto napkin to draw out oil. Then gently open taco and insert lettuce and tomatoes and cotija cheese. Add salsa of choice to taco as desired (see recipe above). Enjoy with side of refried beans and Spanish rice.

NENA'S RED OR GREEN ENCHILADAS (NO OVEN NEEDED)

1. Start with commercial corn tortillas
2. Store bought enchilada sauce (red or green, amount as desired)
3. Diced tomatoes and finely shredded cabbage, or lettuce. (Nena preferred cabbage)
4. Powdered cotija Mexican cheese
5. Use two large pans
   - Place olive oil or grape seed oil in one pan, heat to medium high, place tortilla and slightly fry on both sides. (Use tongs or a glove)
   - Place the fried tortilla individually onto hot enchilada sauce in the second pan and bathe (hold with tongs and gently remove and place onto flat plate), then while open add tomatoes, cabbage, (lettuce), and cotija cheese. Then roll enchiladas. Repeat 1,2,3 for four enchiladas. Then add additional diced tomatoes and cabbage on top of rolled enchilada. Add additional enchilada sauce on top, then sprinkle cotija cheese, then serve hot! No oven!

When doing chicken or beef enchiladas you do the same except add shredded chicken or beef into the ingredients then roll.

To prepare chicken and beef

Prepare the shredded chicken or beef stuffing. Mix shredded chicken with a tinge of vinegar to moist chicken then sprinkle with oregano then mix. Place onto the mixture above. Shredded beef does not need vinegar or oregano. Enjoy hot with refried beans and Spanish rice.

NENA'S CHILE RELLENO AND RANCHERO SOUP

1. Start with an assortment of either ortega or pasilla chilis (as many as desired)
2. Roast chilis on hot plate, then wrap on moist towel for thirty minutes to allow easy peeling of skin. After peeling, slit the side of the chili and pull out seeds. Leave stem in place (Becomes a valuable handle while enjoying your meal), stack the chilis and set aside.
3. Dice tomatoes and white onion and small segments of shrimp (boil shrimp for 10 minutes and then cut into small pieces). Then mix all three items and add ¼ tsp of oregano depending on amount of chili rellenos to be served. Also add powdered cotija Mexican cheese to the mix then set aside-called "total relleno stuffing." May leave shrimp out if desired (Nena preferred shrimp also).
4. Egg batter (as many eggs as needed). Place in sauce pan. On a flat plate place regular cooking flour.
5. Slit chilis on the side and add "total relleno stuffing". Then bathe them in the egg batter then onto the flour to cover egg batter. Place the stuffed chilis into a pan with olive oil or grape seed oil and fry until slightly brown. Then place on napkins to draw out oil. Then set aside.

NENA'S RANCHERO SOUP

1. Start with commercial chicken stock or fresh chicken stock (Nena preferred fresh stock), place in a large soup pot and warm. Usually 6-8 cups of stock. Makes about 6-8 bowls of soup.

2. Dice ½ to whole white onion as per amount of soup to be made. Dice tomatoes also to amount of soup to be made. 4-5 Ortega fresh chilis, cut into ring size segments (pull out seeds). Place in hot soup pot with slight olive or grape seed oil, add a sprinkle of salt, and two small diced pieces of garlic. Fry until soft, then add above broth to mixture. Stir and let sit. Take two spoons of flour and brown in small pan, then mix into ½ cup of warm stock and stir. Then gradually add this to above and stir. (This will thicken the soup). Increase heat to boil. Be careful not to put too much flour mixture because it will turn into oatmeal. Do it slowly! Add a few sprinkles of oregano then gently mix and set to boil for 15-20 minutes, then set back and enjoy your chili relleno with ranchero soup, while engaged in a lengthy conversation the Nena way!

In a bowl, ladle out soup, then add one or two chili rellenos into the soup. Use a spoon to cut the chili in segments and enjoy this flavorful meal. Don't forget to use the chili stem to hold chili while you cut with spoon. To add more taste, use warm commercial corn tortilla on your left hand or right hand and moisten in soup as you savor this fine meal prepared by Nena for over 60 years. You could also make a bold move and use gorditas instead of tortillas.

NENA'S CHICKEN MOLÉ WITH GORDITAS

Buy molé from local Mexican grocery store. They come in various brand names, most are suitable (get the one with glass container) which generally will feed 5-6 people.

Once you have placed the molé into a deep pan, gradually dissolve (it's very thick) by adding chicken stock (Nena preferred fresh chicken broth since you are making chicken molé). Use about three cups of broth. Once you make it for more than four people, you will be an expert as to how much you need. Stir until it becomes slightly thick, like a gravy. Since molé contains multiple ingredients it's better to use commercially available because making it from scratch is very time consuming (something Nena did for many years) and it tastes much the same when modified as follows.

Take one banana, 2 cloves of garlic, one fresh ripe tomato (small) and a spoon of sesame seeds (place seeds on hot plate and brown) then place into blender and add a cup of chicken broth and blend until complete liquid. Then add to molé and stir over low flame (prefer flame vs electric stove-Nena's preference-but electric stove will do. Recall that Nena cooked on open flame from logs on fire for many years, then in 1966 had a gas stove). The molé will start taking a bright chocolate brown color. Boil for 10 minutes then set aside.

Shred chicken (previously freshly boiled) or use chunks. No salt or pepper. Add chicken to molé and stir while molé is hot, set on stove on low heat for 15-20 minutes then serve. When you serve on flat place sprinkle sesame seeds on molé. (Don't need to roast)

Usually molé can be served on a flat plate accompanied by a side of refried beans and a portion of Spanish rice (easy to make). Nena made gorditas instead of tortillas or bread to go along with the molé.

Gorditas are simple to make. You can buy the fresh masa (corn dough) at a tortilla shop or you can make your own by buying commercial bags of masa powder (Maseca), add water until you make a dough. Form the gorditas with your hands like making a very thick tortilla a little over a quarter of an inch in thickness and the size of a very small tortilla. Place on hot plate and let it slightly develop brown dark spots on both sides then enjoy by taking a knife and splitting the gordita (like butterflying it). A slit on side of the gordita allows stuffing with molé, beans and rice or simply our tradition is to slit in half or just cut into pieces and dip or use a fork. Enjoy!

NENA'S STUFFED GORDITAS WITH BEANS OR CHORIZO

Buy fresh masa from a Mexican grocery store (where they make fresh tortillas (many southwestern states) or Maseca powder corn flour. Add water to make dough. Make the gorditas by working a clump of dough and making a thick tortilla ¼ or so in thickness (hence word gordita means slightly fat) ¾ the size of a regular round disc tortilla. Place onto hot flat plate and cook until you see brown or black spots. Make sure you turn over to cook both sides. While warm, slit on the side with a knife and open the walls of the hot gordita to accommodate stuffing with refried beans and cotija powder Mexican cheese or American cheese or chorizo or scrambled eggs, then add salsa of your choice. You can also simply stuff with cheese, add lettuce and tomatoes and salsa of choice-vegetarian type.

NENA'S TOREJAS

1. Take several boiled soft potatoes and mash them like making mashed potatoes.
2. Add diced tomatoes and tiny segments of green scallion (use the green part only) to potatoes.
3. Add small size pieces of pre-boiled shrimp, and a tiny sprinkle cotija powder cheese, then mix.
4. Make patties like crab cakes (these are the torejas), dip the torejas in egg batter, then coat with flour to cover egg batter (like the chili relleno). Fry until brown. Set aside on napkin to draw out oil.
5. Consider adding torejas to ranchero soup!

ACKNOWLEDGMENTS

Thank you to my sisters—Surama, Lupe, Asunción, and Reyna. To my brothers—Pedro, Jorge, Manuel, Jose Angel, and Salvador. To my wife, Lupe, and to our children—Marisa, Miguel, and Carlos, and their spouses, Kara and Graciela. To Dr. Billy Cox, Shanna Hardman, and Nancy Pile.

About the Author

Edgar H. Hernández, M.D., M.S., F.A.C.S., lives in Tempe, Arizona. In addition to being a proud husband and father, he is now a happy grandfather of six granddaughters from the ages of two years to 17 years and a grandson who's only a few months old.

For over thirty years he has been a surgeon in private practice. Additionally, he has served as chief of surgery, chief of staff, and member of the board at Chandler Regional Medical Center in Chandler, Arizona.

For over 20 years Dr. Hernández has practiced general surgery. In the last twelve years, Dr. Hernández has dedicated himself to the field of breast surgery. He cares for women with minimal to devastating breast cancers. Recently Dr. Hernández joined the Ironwood Cancer and Research Center, a renowned oncology center in Arizona. He is a diplomate of the American Board of Surgery, a fellow of the American College of Surgeons, and a practicing oncoplastic breast surgeon.

Over the course of his career, Dr. Hernández has worked with charitable groups and various foundations. He has led and participated in many mission trips to Mexico to perform surgeries, teach and train Mexican surgeons, and bring medical equipment and supplies to underfunded Mexican hospitals. In 2000, the Phoenix Hispanic community awarded him its "Humanitarian Award" for his mission work in Mexico. In 2011, Dr. Hernández was named

"Man of the Year," a humanitarian distinction, by Fresh Start Women's Foundation of Arizona for his treatment of uninsured women in need of surgeries for breast disorders, including breast cancers. The Desert Cancer Foundation of Arizona also honored Dr. Hernández with a humanitarian award. South Mountain Community College of Arizona has selected Dr. Hernández to speak at their 2017 commencement ceremony. He has been selected to speak at the Fourth of July 2018 Naturalization (Citizenship) ceremonies in Phoenix, Arizona.

Nena, age 33
in La Mira circa 1954

Family (Edgar lower left)
in La Mira circa 1956

Miguel Sr. and family
(approx. 1 yr before his passing)
in La Mira circa 1958

Nena's parents in La Mira circa 1957

Nena w/Edgar(l) & Pedro(r)
in Phoenix circa 1967

Nena & Salvador
(green card photo)
in Nogales circa 1966

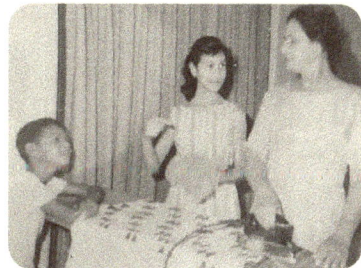

Nena with Reyna & Manuel
in Phoenix circa 1970